basic russian
vocabulary

A Handy Reference of Everyday

Words Arranged by Topic

ANN ROLBIN

PASSPORT BOOKS
NTC/Contemporary Publishing Group

Library of Congress Cataloging-in-Publication Data

Rolbin, Ann.
    Basic Russian vocabulary : a handy reference of everyday words arranged by topic / Ann Rolbin.
      p.   cm.
    ISBN 0-8442-4297-7
    1. Russian language—Glossaries, vocabularies, etc.   2. English language—Dictionaries—Russian.   I. Title.
    PG2680.R65   1998
    491.782'421—dc21   98-22737
                                                CIP

Cover design by Mary Lockwood
Interior design and production by VARDA Graphics, Inc.

Published by Passport Books
A division of NTC/Contemporary Publishing Group, Inc.
4255 West Touhy Avenue, Lincolnwood (Chicago), Illinois 60646-1975 U.S.A.
Copyright © 1998 by Ann Rolbin
English Vocabulary Topic Lists copyright © Addison Wesley Longman Australia
All rights reserved. No part of this book may be reproduced, stored in a retrieval system, or transmitted in any form or by any means, electronic, mechanical, photocopying, recording, or otherwise, without the prior permission of NTC/Contemporary Publishing Group, Inc.
Printed in the United States of America
International Standard Book Number: 0-8442-4297-7
18   17   16   15   14   13   12   11   10   9   8   7   6   5   4   3   2   1

Contents

Contents

Appendices

Introduction

Basic Russian Vocabulary is designed to help you communicate in Russian and "survive" in real-life language situations. Basic words considered necessary for communication in Russian are given with their English translations. A transliteration, or phonetic transcription, is also supplied.

The vocabulary has been grouped into 19 essential topics, each divided into subsections containing entries ordered alphabetically by the English translation. The Russian term appears first in Cyrillic, then as a transliteration into the Latin alphabet.

The transliteration system used is based on the one devised by the U.S. Board on Geographic Names, with a few minor variations geared toward the general reader. It is designed to enable correct pronunciation by reading the transliteration as if it were English. For further guidelines, consult the Cyrillic Alphabet table and Pronunciation Tips below.

The vocabulary topic lists are followed by Russian-English and English-Russian Glossaries, complete alphabetical orderings of all the terms appearing in the thematic lists. Both glossaries also cross-reference each term to the section(s) where it appears in the thematic lists. This provides the user with a helpful index to locate related vocabulary.

The Russian Language

The Russian language belongs to the Slavic language family, which also includes Ukrainian, Belorusian, Polish, Bulgarian, and Czech. The Cyrillic alphabet was created by Saint Cyril and his brother Saint Methodius about 860 A.D. After the Bolshevik Revolution of 1917, the alphabet was simplified.

Russian is the primary language of Russia and is now the secondary language in other countries of the CIS (Commonwealth of Independent States), which now consists of 12 of the 15 republics of the former Soviet Union.

The Russian (Cyrillic) Alphabet

Russian letter (upper & lower case)	Transliteration	Sound
А а	a	a as in father
Б б	b	b as in baby
В в	v	v as in victory
Г г	g	g as in garden
Д д	d	d as in dad
Е е	ye	ye as in yes
Ё ё	yo	yo as in yogurt
Ж ж	zh	s as in pleasure
З з	z	z as in zoo
И и	i	i as in marine
Й й	y	y as in boy
К к	k	k as in make
Л л	l	l as in light
М м	m	m as in map
Н н	n	n as in never
О о	o	o as in phone
П п	p	p as in plan
Р р	r	rolled like the Spanish r
С с	s	s as in sad
Т т	t	t as in tomato
У у	u	u as in flute
Ф ф	f	f as in five
Х х	kh	like ch in the Scottish loch or the German Bach
Ц ц	ts	ts as in melts
Ч ч	ch	ch as in cheese
Ш ш	sh	sh as in show
Щ щ	shch	sh followed by ch, as in fresh cheese
Ъ ъ	”	(hard sign) no sound value; separates the letters before and after it
Ы ы	y	similar to the short i in hit but with the tongue positioned higher
Ь ь	’	(soft sign) no sound value; makes the preceding consonant soft
Э э	e	e as in met
Ю ю	yu	yu as in yule
Я я	ya	ya as in yacht

Pronunciation Tips

The following tips will help you pronounce standard Russian more accurately. They reflect cases where the transliteration system used in this book diverges from the transliteration in the Alphabet table above.

Vowels

(i) The Russian letter **e** is transliterated as **ye** at the beginning of a word, after vowels, and after the soft sign (**ь**) and the hard sign (**ъ**). In all other (unstressed) positions, it is transliterated either as **e** or **i** to aid the reader in pronouncing a word fluently and accurately.

(ii) The letter **й** is transliterated as **y**, as is the vowel **ы**. However, for proper nouns and names appearing in English dictionaries, conventional spellings are followed (e.g., Tchaikovsky, Bolshoi). To more closely parallel English diphthongs, the letter **й** appears as **i** when it falls next to a vowel in the middle of a transliterated word (e.g., **тайга** is transliterated as *taiga*). Word endings in -**ый** and -**ий** are transliterated simply as -**iy**, and those ending in -**ые** and -**ие** as -**iye**.

(iii) When unstressed, the letter **o** is pronounced like the Cyrillic **a**. The vowel **я** becomes shortened or reduced when it occurs in unstressed syllables. It is then transliterated either as **i** or **a**.

Consonants

(i) Consonants at the end of Russian words are pronounced unvoiced, for example, a **д** (d) is pronounced like a **т** (t), a **б** (b) is pronounced like a **п** (p), and **г** (g) is pronounced like a **к** (k). Devoicing also occurs when consonants occur next to unvoiced consonants, for example, **вторник** (Tuesday) is pronounced *ftornik*.

(ii) Silent consonants occur in Russian only in some isolated words, such as the **л** in **солнце** *(sontse)*. The prepositions **в** (v), **к** (k), and **с** (s) are pronounced as though they were part of the following word.

(iii) An apostrophe (') represents the soft sign (**ь**) and indicates that the consonant is soft. A quotation mark (") represents the hard sign (**ъ**).

Notes

Stress

Stress, or emphasis, in Russian words can fall on any syllable. Since stress is arbitary, it is marked throughout the book in the Cyrillic form of the Russian word. Although this is a helpful device for learners of Russian, stress marks do not appear in standard Russian print. It is important to pay attention to where the stress falls in a word, because it may affect the meaning. Note that the letter ё is always stressed.

Gender

Russian nouns are either masculine (*m*), feminine (*f*), or neuter (*n*). In general, nouns that end in a consonant are masculine, those ending in -**a** are feminine, and those ending in -**o** are neuter. Nouns that end in -**ь**, the soft sign, may be masculine or feminine. For clarification, the gender is indicated after every noun.

However, for simplicity, note that in this book adjectives are usually shown only in their masculine form, ending in -**ый** or -**ий**.

Verbs

Verbs in this book are shown in the infinitive form of the imperfective aspect, unless it is indicated that the perfective infinitive is shown (*perf.*).

Prepositions

Prepositions in Russian govern the case of the following noun or noun phrase. The abbreviations used to indicate case are as follows: (+ *acc.*) for the accusative, (+ *gen.*) for the genitive, (+ *dat.*) for the dative, (+ *inst.*) for the instrumental, and (+ *prep.*) for the prepositional case.

Vocabulary Topics

1. Nature

1.1 Sky	Нéбо	Nyeba
air	вóздух *(m)*	vozdukh
bright	я́ркий	yarkiy
dark	тёмный	tyomniy
day	день *(m)*	dyen'
light	свет *(m)*	svyet
moon	лунá *(f)*	luna
shine, to	свети́ть	svitit'
sky	нéбо *(n)*	nyeba
star	звездá *(f)*	zvyezda
sun	сóлнце *(n)*	sontse
sunlight	сóлнечный свет *(m)*	solnichniy svyet

1.2 Earth	Зéмля	Zimlya
bay	зали́в *(m)*	zalif
continent	континéнт *(m)*	kantinyent
desert	пусты́ня *(f)*	pustynye
earth; land	земля́ *(f)*	zimlya
hill	холм *(m)*	kholm
island	óстров *(m)*	ostraf
mainland	матери́к *(m)*	matirik
mountain	горá *(f)*	gora

| soil | пóчва (f) | pochva |
| stone | кáмень (m) | kamin' |

1.3 Water

1.3 Water	Водá	Vada
beach	пляж (m)	plyazh
creek	ручéй (m)	ruchyei
flow, to	течь	tyech'
lake	óзеро (n)	ozira
ocean	океáн (m)	akian
pond	пруд (m)	prut
river	рекá (f)	rika
shore	бéрег (m)	berik
water	водá (f)	vada
wave	волнá (f)	valna

1.4 Climate	Клúмат	Klimat
blow, to	дуть	dut'
clear	я́сно	yasna
climate	клúмат (m)	klimat
cloud	óблако (n)	oblaka
cloudy	óблачно	oblachna
cold	хóлодно	kholadna
drizzle	морося́щий дождь (m)	marasyashchiy dozhd'
dry	сýхо	sukha
fog	тумáн (m)	tuman
hail	град (m)	grat
hot	жáрко	zharka
lightning	мóлния (f)	molniya
mist	мгла (f)	mgla
rain	дождь (m)	dozhd'
rainy	дождлú́вый	dazhdliviy
rainy season	дождлú́вый сезóн (m)	dazhdliviy sizon

snow	снег *(m)*	snyek
sultry	ду́шный	dushniy
temperature	температу́ра *(f)*	timpiratura
thermometer	термо́метр *(m)*	termometr
thunder	гром *(m)*	grom
warm	тепло́	tiplo
weather	пого́да *(f)*	pagoda
weather report	сво́дка *(f)* пого́ды	svotka pagody
wet	мо́крый	mokriy

1.5 Natural disasters — Стихи́йные бе́дствия — Stikhiyniye byetstviya

avalanche	снѐжный обва́л *(m)*	snyezhniy abval
burn, to	горе́ть	garyet'
catch fire, to	загоре́ться *(perf.)*	zagaryet'sa
danger	опа́сность *(f)*	apasnast'
disaster	бе́дствие *(n)*	byetstviye
earthquake	землетрясе́ние *(n)*	zimlitrisyeniye
fire	пожа́р *(m)*	pazhar
flood	наводне́ние *(n)*	navadnyeniye
happen, to	случа́ться	sluchat'sa
hurricane	урага́н *(m)*	uragan
injured	ра́неный	raniniy
natural	приро́дный	prirodniy
storm	шторм *(m)*	shtorm
strong wind	си́льный ве́тер *(m)*	sil'niy vyetir
suffer, to	страда́ть	stradat'
unexpected	неожи́данный	niazhidanniy
wind	ве́тер *(m)*	vyetir

1.6 Seasons — Времена́ го́да — Vrimina goda

| four seasons | четы́ре вре́мени го́да | chityri vryemini goda |

1.7 Plants

season	вре́мя го́да (n)	vryemye goda
spring	весна́ (f)	visna
summer	ле́то (n)	lyeta
fall	о́сень (f)	osen'
winter	зима́ (f)	zima

1.7 Plants	Расте́ния	Rastyeniye
alive	живо́й	zhivoy
botanical garden	ботани́ческий сад (m)	batanichiskiy sat
branches	ве́тки (pl)	vyetki
bush	куст (m)	kust
dead	мёртвый	myortviy
flower	цвето́к (m)	tsvitok
forest	лес (m)	lyes
garden	сад (m)	sat
grass	трава́ (f)	trava
lawn	газо́н (m)	gazon
leaf	лист (m)	list
orchard	фрукто́вый сад (m)	fruktoviy sat
plant	расте́ние (n)	rastyeniye
root	ко́рень (m)	koren'
seeds	семена́ (pl)	simina
tree	де́рево (n)	dyereva

1.8 Animals (general)	Живо́тные	Zhivotniye
animal	живо́тное (n)	zhivotnoye
bark, to	ла́ять	layet'
bite, to	куса́ть	kusat'
fly	лета́ть	litat'
hide	шку́ра (f)	shkura
pet	дома́шнее живо́тное (n)	damashniye zhivotnaye

raise animals, to	выра́щивать живо́тных	vyrashchivat' zhivotnykh
run, to	бежа́ть	bizhat'
skin	ко́жа *(f)*	kozha
sting, to	ужа́лить *(perf.)*	uzhalit'
walk the dog, to	прогу́ливать соба́ку	pragulivat' sabaku
wild animals	ди́кие живо́тные *(pl)*	dikiye zhivotniye
zoo	зоопа́рк *(m)*	zaapark

1.9 Animals (specific)	Живо́тные	Zhivotniye
ant	мураве́й *(m)*	muravyei
bear	медве́дь *(m)*	midvyet'
bee	пчела́ *(f)*	pchila
bird	пти́ца *(f)*	ptitsa
cat	ко́шка *(f)*	koshka
chicken	ку́рица *(f)*	kuritsa
cow	коро́ва *(f)*	karova
deer	оле́нь *(m)*	alyen'
duck	у́тка *(f)*	utka
elephant	слон *(m)*	slon
fish	ры́ба *(f)*	ryba
horse	ло́шадь *(f)*	loshad'
insect	насеко́мое *(n)*	nasikomaye
pig	свинья́ *(f)*	svin'ya
rabbit	кро́лик *(m)*	krolik
sheep	овца́ *(f)*	avtsa
wolf	волк *(m)*	volk

2. People

2.1 People	Лю́ди	Lyudi
adult	взро́слый	vzrosliy
baby	младе́нец *(m)*	mladyenits
boy	ма́льчик *(m)*	mal'chik
child	ребёнок *(m)*	rebyonak
girl	де́вочка *(f)*; де́вушка *(f)*	dyevachka; dyevushka
man	мужчи́на *(m)*	muzhchina
middle-aged person	челове́к *(m)* сре́днего во́зраста	chilavyek sryedneva vozrasta
old person	пожило́й челове́к *(m)*	pazhiloy chilavyek
people	лю́ди *(pl)*	lyudi
person	челове́к *(m)*	chilavyek
woman	же́нщина *(f)*	zhenshchina
young person	молодо́й челове́к *(m)*	maladoy chilavyek

2.2 Parts of the body	Ча́сти те́ла	Chasti tyela
abdomen	живо́т *(m)*	zhivot
arm	рука́ *(f)*	ruka
beard	борода́ *(f)*	barada
blood	кровь *(f)*	krov'
body	те́ло *(n)*	tyela
bone	кость *(f)*	kost'
brain	мозг *(m)*	mozg
breast	грудь *(f)*	grud'
buttocks	я́годицы *(f)*	yagaditsy
chest	грудна́я кле́тка *(f)*	grudnaya klyetka
develop, to	развива́ть	razvivat'

ear	у́хо (*n*)	ukha
eye	глаз (*m*)	glaz
eyebrow	бровь (*f*)	brov'
face	лицо́ (*n*)	litso
fat	то́лстый	tolstiy
flesh	плоть (*f*)	plot'
foot	нога́ (*f*)	naga
gain weight, to	поправля́ться	papravlyat'sa
grow, to	расти́	rasti
hair	во́лосы (*pl*)	volosy
hand	рука́ (*f*)	ruka
heart	се́рдце (*n*)	sertse
leg	нога́ (*f*)	naga
lose weight, to	худе́ть	khudyet'
lungs	лёгкие (*pl*)	lyokiye
mouth	рот (*m*)	rot
muscle	му́скул (*m*)	muskl
nail	но́готь (*m*)	nogat'
nerves	не́рвы (*pl*)	nyervy
nose	нос (*m*)	nos
short	коро́ткий, ма́ленький	karotkiy, malin'kiy
shoulder	плечо́ (*n*)	plicho
skin	ко́жа (*f*)	kozha
stomach	желу́док (*m*)	zhiludak
tall	высо́кий	vysokiy
teeth	зу́бы (*pl*)	zuby
thigh	бедро́ (*n*)	bidro
thin	худо́й	khudoy
throat	го́рло (*n*)	gorla
tongue	язы́к (*m*)	yezyk
waist	та́лия (*f*)	taliya

2.3 Life	Жизнь	Zhizn'
alive	живо́й	zhivoy
birthday	день (m) рожде́ния	dyen' razhdyeniye
born, to be	роди́ться	radit'sa
dead, to be	мёртвый	myortviy
die, to	умере́ть (perf.)	umiryet'
divorce, to	разводи́ться	razvodit'sa
marry, to	жени́ться	zhinit'sa
old age	пожило́й во́зраст (m)	pazhiloy vozrast
young	молодо́й	maladoy

2.4 Day	День	Dyen'
asleep, to be; sleep, to	спать	spat'
dream, to	мечта́ть	michtat'
get up, to	встава́ть	vstavat'
go to bed, to	ложи́ться спать	lazhit'sa spat'
go to sleep, to	засыпа́ть	zasypat'
lie down, to	ложи́ться	lazhitsa
sleepy	со́нный	sonniy
tired	уста́лый	ustaliy
wake up, to	буди́ть	budit'

2.5 Personal hygiene	Ли́чная гигие́на	Lichnaya gigiyena
brush one's teeth, to	чи́стить зу́бы	chistit' zuby
cold water	холо́дная вода́ (f)	khalodnaya vada
comb one's hair, to	причёсывать во́лосы	prichyosyvat' volosy
gargle, to	полоска́ть го́рло	palaskat' gorla
go to the bathroom, to	идти́ в туале́т	iti f tualyet
hot water	горя́чая вода́ (f)	garyachaya vada
hygiene	гигие́на (f)	gigiyena

shampoo one's hair, to	мыть го́лову	myt' golavu
shave, to	бри́ться	britsa
shower, to	принима́ть душ (m)	prinimat' dush
soap	мы́ло (n)	myla
take a bath, to	принима́ть ва́нну	prinimat' vannu
toilet paper	туале́тная бума́га (f)	tualyetnaya bumaga
toothbrush	зубна́я щётка (f)	zubnaya shchyotka
toothpaste	зубна́я па́ста (f)	zubnaya pasta
towel	полоте́нце (n)	palatyentse
warm water	тёплая вода́ (f)	tyoplaya vada
wash one's face, to	умыва́ться; мыть лицо́	umyvat'sya; myt' litso

2.6 Health	Здоро́вье	Zdarovye
blood pressure	давле́ние (n)	davlyeniye
catch a cold, to	простуди́ться (perf.)	prastudit'sa
cough, to	ка́шлять	kashlyat'
diarrhea	поно́с (m)	panos
feel, to	чу́вствовать	chustvavat'
fever	жар (m)	zhar
go to the doctor, to	идти́ к врачу́	iti k vrachu
good spirits/mood	хоро́шее настрое́ние (n)	kharoshiye nastrayeniye
headache	головна́я боль (f)	galavnaya bol'
health	здоро́вье (n)	zdarov'ye
healthy	здоро́вый	zdaroviy
influenza	грипп (m)	gripp
injure, to	ра́нить; повреди́ть (perf.)	ranit'; pavridit'
pain	боль (f)	bol'
painfully	бо́льно	bol'na
prescription	реце́пт (m)	ritsept
sick, to be	быть больны́м	byt' bol'nym
sickness; illness	боле́знь (f)	balyezn'
sore throat, to have a	боли́т го́рло (n)	balit gorla

| temperature | температу́ра *(f)* | timpiratura |
| well, to be/feel | чу́вствовать себя́ хорошо́ | chustvavat' sebya kharasho |

2.7 **Medicine**	**Медици́на**	**Miditsina**
clinic	поликли́ника *(f)*	paliklinika
dentist	зубно́й врач *(m)*	zubnoy vrach
doctor; physician	до́ктор *(m)*; врач *(m)*	doktr; vrach
fracture (of the bone)	перело́м *(m)*	pirilom
hospital	больни́ца *(f)*	bol'nitsa
internal	вну́тренний	vnutriniy
nurse	медсестра́ *(f)*	medsistra
operation	опера́ция *(f)*	apiratsiya
patient	пацие́нт *(m)*, пацие́нтка *(f)*	patsiyent, patsiyentka
pharmacy	апте́ка *(f)*	aptyeka
physical therapy	физиотерапи́я *(f)*	fizioterapiya
sleeping pill	снотво́рное *(n)*	snatvornaye
surgery	опера́ция *(f)*	apiratsiya
take medicine, to	принима́ть лека́рство	prinimat' likarstva
Western medicine	за́падная медици́на *(f)*	zapadnaya miditsina
X ray	рентге́н *(m)*	rentgen

2.8 **Emotions**	**Эмо́ции**	**Imotsii**
admire, to	восхища́ться	vaskhishchat'sa
angry	серди́тый	serditiy
annoy, to	раздража́ть	razdrazhat'
boring	ску́чный	skuchniy
careful	осторо́жный	astarozhniy
cry, to	крича́ть; пла́кать	krichat'; plakat'
disappoint, to	разочарова́ть *(perf.)*	razachiravat'
embarrass, to	смуща́ть	smushchat'
excite, to	возбужда́ть	vazbuzhdat'
exhaust, to	истоща́ть	istashchat'

feel, to	чу́вствовать	chustvavat'
funny	смешно́й	smishnoy
happy	счастли́вый	schastliviy
hope, to	наде́яться	nadyeyatsa
intention	наме́рение *(n)*	namyereniye
jealous	ревни́вый	rivniviy
laugh, to	смея́ться	smiyatsa
lonely	одино́кий	adinokiy
long for, to	тоскова́ть	taskavat'
lose, to	теря́ть	tiryat'
nervous	не́рвный	nyervniy
regret, to	сожале́ть	sazhalyet'
regrettable	приско́рбный	priskorbniy
relieve, to	облегча́ть	ablikhchat'
sad	гру́стный	grustniy
take care of, to	забо́титься	zabotitsa
temperament	темпера́мент *(m)*	temperament
terrible	ужа́сный	uzhasniy
unexpected	неожи́данный	niazhidanniy
worry, to	беспоко́иться	bispakoitsa

2.9 Attitudes — Отноше́ния — Atnasheniya

all right; that's all right	всё в поря́дке	vsyo v paryatke
bad	плохо́й	plakhoy
bad luck	неуда́ча *(f)*	niudacha
boast, to	хва́статься	khvastatsa
comfortable; contented	дово́льный	davol'niy
enthusiasm	энтузиа́зм *(m)*	entuziazm
flatter, to	льстить	l'stit'
forgive, to	проща́ть	prashchat'
good	хоро́ший	kharoshiy
good luck	уда́ча *(f)*	udacha

2.10 Perceptions

how terrible	как ужа́сно	kak uzhasna
important	ва́жный	vazhniy
interesting	интере́сный	intiryesniy
like, to; I like	нра́виться; мне нра́вится	nravit'sa; mnye nravitsa
lovable	ми́лый	miliy
love	любо́вь (f)	lyubov'
love, to	люби́ть	lyubit'
luck; success	уда́ча (f)	udacha
praise, to; commend, to	хвали́ть	khvalit'
terrific	великоле́пный	vilikalyepniy
trouble	неприя́тности (pl)	nipriyatnasti
unimportant	нева́жный	nivazhniy
unsuccessful	неуда́чный	niudachniy
very bad	о́чень пло́хо	ochin' plokha
wonderful	прекра́сный	prikrasniy

2.10 Perceptions	Восприя́тия	Vaspriyatiya
clear	я́сный	yasniy
consider, to	учи́тывать	uchityvat'
hear, to	слы́шать	slyshat'
know, to	знать	znat'
listen, to	слу́шать	slushat'
realize, to	осознава́ть	asaznavat'
see, to	ви́деть	vidit'
think, to	ду́мать	dumat'
understand, to	понима́ть	panimat'

2.11 Character and capabilities	Хара́ктер и спосо́бности	Kharakter i spasobnasti
arrogant	высокоме́рный	vysakomyerniy
capable	спосо́бный	spasobniy

careful	осторо́жный	astarozhniy
careless	беззабо́тный	bizzabotniy
clever; intelligent	у́мный	umniy
conscientious	созна́тельный	saznatel'niy
especially	специа́льно	spitsial'na
forceful	си́льный; убеди́тельный	sil'niy; ubiditel'niy
friendly	дружелю́бный	druzhilyubniy
gentle	мя́гкий; кро́ткий	myakhkiy; krotkiy
get used to, to	привы́кнуть *(perf.)*	privyknut'
hardworking	трудолюби́вый	trudalyubiviy
honest	че́стный	chyestniy
important	ва́жный	vazhniy
kind	до́брый	dobriy
lazy	лени́вый	liniviy
lively	живо́й	zhivoy
lovable	ми́лый	miliy
methodical	методи́чный	mitadichniy
mischievous	озорно́й	azarnoy
modest	скро́мный	skromniy
nice	ми́лый	miliy
obedient	послу́шный	paslushniy
patient	терпели́вый	tirpiliviy
reasonable	разу́мный	razumniy
reliable	надёжный	nadyozhniy
sharp	проница́тельный	pranitsatel'niy
shrewd	хи́трый	khitriy
spoiled	избало́ванный	izbalovanniy
stern	неумоли́мый	niumalimiy
straightforward	прямо́й	primoi
strict	стро́гий	strogiy
studious	приле́жный	prilyezhniy
stupid	глу́пый	glupiy
timid; shy	ро́бкий	robkiy

untrustworthy	ненадёжный	ninadyozhniy
warmhearted	добросердéчный	dabrasirdyechniy
wicked	злóбный	zlobniy

2.12 Family and relations	Семьá и рóдственники	Sim'ya i rotstviniki
ancestors	прéдки (pl)	pretki
aunt	тётя (f)	tyotya
brother	брат (m)	brat
dad	пáпа (m)	papa
daughter	дочь (f)	doch
family	семьá (f)	sem'ya
father	отéц (m)	atyets
first name	ѝмя (n)	imya
full name	пóлное ѝмя (n)	polnaye imya
generation	поколéние (n)	pakalyeniye
granddaughter	внýчка (f)	vnuchka
grandfather	дéдушка (m)	dyedushka
grandpa	дед (m)	dyed
grandson	внук (m)	vnuk
husband	муж (m)	muzh
last name	фамѝлия (f)	familiye
mom	мáма (f)	mama
mother	мать (f)	mat'
parents	родѝтели (pl)	raditili
relative; relation	рóдственник (m)	rotstvennik
sister	сестрá (f)	sistra
son	сын (m)	syn
stepfather	óтчим (m)	ochim
stepmother	мáчеха (f)	machikha
twins	близнецы́ (pl)	bliznitsy
uncle	дя́дя (m)	dyadya
wife	женá (f)	zhina

2.13 Pronouns	Местоиме́ния	Mistaimyeniya
everyone	ка́ждый	kazhdiy
he, him, (to) him	он, его́, ему́	on, yevo, yemu
I, me, (to) me	я, меня́, мне	ya, minya, mnye
she, her, (to) her	она́, её, ей	ana, yeyo, yey
they, them, (to) them	они́, их, им	ani, ikh, im
we, us, (to) us	мы, нас, нам	my, nas, nam
who, whom, (to) whom	кто, кого́, кому́	kto, kavo, kamu
you (plural), you, (to) you	вы, вас, вам	vy, vas, vam
you (polite), you, (to) you	Вы, Вас, Вам	vy, vas, vam
you (singular), you, (to) you	ты, тебя́, тебе́	ty, tibya, tibye

2.14 Professions	Профе́ссии	Prafyesii
actor	актёр (m)	aktyor
architect	архите́ктор (m)	arkhityektar
artist	худо́жник (m)	khudozhnik
barber	парикма́хер (m)	parikmakher
bricklayer	ка́менщик (m)	kamin'shchik
businessman	бизнесме́н (m)	biznismyen
cashier	касси́р (m), касси́рша (f)	kasir, kasirsha
civil engineer	инжене́р-строи́тель (m)	inzhinyer-straityel'
computer specialist	специали́ст (m) по компью́терам	spitsialist pa kamp'uteram
conductor (of orchestra/band)	дирижёр (m)	dirizhyor
conductor (ticket seller)	конду́ктор (m), конду́кторша (f)	kanduktar, kanduktarsha
contractor	подря́дчик (m)	padryadchik
cook	по́вар (m)	povar
dentist	зубно́й врач (m)	zubnoy vrach

diplomat	диплома́т *(m)*	diplamat
doctor	врач *(m)*, до́ктор *(m)*	vrach, doktar
electrician	эле́ктрик *(m)*	elyektrik
engineer	инжене́р *(m)*	inzhinyer
farmer	фе́рмер *(m)*	fyermer
fisherman	рыба́к *(m)*	rybak
gardener	садо́вник *(m)*	sadovnik
guide	гид *(m)*	git
hairdresser	парикма́хер *(m)*	parikmakher
housewife	домохозя́йка *(f)*	damakhazyaika
intellectual	интеллектуа́л *(m)*	intiliktual
judge	судья́ *(m)*	sud'ya
lawyer	юри́ст *(m)*	yurist
lecturer	ле́ктор *(m)*	lyektar
librarian	библиоте́карь *(m)*, библиоте́карша *(f)*	bibliatyekar', bibliatyekarsha
mailman	почтальо́н *(m)*	pachtal'on
mechanic	меха́ник *(m)*	mikhanik
miner	шахтёр *(m)*	shakhtyor
musician	музыка́нт *(m)*	muzykant
nurse	медсестра́ *(f)*	medsistra
operator	опера́тор *(m)*	apiratr
peasant	крестья́нин *(m)*, крестья́нка *(f)*	krist'yanin, krist'yanka
photographer	фото́граф *(m)*	fatograf
pilot	пило́т *(m)*	pilot
policeman	милиционе́р *(m)*	militsianyer
politician	поли́тик *(m)*	palitik
publisher	изда́тель *(m)*	izdatil'
reporter	репортёр *(m)*	ripartyor
researcher	иссле́дователь *(m)*	isslyedavatil'
retiree	пенсионе́р *(m)*	pinsianyer
sailor	матро́с *(m)*	matros

salesclerk	продаве́ц (m), продавщи́ца (f)	pradavyets, pradavshchitsa
scientist	учёный (m)	uchyoniy
secretary	секрета́рь (m), секрета́рша (f)	sikritar', sikritarsha
singer	певе́ц (m), певи́ца (f)	pivyets, pivitsa
soldier	солда́т (m)	saldat
surgeon	хиру́рг (m)	khirurk
tailor	портно́й (m)	partnoy
teacher	учи́тель (m), учи́тельница (f)	uchitil', uchitil'nitsa
technician	те́хник (m)	tyekhnik
unemployed (noun and adj.)	безрабо́тный (m)	bezrabotniy
worker	рабо́чий (m)	rabochiy
writer	писа́тель (m), писа́тельница (f)	pisatel', pisatel'nitsa

2.15 Common forms of address	Фо́рма обраще́ния	Forma obrashchyeniya
boys	ма́льчики (pl)	mal'chiki
dear friends	дороги́е друзья́ (pl)	daragiye druz'ya
girls	де́вочки (pl)	dyevachki
grandfather	де́душка (m)	dyedushka
grandmother	ба́бушка (f)	babushka
guys; kids	ребя́та (pl)	ribyata
madam	мада́м (f)	madam
Miss	де́вушка (f)	dyevushka
Mr.	господи́н (m)	gaspadin
Mrs.	госпожа́ (f)	gaspazha

3. Russia

3.1 General	Óбщее	Opshchiye
city	гóрод *(m)*	gorat
Commonwealth of Independent States	Содрýжество *(n)* Незави́симых Госудáрств	Sadruzhistva Nizavisimykh Gasudarstf
downtown	центр *(m)*	tsyentr
Duma *(parliament)*	Дýма *(f)*	Duma
International Woman's Day	Междунарóдный жéнский день *(m)*	Mezhdunarodniy zhenskiy dyen'
Labor Day	День *(m)* Трудá	Den' Truda
metro	метрó *(n)*	metro
Moscow	Москвá *(f)*	Maskva
October Revolution Day	День Октя́брьской Револю́ции	Den' Oktyabr'skoy Revolyutsie
president	президéнт *(m)*	prezidyent
village	дерéвня *(f)*	deryevnya

3.2 Russia— tourism	Росси́я— тури́зм	Rassiya— turizm
ballet	балéт *(m)*	balyet
Bolshoi Theater	Большóй теáтр *(m)*	Bol'shoi tiatr
Boulevard Ring	Садóвое кольцó *(n)*	Sadovaye kal'tso
Central Puppet Theater	Центрáльный теáтр *(m)* кýкол	Tsintral'niy tiatr kukal
Golden Ring	Золотóе кольцó *(n)*	Zalatoye kal'tso
Hermitage Museum	Эрмитáж *(m)*	Ermitazh
Kremlin	Кремль *(m)*	Kreml'
Lenin's tomb	Мавзолéй *(m)* Лéнина	Mavzalyei Lenina
Maly Theater	Мáлый теáтр *(m)*	Maliy tiatr
Moscow University	Москóвский университéт *(m)*	Maskofskiy univirsityet

opera	о́пера *(f)*	opira
Palace of Congresses	Дворе́ц *(m)* съе́здов	Dvaryets s'yezdof
Petrodvorets	Петродворе́ц *(m)*	Pitradvaryets
Pushkin Museum	музе́й *(m)* Пу́шкина	muzey Pushkina
Summer Palace	Ле́тний дворе́ц *(m)*	Letniy dvaryets
Tchaikovsky Concert Hall	Конце́ртный зал *(m)* и́мени Чайко́вского	Kantsertniy zal imeni Chaikovskava
Tretyekov Art Gallery	Третьяко́вская галере́я *(f)*	Tret'yakofskaya galeryeya
Tsar Bell	Царь-ко́локол	Tsar'-kolakal
Tsar Cannon	Царь-пу́шка	Tsar'-pushka
Winter Palace	Зи́мный дворе́ц *(m)*	Zimniy dvaryets
Yasnaya Polyana Estate Museum	музе́й-уса́дьба *(m)* Я́сная Поля́на	Muzey-usat'ba Yasnaya Palyana

3.3 Russian language	**Ру́сский язы́к**	**Russkiy yezyk**
alphabet	алфави́т *(m)*	alfavit
case	паде́ж *(m)*	padyezh
consonant: hard, soft, voiced, unvoiced	согла́сный звук *(m):* твёрдый, мя́гкий, зво́нкий, глухо́й	saglasniy zvuk: tvyordiy, myakhkiy, zvonkiy, glukhoy
ending	оконча́ние *(n)*	akanchaniye
gender: masculine, feminine, neuter	род *(m):* мужско́й, же́нский, сре́дний	rot: muzhskoi, zhenskiy, sredniy
hard sign	твёрдый знак *(m)*	tvyordiy znak
letter	бу́ква *(f)*	bukva
plural	мно́жественное число́ *(n)*	mnozhistvennoye chislo
Russian *(language)*	Ру́сский язы́к *(m)*	Russkiy yezyk
singular	еди́нственное число́ *(n)*	yedinstvinnoye chislo
Slavic language family	гру́ппа *(f)* славя́нских языко́в	gruppa slavyanskikh yezykov
soft sign	мя́гкий знак *(m)*	myakhkiy znak
sound	звук *(m)*	zvuk

stress	ударе́ние (*n*)	udaryeniye
syllable	слог (*m*)	slok
verb tense	вре́мя (*n*) глаго́ла	vryemya glagola
vowel: stressed, unstressed	гла́сный звук (*m*): уда́рный, безуда́рный	glasniy zvuk: udarniy, bezudarniy

3.4 Geography of Russia — Геогра́фия Росси́и — Giografiya Rassii

Baltic Sea	Балти́йское мо́ре (*n*)	Baltiyskaye morye
Black Sea	Чёрное мо́ре (*n*)	Chyornoye morye
Caucasus Mountains	Кавка́зские го́ры (*pl*)	Kavkazskiye gory
Lake Baikal	О́зеро (*n*) Байка́л	Ozero Baikal
Moskva River	Москва́-река́ (*f*)	Maskva-rika
Neva	Нева́ (*f*)	Neva
Siberia	Сиби́рь (*f*)	Sibir'
taiga	тайга́ (*f*)	taiga
tundra	ту́ндра (*f*)	tundra
Ural Mountains	Ура́льские го́ры (*pl*)	Ural'skiye gory
Volga River	река́ Во́лга (*f*)	rika Volga

Countries of the former Soviet Union — Стра́ны бы́вшего Сове́тского Сою́за — Strany byvshiva Savetskava Sayuza

Armenia	Арме́ния (*f*)	Armyeniya
Azerbaijan	Азербайджа́н (*m*)	Azirbaidzhan
Belarus	Белару́сь (*f*)	Bilarus'
Estonia*	Эсто́ния (*f*)	Estoniya
Georgia	Гру́зия (*f*)	Gruziya
Kazakhstan	Казахста́н (*m*)	Kazakhstan
Kyrgyzstan	Кыргызста́н (*m*)	Kyrgystan
Latvia*	Ла́твия (*f*)	Latviya
Lithuania*	Литва́ (*f*)	Litva
Moldova	Молдо́ва (*f*)	Maldova

* All the above except these three are members of the CIS.

Russia	Росси́я *(f)*	Rassiya
Tajikistan	Таджикиста́н *(m)*	Tadzhikistan
Turkmenistan	Туркмениста́н *(m)*	Turkministan
Ukraine	Украи́на *(f)*	Ukraina
Uzbekistan	Узбекиста́н *(m)*	Uzbekistan
Commonwealth of Independent States (CIS)	Содру́жество *(n)* Незави́симых Госуда́рств (СНГ)	Sadruzhistva Nizavisimykh Gasudarstf (SNG)

Capitals   Столи́цы   Stalitsi

Almaty (Kazakhstan)	Алматы́ *(f)*	Almaty
Ashkhabad (Turkmenistan)	Ашхаба́д *(m)*	Ashkhabat
Baku (Azerbaijan)	Баку́ *(m)*	Baku
Bishkek (Kyrgyzstan)	Бишке́к *(m)*	Bishkek
Dushanbe (Tajikistan)	Душанбе́ *(m)*	Dushanbe
Kiev (Ukraine)	Ки́ев *(m)*	Kiyef
Kishinev (Moldova)	Кишинёв *(m)*	Kishinyov
Minsk (Belarus)	Минск *(m)*	Minsk
Moscow (Russia)	Москва́ *(f)*	Maskva
Riga (Latvia)	Ри́га *(f)*	Riga
Tallinn (Estonia)	Та́ллин *(m)*	Tallin
Tashkent (Uzbekistan)	Ташке́нт *(m)*	Tashkyent
Tbilisi (Georgia)	Тбили́си *(m)*	Tbilisi
Vilnius (Lithuania)	Ви́льнюс *(m)*	Vil'nyus
Yerevan (Armenia)	Ерева́н *(m)*	Yerivan

3.5 History of Russia   Исто́рия Росси́и   Istoriya Rassii

Decembrist Revolt	восста́ние *(n)* декабри́стов	vasstaniye dikabristof
democracy	демокра́тия *(f)*	dimakratiya
dictatorship	диктату́ра *(f)*	diktatura
dynasty	дина́стия *(f)*	dinastiya

emperor	импера́тор *(m)*	impiratar
evacuation	эвакуа́ция *(f)*	evakuatsiya
government	прави́тельство *(n)*	pravitil'stva
Great Patriotic War	Вели́кая Оте́чественная война́ *(f)*	Velikaya Atechistvinnaya voina
historical period	истори́ческий пери́од *(m)*	istarichiskiy piriot
Kievan Rus	Ки́евская Русь *(f)*	Kiyevskaya Rus'
liberation	освобожде́ние *(n)*	asvabazhdyeniye
nobleman	дворяни́н *(m)*	dvarinin
occupation	оккупа́ция *(f)*	akupatsiya
October Revolution	Октя́брьская револю́ция *(f)*	Aktyabr'skaya rivalutsiya
republic	респу́блика *(f)*	rispublika
revolt	восста́ние *(n)*	vasstaniye
revolution	револю́ция *(f)*	rivalutsiya
Romanov dynasty	дина́стия *(f)* Рома́новых	dinastiya Romanavykh
rule, to	пра́вить	pravit'
serfdom	крепостно́е пра́во *(n)*	kripastnoye prava
tsar	царь *(m)*	tsar'
tsarina	цари́ца *(f)*	tsaritsa
World War I	Пе́рвая мирова́я война́ *(f)*	Pervaya miravaya vaina
World War II	Втора́я мирова́я война́ *(f)*	Vtaraya miravaya vaina

4. Social Expressions

4.1 Greetings	Приве́тствия	Privyetstviya
hello	здра́вствуйте	zdrastvuite
good morning	до́брое у́тро *(n)*	dobraye utra
good afternoon	до́брый день *(m)*	dobriy dyen'
good evening	до́брый ве́чер *(m)*	dobriy vyecher
good night	споко́йной но́чи	spakoynoy nochi
how are you? And you?	как пожива́ете? А вы?	kak pazhivaite? A vy?
how are things?	как дела́?	kak dela?
how about you?	а как вы?	a kak vy?
haven't seen you for ages	я вас сто лет не ви́дел	ya vas sto lyet ni vidil
where are you from?	отку́да вы?	atkuda vy?

4.2 Colloquial expressions	Разгово́рные выраже́ния	Razgavorniye vyrazhyeniya
as you wish	как хоти́те	kak khatite
cheers!	на здоро́вье!	na zdarov'ye!
congratulations	поздравля́ем	pazdravlyayem
excuse me	извини́те	izvinitye
I don't deserve it	я э́того не заслу́живаю	ya etova ni zasluzhivayu
I'm glad to see you	рад вас ви́деть	rat vas vidit'
is it all right?	э́то хорошо́?	eta kharasho?
let me help you	разреши́те вам помо́чь	razrishiti vam pamoch
make a toast, to	предложи́ть *(perf.)* тост	pridlazhit' tost
may I trouble you?	мо́жно вас побеспоко́ить?	mozhna vas pabispakoit'?
never mind, that's all right	ничего́	nichivo
no	нет	nyet
no more	бо́льше нет	bol'she nyet

no problem	нет проблём	nyet prablyem
O.K.	хорошо́	kharasho
please come in	пожа́луйста, заходи́те	pazhalsta, zakhaditye
so-so	так себе́	tak sibye
suit yourself	как вам подхо́дит	kak vam padkhodit
take a seat, please	сади́тесь, пожа́луйста	saditis', pazhalsta
thank you	спаси́бо	spasiba
thank you very much	большо́е спаси́бо	bal'shoye spasiba
wait a minute	подожди́те мину́тку	padazhditye minutku
what happened?	что случи́лось?	shto sluchilas'?
yes	да	da

4.3 Thanks and apologies	Благода́рность и извине́ния	Blagadarnast' i izvinyeniya
don't mention it	не сто́ит благода́рности	ni stoit blagadarnasti
gift; present	пода́рок (m)	padarak
please	пожа́луйста	pazhalsta
polite	ве́жливо	vyezhliva
politeness	ве́жливость (f)	vyezhlivast'
sorry	прости́те	prastite
souvenir	сувени́р (m)	suvinir
thank, to	благодари́ть	blagadarit'
you are too kind	вы о́чень добры́	vy ochin' dabry

4.4 Arrivals	Прибы́тие	Pribytie
how are you?	как вы пожива́ете?	kak vy pazhivaite?
introduce, to	предста́вить (perf.)	pridstavit'
may I introduce (to you) …?	разреши́те вам предста́вить …?	razryeshitye vam pridstavit' …?
my name is …	меня́ зову́т …	minya zavut …
pleased to meet you	прия́тно познако́миться	priyatna paznakomit'sa

| welcome | добро́ пожа́ловать | dabro pazhalavat' |
| what is your name? | как вас зову́т? | kak vas zavut? |

4.5 Departures   Отъе́зд   At"yezd

bon voyage!; have a good trip!	счастли́вого пути́!	schastlivava puti!
drive safely	веди́те маши́ну осторо́жно	viditye mashinu astarozhna
good-bye	до свида́ния	da svidaniya
give my regards to ...	переда́йте приве́т ...	piridaite privyet ...
see you soon	до ско́рого	da skorava
see you tomorrow	до за́втра	da zaftra
thank you for your hospitality	спаси́бо за гостеприи́мство	spasiba za gastipriimstva

5. Food and Drink

5.1 General	Общее	Opshchiye
buffet	шве́дский стол (m)	shvyetskiy stol
(cold) appetizers	(холо́дные) заку́ски (pl)	(khalodniye) zakuski
cold dish	холо́дное блю́до (n)	khalodnaye blyuda
delicacies	деликате́сы (pl)	dilikatyesy
dish	блю́до (n)	blyuda
drink to, to	пить за (+ acc.)	pit' za
eat	есть	yest'
food	еда́ (f)	yeda
help yourself	угоща́йтесь	ugashchaytes'
host, to be a	быть хозя́йкой	byt' khazyaykay
hungry	голо́дный	galodniy
invite to dinner, to	пригласи́ть (perf.) на обе́д	priglasit' na abyet
meal	еда́	yeda
set the table, to	накрыва́ть на стол	nakryvat' na stol
snack, to have a	перекуси́ть	pirikusit'
tasty, it's	вку́сно	fkusna
thirsty, to be	хоте́ть пить	khatyet' pit'

5.2 Mealtimes	Вре́мя приёма пи́щи	Vryemya priyoma pishchi
afternoon snack	по́лдник (m)	poldnik
breakfast	за́втрак (m)	zaftrak
dinner	обе́д (m)	abyet
supper	у́жин (m)	uzhin

5.3 At a restaurant	В рестора́не	V ristaranye
bakery (sweets)	конди́терская (f)	kanditerskaya
bar	бар (m)	bar
café	кафе́ (n)	kafye
cafeteria	кафете́рий (m)	kafityeriy
check; bill	счёт (m)	schyot
dining hall (in a school)	столо́вая (f) (в школе)	stalovaya (f shkole)
dining room (in a home)	столо́вая (дома)	stalovaya (doma)
go to a restaurant, to	пойти́ (perf.) в рестора́н	paiti v ristaran
menu	меню́ (n)	minyu
order food, to	заказа́ть еду́	zakazat' yedu
pay, to	плати́ть	platit'
restaurant	рестора́н (m)	ristaran
tip	чаевы́е (pl)	chaiviye
waiter	официа́нт (m)	afitsiant

5.4 Kinds of food	Разли́чные ви́ды еды́	Razlichniye vidy edy
beef	говя́дина (f)	govyadina
bread	хлеб (m)	khlep
butter	ма́сло (n)	masla
cake	пиро́г (m)	pirok
candy	конфе́та (f)	kanfyeta
cheese	сыр (m)	syr
chewing gum	жва́чка (f)	zhvachka
chicken	ку́рица (f)	kuritsa
chocolate	шокола́д (m)	shikalat
cream	крем (m)	kryem
egg	яйцо́ (n)	yaitso
fish	ры́ба (f)	ryba
fried eggs	яи́чница (f)	yaichnitsa
frozen	заморо́женный	zamarozhenniy

5.5 Fruit

garlic	чесно́к *(m)*	chisnok
ham	ветчина́ *(f)*	vichina
hard-boiled egg	яйцо́ вкруту́ю	yaitso vkrutuyu
ice cream	моро́женое *(n)*	marozhinaye
jam	пови́дло *(n)*	pavidla
lamb	бара́нина *(f)*	baranina
meat	мя́со *(n)*	myasa
nuts	оре́хи *(pl)*	aryekhi
oil *(cooking)*	расти́тельное ма́сло *(n)*	rastitel'naye masla
pepper	пе́рец *(m)*	pyerits
pork	свини́на *(f)*	svinina
potato	карто́шка *(f)*	kartoshka
salad	сала́т *(m)*	salat
salt	соль *(f)*	sol'
sandwich	бутербро́д *(m)*	buterbrot
soup	суп *(m)*	sup
sugar	са́хар *(m)*	sakhar
sweets	сла́дости *(pl)*	sladasti
toast	тост *(m)*	tost
torte	торт *(m)*	tort
vinegar	у́ксус *(m)*	uksus

5.5 Fruit	**Фру́кты**	**Frukty**
apple	я́блоко *(n)*	yablaka
apricot	абрико́с *(m)*	abrikos
banana	бана́н *(m)*	banan
grapes	виногра́д *(m)*	vinagrat
lemon	лимо́н *(m)*	limon
mandarin *(orange)*	мандари́н *(m)*	mandarin
mango	ма́нго *(n)*	manga
melon	ды́ня *(f)*	dynya
orange	апельси́н *(m)*	apil'sin

peach	пéрсик (*m*)	persik
pear	грýша (*f*)	grusha
pineapple	ананáс (*m*)	ananas
plum	слúва (*f*)	sliva
raspberry	малúна (*f*)	malina
strawberry	клубнúка (*f*)	klubnika
watermelon	арбýз (*m*)	arbuz

5.6 Vegetables   Óвощи   Ovoshchi

asparagus	спáржа (*f*)	sparzha
cabbage	капýста (*f*)	kapusta
carrots	моркóвь (*f*)	morkov'
celery	сельдерéй (*m*)	sildiryey
corn	кукурýза (*f*)	kukuruza
cucumber	огурéц (*m*)	aguryets
eggplant	баклажáн (*m*)	baklazhan
green peas	зелёный горóшек (*m*)	zilyoniy garoshik
lettuce	салáт (*m*)	salat
mushrooms	грибы́ (*pl*)	griby
onion	лук (*m*)	luk
potato	картóшка (*f*)	kartoshka
pumpkin	ты́ква (*f*)	tykva
spinach	шпинáт (*m*)	shpinat
tomato	помидóр (*m*)	pamidor
turnip	рéпа (*f*)	ryepa
vegetable dish	овощнóе блю́до (*n*)	avoshchnoye blyuda
vegetables	óвощи (*pl*)	ovashchi

5.7 Russian cuisine   Рýсская кýхня   Russkaya kukhnya

| black caviar with blinis | чёрная икрá (*f*) с блинáми | chyornaya ikra s blinami |
| borshch | борщ (*m*) | borshch |

5.8 Taste

cold appetizers	холо́дные заку́ски (pl)	khalodnye zakuski
cucumber salad	сала́т (m) из огурцо́в	salat iz agurtsof
fish soup	ры́бный суп (m)	ribniy sup
golubtsi (stuffed cabbage)	голубцы́ (pl)	golubtsy
goulash	гуля́ш (m)	gulyash
kulibyaka (cabbage bread)	кулебя́ка (f)	kulibyaka
meat salad	мясно́й сала́т (m)	misnoy salat
mushrooms	грибы́ (pl)	griby
pelmeni (ravioli)	пельме́ни (pl)	pil'myeni
pirogi with meat	пироги́ (pl) с мя́сом	piragi s myasam
pirogi with mushrooms	пироги́ с гриба́ми	piragi s gribami
pirogi with potatoes	пироги́ с карто́шкой	piragi s kartoshkoy
red caviar with blinis	кра́сная икра́ (f) с блина́ми	krasnaya ikra s blinami
shchi (fish soup)	щи (pl)	shchi
tomato juice	тома́тный сок (m)	tamatniy sok
tomato salad	сала́т из помидо́р	salat iz pamidor

5.8 Taste	Вкусовы́е ощуще́ния	Fkusaviye ashchushchyeniya
aromatic	арома́тный	aramatniy
bitter	го́рький	gor'kiy
delicious	вку́сный	fkusniy
dry	сухо́й	sukhoy
hot (boiling)	горя́чий	garyachiy
hot (spicy)	о́стрый	ostriy
oily	жи́рный	zhirniy
salty	солёный	salyoniy
smell, to	па́хнуть	pakhnut'
it smells good	хорошо́ па́хнуть	kharasho pakhnut'
sour	ки́слый	kisliy
strong	кре́пкий	krepkiy
sweet	сла́дкий	slatkiy
tasty	вку́сный	fkusniy

tender	мя́гкий	myakhkiy
tough	твёрдый	tvyordiy
weak *(of a drink)*	сла́бый	slabiy

5.9 Drinks   Напи́тки   Napitki

beer	пи́во *(n)*	piva
boiled water	кипячёная вода́ *(f)*	kipachyonaya vada
brandy	бре́нди *(n)*	brendi
Coca-Cola®	ко́ка-ко́ла *(f)*	koka-kola
cold drink	холо́дный напи́ток *(m)*	khalodniy napitak
drunk; tipsy	пья́ный	p'yaniy
fruit drink	фрукто́вый напи́ток *(m)*	fruktoviy napitak
hot tea	горя́чий чай *(m)*	garyachiy chay
ice	лёд *(m)*	lyot
iced tea	чай со льдом	chay so l'dom
lemonade	лимона́д *(m)*	limanat
make coffee, to	вари́ть ко́фе	varit' kofe
make tea, to	пригото́вить чай	prigatovit' chay
milk	молоко́ *(n)*	malako
mineral water	минера́льная вода́ *(f)*	miniral'naya vada
orange drink	апельси́новый напи́ток *(m)*	apil'sinaviy napitak
orange juice	апельси́новый сок *(m)*	apil'sinaviy sok
soda water	со́довая вода́ *(f)*	sodavaya vada
tea	чай *(m)*	chay
teapot	ча́йник *(m)*	chaynik
thirsty, to be	хоте́ть пить	khatyet' pit'
water	вода́ *(f)*	vada
whiskey	ви́ски *(n)*	viski
wine:	вино́ *(n)*:	vino:
red wine, white wine	кра́сное вино́, бе́лое вино́	krasnaye vino, byelaye vino

5.10 Cooking	Приготовле́ние пи́щи	Prigatavlyeniye pishchi
bake	печь	pyech'
cook a meal, to	пригото́вить еду́	prigatovit' yedu
cookbook	пова́ренная кни́га (f)	pavarennaya kniga
fry, to	жа́рить	zharit'
simmer, to	туши́ть	tushit'
steam, to	вари́ть на пару́	varit' na paru

5.11 Utensils	Прибо́ры	Pribory
bowl	ми́ска (f)	miska
cup	ча́шка (f)	chashka
fork	ви́лка (f)	vilka
glass	стака́н (m)	stakan
kettle	ча́йник (m)	chaynik
knife	нож (m)	nozh
microwave oven	ми́кроволно́вая печь (f)	mikravalnovaya pech
napkin	салфе́тка (f)	salfyetka
plate	таре́лка (f)	taryelka
sauce	блю́дце (n)	blyutse
spoon	ло́жка (f)	lozhka
stove	плита́ (f)	plita
teacup	ча́шка (f)	chashka
thermos	те́рмос (m)	tyermos

5.12 Smoking	Куре́ние	Kuryeniye
ashtray	пе́пельница (f)	pyepilnitsa
cigarettes	сигаре́ты (pl)	sigaryety
cigars	сига́ры (pl)	sigary
lighter	зажига́лка (f)	zazhigalka
lung cancer	рак (m) лёгких	rak lyokhkikh

matches	спи́чки *(pl)*	spichki
pipe	тру́бка *(f)*	trupka
smoke, to	кури́ть	kurit'
smoke	дым *(m)*	dym
tobacco	таба́к *(m)*	tabak

6. Apparel

6.1 Clothing	Одéжда	Adyezhda
buckle	пря́жка *(f)*	pryazhka
button	пу́говица *(f)*	pugavitsa
button, to	застёгивать	zastyogivat'
change (clothes), to	переодéть	piriadyet'
clean	чи́стый	chistiy
clothes	одéжда *(f)*	adyezhda
collar	воротни́к *(m)*	varatnik
dirty	гря́зный	gryazniy
dry cleaning	химчи́стка *(f)*	khimchistka
fashionable	мо́дный	modniy
fit, to	хорошо́ сидéть	kharasho sidyet'
long	дли́нный	dlinniy
loose	свобо́дный	svabodniy
made of …	сдéланный из … *(+ gen.)*	sdelanniy iz …
needle	игла́ *(f)*	igla
pocket	карма́н *(m)*	karman
scissors	но́жницы *(pl)*	nozhnitsy
sew, to	шить	shit'
sewing machine	швéйная маши́на *(f)*	shveynaya mashina
short	коро́ткий	karotkiy
size	размéр *(m)*	razmyer
sleeve	рука́в *(m)*	rukaf
tailor	портно́й *(m)*	partnoy
take off *(undress)*, to	раздева́ть	razdivat'
thread	ни́тка *(f)*	nitka
ugly	некраси́вый	nikrasiviy
uniform	фо́рма *(f)*	forma

| wash, to | стира́ть | stirat' |
| wear, to | носи́ть | nasit' |

6.2 Articles of clothing	**Ви́ды оде́жды**	**Vidy adyezhdy**
blouse	блу́зка (f)	bluzka
coat	пальто́ (n)	pal'to
dress	пла́тье (n)	plat'ye
evening gown	вече́рнее пла́тье (n)	vichyerniye plat'ye
jeans	джи́нсы (pl)	dzhinsy
pajamas	пижа́ма (f)	pizhama
pullover	пуло́вер (m)	pulovyer
raincoat	плащ (m)	plashch
shirt	руба́шка (f)	rubashka
shorts	шо́рты (pl)	shorty
skirt	ю́бка (f)	yupka
socks	носки́ (pl)	naski
stockings	чулки́ (pl)	chulki
suit	костю́м (m)	kastyum
sweat suit	спорти́вный костю́м (m)	spartivniy kastyum
trousers	брю́ки (pl)	bryuki
T-shirt	ма́йка (f)	mayka
underpants	трусы́ (pl)	trusy
undershirt	ма́йка (f)	mayka
underwear	бельё (n)	bel'yo

6.3 Shoes and accessories	**О́бувь и предме́ты туале́та**	**Obuf' i pridmyety tualyeta**
bag; handbag	су́мка (f)	sumka
boots	сапоги́ (pl)	sapagi
bracelet	брасле́т (m)	braslyet
cufflinks	за́понки (pl)	zapanki

earrings	се́рьги *(pl)*	syer'gi
glasses	очки́ *(pl)*	achki
gloves	перча́тки *(pl)*	pirchatki
handkerchief	носово́й плато́к *(m)*	nasavoy platok
jewelry	ювели́рные изде́лия *(pl)*	yuvilirnye izdyeliya
necklace	цепо́чка *(f)*	tsipochka
pair	па́ра *(f)*	para
ring	кольцо́ *(n)*	kal'tso
sandals	санда́лии *(pl)*	sandalii
scarf	шарф *(m)*	sharf
shoelaces	шнурки́ *(pl)*	shnurki
shoe polish	крем *(m)* для боти́нок	kryem dlya batinak
slippers	та́почки *(pl)*	tapachki
sunglasses	очки́ *(pl)* от со́лнца	achki at sontsa
tennis shoes	ке́ды *(pl)*	kyedy
tie	га́лстук *(m)*	galstuk
tie, to	завяза́ть *(perf.)*	zavyazat'
umbrella	зонт *(m)*	zont
wallet	бума́жник *(m)*	bumazhnik
watch	часы́ *(pl)*	chasy

6.4 Fabrics — Тка́ни — Tkani

6.4 Fabrics	Тка́ни	Tkani
cloth; fabric	ткань *(f)*	tkan'
cotton	хло́пок *(m)*	khlopak
fabric	материа́л *(m)*	matirial
lace	кру́жево *(n)*	kruzhivo
leather	ко́жа *(f)*	kozha
linen	лён *(m)*	lyon
nylon	нейло́н *(m)*	neilon
plastic	пла́стик *(m)*	plastik
rayon	виско́за *(f)*	viskoza
satin	сати́н *(m)*	satin

silk	шёлк *(m)*	shyolk
synthetic	синтéтика *(f)*	sintyetika
velvet	бáрхат *(m)*	barkhat
wool	шерсть *(f)*	sherst'

6.5 Colors	**Цветá**	**Tsveta**
beige	бéжевый	bezhiviy
black	чёрный	chyorniy
blue	голубóй	galuboy
brown	корúчневый	karichniviy
color	цвет *(m)*	tsvet
cream	крéмовый	kryemaviy
dark	тёмный	tyomniy
golden	золотóй	zalatoy
green	зелёный	zilyoniy
gray	сéрый	seriy
light	свéтлый	svetliy
orange	орáнжевый	aranzhiviy
pink	рóзовый	rozaviy
purple	фиолéтовый	fialyetaviy
red	крáсный	krasniy
silver	серéбряный	siryebriniy
white	бéлый	beliy
yellow	жёлтый	zhyoltiy

7. Shopping

7.1 Shops	Магази́ны	Magaziny
antiques; antique store	антиква́рные това́ры *(pl)*	antikvarniye tavary
bakery *(bread)*	бу́лочная *(f)*	bulachnaya
bank	банк *(m)*	bank
barber shop	парикма́херская *(f)*	parikmakherskaya
bookstore	кни́жный магази́н *(m)*	knizhniy magazin
butcher shop	мясно́й магази́н *(m)*	myasnoy magazin
department store	универса́льный магази́н *(m)*	universal'niy magazin
dry cleaner's	химчи́стка *(f)*	khimchistka
fish shop	ры́бный магази́н *(m)*	ribniy magazin
furniture store	ме́бельный магази́н *(m)*	myebil'niy magazin
grocery store	гастроно́м *(m)*	gastranom
hardware store	хозя́йственный магази́н *(m)*	khazyaistvenniy magazin
jewelry shop	ювели́рный магази́н *(m)*	yuvelirniy magazin
market	ры́нок *(m)*	rinak
pharmacy; drugstore	апте́ка *(f)*	aptyeka
photo shop	фототова́ры *(pl)*	fototavary
post office	по́чта *(f)*	pochta
shoe shop	о́бувь *(f)*	obuv'
souvenir shop	сувени́ры *(pl)*	suviniry
sporting goods store	спорти́вные това́ры *(pl)*	spartivniye tavary
stationery shop	канцеля́рские това́ры *(pl)*	kantsilyarskiye tavary
supermarket	суперма́ркет *(m)*	supermarkit
tailor's	ателье́ *(n)*	atel'ye
tobacco shop	таба́чная ла́вка *(f)*	tabachnaya lavka
toy store	игру́шки *(pl)*	igrushki
watches	часы́ *(pl)*	chisy

7.2 Shopping — Покупки — Pakupki

English	Русский	Transliteration
bargain, to	торговáться	targavat'sa
bill	счёт *(m)*	schyot
borrow, to	одáлживать	adalzhivat'
buy, to	покупáть	pakupat'
cashier	кассúр *(m)*	kassir
customer	покупáтель *(m)*	pakupatil'
deliver	доставлять	dastavlyat'
discount	скúдка *(f)*	skitka
exchange, to	менять	minyat'
fitting room	примéрочная *(f)*	primyerachnaya
let me pay	я заплачý	ya zaplachu
make a list, to	записáть *(perf.)*	zapisat'
order, to	заказáть *(perf.)*	zakazat'
pay, to	платúть	platit'
… percent off	… процéнтов скúдка *(f)*	… pratsyentaf skitka
purse	сýмка *(f)*	sumka
receipt	квитáнция *(f)*	kvitantsiya
receive, to	получáть	paluchat'
sale	распродáжа *(f)*	raspradazha
salesperson	продавéц *(m)*	pradavyets
sell, to	продавáть	pradavat'
shop; store	магазúн *(m)*	magazin
sold out	распрóдан	rasprodan
tip	чаевы́е *(pl)*	chayeviye
wrap, to	завёртывать	zavyortyvat'

7.3 Money — Дéньги — Dyen'gi

English	Русский	Transliteration
cash	налúчные дéньги *(pl)*	nalichniye dyen'gi
cent	цент *(m)*	tsyent
change	мéлочь *(f)*; сдáча *(f)*	myeloch; sdacha

7.3   Money

check	чек *(m)*	chyek
credit card	креди́тная ка́рточка *(f)*	kriditnaya kartochka
currency	валю́та *(f)*	valyuta
dollar	до́ллар *(m)*	dollar
exchange	обме́н *(m)*	abmyen
expensive	дорого́й	daragoy
how much is it?	ско́лько сто́ит?	skol'ka stoit?
money	де́ньги *(pl)*	dyen'gi
money exchange	обме́н де́нег	abmyen dyenig
paper money	бума́жные де́ньги *(pl)*	bumazhniye dyen'gi
price	цена́ *(f)*	tsina
ruble	рубль *(m)*	rubl'
Russian currency	ру́сская валю́та *(f)*	russkaya valyuta

8. Accommodations

apartment	кварти́ра (f)	kvartira
build, to	стро́ить	stroit'
building	зда́ние (n)	zdaniye
construction site	строи́тельная площа́дка (f)	straitel'naya plashchatka
floor	эта́ж (m)	etazh
garage	гара́ж (m)	garazh
house	дом (m)	dom
skyscraper	небоскрёб (m)	nibaskryop
story	эта́ж (m)	etazh

bathroom	ва́нная (f)	vannaya
bedroom	спа́льня (f)	spal'nya
corridor	коридо́р (m)	karidor
dining room	столо́вая (f)	stalovaya
double room (in a hotel)	но́мер (m) на двои́х	nomir na dvoikh
guest room	ко́мната (f) для госте́й	komnata dlya gostey
kitchen	ку́хня (f)	kukhnya
laundry	пра́чечная (f)	prachichnaya
living room	гости́ная (f)	gastinaya
pool room	билья́рдная (f)	bil'yardnaya
room (in a hotel)	но́мер (m)	nomir
single room (in a hotel)	но́мер (m) на одного́	nomir na adnovo
spare room	свобо́дная ко́мната (f)	svabodnaya komnata
study	кабине́т (m)	kabinet
toilet	туале́т (m)	tualyet

8.3 Furniture	Мебель	Myebil'
armchair	кре́сло (n)	kryesla
bed	крова́ть (f)	kravat'
bedspread	покрыва́ло (n)	pakryvala
blanket	одея́ло (n)	adiyala
bookcase	кни́жный шкаф (m)	knizhniy shkaf
chair	стул (m)	stul
closet	шкаф (m)	shkaf
coffee table	журна́льный стол (m)	zhurnal'niy stol
desk	пи́сьменный стол	pis'menniy stol
furniture	ме́бель (f)	myebil'
pillow	поду́шка (f)	padushka
shelves	по́лки (pl)	polki
sofa	софа́ (f); дива́н (m)	sofa; divan
stool	табуре́тка (f)	taburyetka
table	стол (m)	stol

8.4 Domestic life	Жизнь в до́ме	Zhizn' v domye
backyard	двор (m)	dvor
close	ря́дом	ryadom
close, to	закры́ть (perf.)	zakrit'
cook, to	вари́ть	varit'
decorate, to	обставля́ть	apstavlyat'
descend to; come down, to	спуска́ться	spuskat'sa
enter, to	входи́ть	vkhadit'
garden	сад (m)	sat
hang, to	ве́шать	vyesht'
home owner	владе́лец (m) до́ма	vladyelets doma
knock, to	стуча́ть	stuchat'
lawn	газо́н (m)	gazon
leave, to	оставля́ть; уходи́ть	astavlyat'; ukhadit'

live, to	жить	zhit'
lock the door, to	запира́ть дверь	zapirat' dvyer'
make the bed, to	убира́ть крова́ть	ubirat' kravat'
neighbors	сосе́ди *(pl)*	sasyedi
open, to	открыва́ть	atkryvat'
path	тропи́нка *(f)*	trapinka
rent	пла́та *(f)* за кварти́ру	plata za kvartiru
rent, to	сдава́ть	sdavat'
ring the doorbell, to	звони́ть в дверь	zvanit' v dvyer'
switch off, to	выключа́ть	vyklyuchat'
switch on, to	включа́ть	vklyuchat'
wash the car, to	мыть маши́ну	myt' mashinu
water the plants, to	полива́ть цветы́	palivat' tsvyety

8.5 Rooms and houses   Ко́мнаты и дома́   Komnaty i dama

back entrance	запасно́й вход *(m)*	zapasnoy vkhot
balcony	балко́н *(m)*	balkon
bathtub	ва́нна *(f)*	vanna
bookshelf	кни́жная по́лка *(f)*	knizhnaya polka
carpet	ковёр *(m)*	kavyor
ceiling	потоло́к *(m)*	patalok
curtain	за́навес *(m)*	zanavyes
cushion	поду́шка *(f)* для дива́на	padushka dlya divana
desk lamp	насто́льная ла́мпа *(f)*	nastol'naya lampa
door	дверь *(f)*	dvyer'
doorbell	дверно́й звоно́к *(m)*	dvernoy zvanok
downstairs	внизу́	vnizu
drawer	я́щик *(m)*	yashchik
elevator	лифт *(m)*	lift
entrance	вход *(m)*	vkhot
escalator	эскала́тор *(m)*	eskalatar
fence	забо́р *(m)*	zabor

front entrance	пара́дный вход *(m)*	paradniy vkhot
keys	ключи́ *(pl)*	klyuchi
light	свет *(m)*	svyet
lock	замо́к *(m)*	zamok
mirror	зе́ркало *(n)*	zyerkala
picture	карти́на *(f)*	kartina
plug	розе́тка *(f)*	razyetka
roof	кры́ша *(f)*	krysha
shower	душ *(m)*	dush
sink	ра́ковина *(f)*	rakovina
stairs	ле́стница *(f)*	lyesnitsa
switch	выключа́тель *(m)*	vyklyuchatel'
toilet	туале́т *(m)*	tualyet
toilet paper	туале́тная бума́га *(f)*	tualyetnaya bumaga
trash can	му́сорное ведро́ *(n)*	musarnaye vidro
upstairs	наверху́	naverkhu
vase	ва́за *(f)*	vaza
veranda	вера́нда *(f)*	veranda
wall	стена́ *(f)*	styena
window	окно́ *(n)*	akno

8.6 Heating and air conditioning	**Отопле́ние и кондициони́рованный во́здух**	**Otaplyeniye i kanditsianiravanniy vozdukh**
air conditioner	кондиционе́р *(m)*	kanditsianyer
central heating	центра́льное отопле́ние *(n)*	tsentral'naye ataplyeniye
cold	хо́лодно	kholadna
electric fan	электри́ческий вентиля́тор *(m)*	eliktrichiskiy vintilyatr
gas	газ *(m)*	gaz
heater	отопи́тельный прибо́р *(m)*	atapityel'niy pribor
hot	жа́рко; горячо́	zharka; garacho
light a fire, to	заже́чь *(perf.)* ого́нь	zazhyech agon'

put out a fire, to	погаси́ть *(perf.)* ого́нь	pagasit' agon'
radiator	радиа́тор *(m)*	radiatar
warm	тепло́	tiplo

8.7 Cleaning and washing   Убо́рка и сти́рка   Uborka i stirka

broom	метла́ *(f)*	mitla
bucket	ведро́ *(n)*	vidro
clean	чи́сто	chista
clean, to	убира́ть	ubirat'
dirty	гря́зно	gryazna
dishcloth	посу́дное полоте́нце *(n)*	pasudnaye palatyentse
dryer	су́шка *(f)*	sushka
dry in the sun, to	суши́ть на со́лнце	sushit' na sontse
dust	пыль *(f)*	pyl'
dust, to	вытира́ть пыль	vitirat' pyl'
hang out the laundry, to	ве́шать бельё	vyeshat' bil'yo
iron	утю́г *(m)*	utyuk
iron (clothes), to	гла́дить	gladit'
launder, to	стира́ть	stirat'
laundry detergent	стира́льный порошо́к *(m)*	stiral'niy parashok
put the garbage out, to	выноси́ть му́сор	vynasit' musar
scrubbing brush	щётка *(f)*	shchyotka
shampoo	шампу́нь *(m)*	shampun'
soap	мы́ло *(n)*	myla
sweep, to	подмета́ть	padmitat'
towel	полоте́нце *(n)*	palatyentse
vacuum cleaner	пылесо́с *(m)*	pylisos
wash, to	мыть; стира́ть	myt'; stirat'
wash dishes, to	мыть посу́ду	myt' pasudu
washing machine	стира́льная маши́на *(f)*	stiral'naya mashina
wipe, to	вытира́ть	vytirat'

8.8 Materials and tools	Материа́лы и инструме́нты	Matirialy i instrumyenty
blunt	тупо́й	tupoy
brick	кирпи́ч *(m)*	kirpich
cement	цеме́нт *(m)*	tsimyent
glass	стекло́ *(n)*	stiklo
hammer	молото́к *(m)*	malatok
hard	твёрдый	tvyordiy
iron	желе́зо *(n)*	zhilyeza
lawnmower	коси́лка *(f)* для травы́	kasilka dlya travy
nail	гвоздь *(m)*	gvozd'
scissors	но́жницы *(pl)*	nozhnitsy
screwdriver	отвёртка *(f)*	atvyortka
sharp	о́стрый	ostriy
soft	мя́гкий	myakhkiy
tool	инструме́нт *(m)*	instrumyent
wood	де́рево *(n)*	dyereva

8.9 Repairs	Ремо́нт, почи́нка	Rimont, pachinka
bend, to	сгиба́ть	sgibat'
break, to	лома́ть	lamat'
broken *(damaged)*	сло́манный	slomanniy
broken *(out of order)*	не рабо́тает	ni rabotayet
broken into pieces	разби́тый на кусо́чки	razbitiy na kusochki
completed	зако́нчен	zakonchin
cut, to	ре́зать	ryezat'
fasten, to	прикрепля́ть	prikreplyat'
fix, to	чини́ть	chinit'
glue	клей *(m)*	klyey
patch, to	ста́вить запла́ту	stavit' zaplatu
pull, to	тяну́ть	tanut'
push, to	толка́ть	talkat'

repair, to	чини́ть	chinit'
snap	застёжка *(f)*	zastyozhka
tear, to	разорва́ть *(perf.)*	razarvat'
tie, to	привя́зывать	privyazivat'
torn	разо́рванный	razorvanniy
unscrew, to	отвёртывать	atvyortyvat'
use, to	испо́льзовать	ispol'zavat'

9. Traveling

9.1 The World	Мир	Mir
country	страна́ (f)	strana
foreigner	иностра́нец (m), иностра́нка (f)	inastranyets, inastranka
local residents	ме́стные жи́тели (pl)	myestniye zhityeli
map	ка́рта (f)	karta
population	населе́ние (n)	nasilyeniye
world	мир (m)	mir

9.2 Countries and peoples	Стра́ны и лю́ди	Strany i lyudi
Africa	А́фрика (f)	Afrika
America	Аме́рика (f)	Amyerika
American	америка́нец (m), америка́нка (f)	amerikanyets, amerikanka
Argentina	Аргенти́на (f)	Argentina
Asia	А́зия (f)	Aziya
Australia	Австра́лия (f)	Avstraliya
Brazil	Брази́лия (f)	Braziliya
Canada	Кана́да (f)	Kanada
Canadian	кана́дец (m), кана́дка (f)	kanadyets, kanadka
Chile	Чи́ли (n)	Chili
China	Кита́й (m)	Kitay
city	го́род (m)	gorat
community	общи́на (f)	abshchina
countryside	се́льская ме́стность (f)	syel'skaya myestnost'
county	гра́фство (n)	grafstva
Cuba	Ку́ба (f)	Kuba
England	А́нглия (f)	Angliya

Englishman, Englishwoman	англича́нин *(m)*, англича́нка *(f)*	anglichanin, anglichanka
Europe	Евро́па *(f)*	Yevropa
France	Фра́нция *(f)*	Frantsiya
Germany	Герма́ния *(f)*	Germaniya
Greece	Гре́ция *(f)*	Gryetsiya
Hong Kong	Гонко́нг *(m)*	Gankonk
Indonesia	Индоне́зия *(f)*	Indanyeziya
Ireland	Ирла́ндия *(f)*	Irlandiya
Italy	Ита́лия *(f)*	Italiya
Japan	Япо́ния *(f)*	Yaponiya
Korea	Коре́я *(f)*	Koryeya
Latin America	Лати́нская Аме́рика *(f)*	Latinskaya Amyerika
Mexico	Ме́ксика *(f)*	Myeksika
New Zealand	Но́вая Зела́ндия *(f)*	Novaya Zilandiya
Philippines	Филиппи́ны *(pl)*	Filippiny
Poland	По́льша *(f)*	Pol'sha
province	прови́нция *(f)*, о́бласть *(f)*	pravintsiya, oblast'
region	райо́н *(m)*	rayon
Russia	Росси́я *(f)*	Rassiya
Russian	ру́сский *(m)*, ру́сская *(f)*	russkiy, russkaya
Scotland	Шотла́ндия *(f)*	Shatlandiya
Singapore	Сингапу́р *(m)*	Singapur
South Africa	Ю́жная А́фрика *(f)*	Yuzhnaya Afrika
Spain	Испа́ния *(f)*	Ispaniya
state	штат *(m)*	shtat
suburb	при́город *(m)*	prigarat
Tanzania	Танза́ния *(f)*	Tanzaniya
USA	США *(pl)*	SShA
village	дере́вня *(f)*	dyeryevnya
Zimbabwe	Зимба́бве *(n)*	Zimbabve

9.3 Roads and streets	Доро́ги и у́лицы	Darogi i ulitsy
bridge	мост *(m)*	most
corner	у́гол *(m)*	ugal
cross the street, to	переходи́ть у́лицу	pikhadit' ulitsu
footpath	доро́жка *(f)*	darozhka
freeway	шоссе́ *(n)*	shasse
intersection	перекрёсток *(m)*	pirikryostak
lane *(highway)*	полоса́ *(f)*, ли́ния *(f)*	palasa, liniya
number *(house)*	но́мер *(m)*	nomir
pedestrian	пешехо́д *(m)*	pishikhot
pedestrian crossing	перехо́д *(m)* для пешехо́дов	pirikhot dlya pishikhodof
road	доро́га *(f)*	daroga
street	у́лица *(f)*	ulitsa
traffic light	светофо́р *(m)*	svitafor
underpass	подзе́мный перехо́д *(m)*	padzyemniy pirikhot

9.4 Oceans and seas	Океа́ны и моря́	Akiany i marya
Antarctic Ocean	Антаркти́ческий океа́н *(m)*	Antarktichiskiy akian
Arctic Ocean	Се́верный Ледови́тый океа́н *(m)*	Syeverniy Lidavitiy akian
Atlantic Ocean	Атланти́ческий океа́н *(m)*	Atlantichiskiy akian
Baltic Sea	Балти́йское мо́ре *(n)*	Baltiyskaye morye
Black Sea	Чёрное мо́ре *(n)*	Chornaye morye
Caspian Sea	Каспи́йское мо́ре *(n)*	Kaspiyskaya morye
Indian Ocean	Инди́йский океа́н *(m)*	Indiyskiy akian
Mediterranean Sea	Средизе́мное мо́ре *(n)*	Sridizyemnaye morye
North Sea	Се́верное мо́ре *(n)*	Syevernaye morye
ocean	океа́н *(m)*	akian
Pacific Ocean	Ти́хий океа́н *(m)*	Tichiy akian
Red Sea	Кра́сное мо́ре *(n)*	Krasnaye morye

| sea | мо́ре *(n)* | morye |
| Yellow Sea | Жёлтое мо́ре *(n)* | Zhyoltaye morye |

9.5 Means of transport	Ви́ды тра́нспорта	Vidy transparta
accident	ава́рия *(f)*	avariya
airplane	самолёт *(m)*	samalyot
airport	аэропо́рт *(m)*	aeroport
bicycle	велосипе́д *(m)*	vilasipyed
boat	ло́дка *(f)*	lotka
break down, to	слома́ть(ся) *(perf.)*	slomat'(sa)
buckle up, to	пристёгивать(ся)	pristyogivat'(sya)
bus	авто́бус *(m)*	aftobus
car	маши́на *(f)*	mashina
gas station	запра́вочная ста́нция *(f)*	zapravachnaya stantsiya
motorcycle	мотоци́кл *(m)*	matatsikl
park, to	оставля́ть маши́ну	astavlyat' mashinu
ride, to	е́здить	yezdit'
seat belt	реме́нь *(m)*	rimyen'
ship	кора́бль *(m)*	karabl'
stop, to	остана́вливаться	astanavlivat'sya
stop (bus, trolley, etc.)	остано́вка *(f)*	ostanofka
streetcar	трамва́й *(m)*	tramvay
subway	метро́ *(n)*	mitro
taxi	такси́ *(n)*	taksi
train	по́езд *(m)*	poyezd
tram	трамва́й *(m)*	tramvay
trolley	тролле́йбус *(m)*	traleybus
underground	подзе́мный	padzyemniy
wharf	верфь *(f)*	vyerf'

9.6 Transport	Транспорт	Transport
car accident	автомоби́льная ава́рия (f)	aftamabil'naya avariya
careful; carefully	осторо́жно	astarozhna
danger	опа́сность (f)	apasnast'
drive, to	вести́ маши́ну	visti mashinu
driver	води́тель (m)	vaditil'
get off, to	выходи́ть	vykhadit'
get on, to	входи́ть	vkhadit'
pedestrian	пешехо́д (m)	pishikhot
safety	безопа́сность (f)	bezapasnost'
traffic	движе́ние (n)	dvizhyeniye

9.7 Travel	Путеше́ствия	Putishyestviya
arrive, to	прибыва́ть	pribyvat'
arrival	прибы́тие (n)	pribitiye
arrival time	вре́мя (n) прибы́тия	vryemye pribytiya
depart, to	отъезжа́ть	at"yezhat'
departure	отъе́зд (m)	at"yezd
departure time	вре́мя (n) отъе́зда	vryemye at"yezda
hotel	гости́ница (f)	gastinitsa
leave, to	уезжа́ть	uyezhat'
luggage	бага́ж (m)	bagazh
pack, to	упако́вывать	upakovyvat'
places of interest	достопримеча́тельности (pl)	dastaprimichatel'nasti
prepare, to	подгото́вить (perf.)	padgatovit'
reserve a room (in a hotel)	заказа́ть (perf.) ко́мнату (в гости́нице)	zakazat' komnatu (v gastinitse)
schedule	расписа́ние (n)	raspisaniye
see someone off, to	провожа́ть	pravazhat'
sightsee, to	смотре́ть достопримеча́тельности	smatryet' dastaprimichatyel'nasti
tour bus	тури́стский авто́бус (m)	turistkiy avtobus

tour group	туристская группа *(f)*	turiskaya grupa
tour guide	гид *(m)*	git
travel, to	путешествовать	putishyestvavat'
traveler	путешественник *(m)*	putishyestvinik
visit, to	посещать	pasishchat'

9.8 Places of interest	**Достопримечательности**	**Dastaprimichatel'nasti**
airport	аэропорт *(m)*	aeraport
art gallery	картинная галерея *(f)*	kartinnaya galiryeya
bank	банк *(m)*	bank
bookstore	книжный магазин *(m)*	knizhniy magazin
botanical garden	ботанический сад *(m)*	batanichiskiy sat
church	церковь *(f)*	zerkaf'
college	институт *(m)*	institut
concert hall	концертный зал *(m)*	kantsyertniy zal
dance hall	танцевальный зал *(m)*	tantsival'niy zal
department store	универсальный магазин *(m)*	universal'niy magazin
disco	дискотека *(f)*	diskatyeka
hospital	больница *(f)*	bol'nitsa
hotel	гостиница *(f)*	gastinitsa
library	библиотека *(f)*	bibliatyeka
movie theater	кинотеатр *(m)*	kinatiatr
museum	музей *(m)*	muzyey
office	кабинет *(m)*, бюро *(n)*	kabinyet, byuro
park	парк *(m)*	park
police station	милиция *(f)*	militsiya
post office	почта *(f)*	pochta
public telephone	телефон-автомат *(m)*	tilifon-avtamat
public toilets; restrooms	туалеты *(pl)*	tualyety
restaurant	ресторан *(m)*	ristaran
school	школа *(f)*	shkola
shop	магазин *(m)*	magazin

9.8   Places of interest

snackbar	закýсочная *(f)*	zakusochnaya
telephone booth	телефóнная бýдка *(f)*	tilifonnaya butka
theater	теáтр *(m)*	tiatr
university	университéт *(m)*	universityet
war memorial	пáмятник *(m)* жéртвам войны́	pamyatnik zhertvam voyny
zoo	зоопáрк *(m)*	zaapark

10. Politics and the Economy

10.1 Society	Общество	Obshistva
culture	культу́ра *(f)*	kul'tura
custom	обы́чай *(m)*	abychay
duty	обя́занность *(f)*	abyazannast'
hold a meeting, to	проводи́ть собра́ние	pravadit' sabraniye
meeting	собра́ние *(n)*	sabraniye
participate, to	принима́ть уча́стие	prinimat' uchastiye
responsibility	обя́занность *(f)*	abyazannast'
society	о́бщество *(n)*	opshistva
system	систе́ма *(f)*	sistyema
tradition	тради́ция *(f)*	traditsiya

10.2 Social problems and change	Социа́льные пробле́мы и измене́ния	Sotsial'niye prablyemy i izmyenyeniya
change	измене́ния *(pl)*	izmenyeniya
freedom	свобо́да *(f)*	svaboda
ideal	идеа́льный	idial'niy
poor	бе́дный	byedniy
population	населе́ние *(n)*	nasilyeniye
problem	пробле́ма *(f)*	prablyema
progress	прогре́сс *(m)*	pragress
progressive	прогресси́вный	pragressivniy
prohibit, to	запреща́ть	zaprishchat'
rich	бога́тый	bagatiy

10.3 Politics and government	Поли́тика и прави́тельство	Palitika i pravitel'stva
agree, to	соглаша́ться	saglashat'sa
capitalism	капитали́зм (m)	kapitalizm
chairman	председа́тель (m)	pridsidatel'
communism	коммуни́зм (m)	kammunizm
democracy	демокра́тия (f)	dimakratiya
Department of Education	Министе́рство (n) образова́ния	Ministyerstva abrazavaniya
Department of Foreign Affairs	Министе́рство (n) иностра́нных дел	Ministyerstva inastrannykh dyel
elect, to	выбира́ть	vybirat'
election(s)	вы́боры (pl)	vybary
freedom	свобо́да (f)	svaboda
government	прави́тельство (n)	pravitel'stva
king	коро́ль (m)	karol'
liberalism	либерали́зм (m)	libiralizm
minister	свяще́нник (m)	svishchyennik
opinion	мне́ние (n)	mnyeniye
oppose, to	возража́ть	vazrazhat'
parliament	парла́мент (m)	parlament
political party	полити́ческая па́ртия (f)	palitichiskaya partiya
politician	поли́тик (m)	palitik
politics	поли́тика (f)	palitika
president	президе́нт (m)	prizidyent
prime minister	премье́р-мини́стр (m)	prim'yer ministr
represent, to	представля́ть	pridstavlyat'
representative	представи́тель (m)	pridstavitil'
socialism	социали́зм (m)	satsializm

10.4 Law	Зако́н	Zakon
decide, to	реша́ть	rishat'

decision	реше́ние (n)	rishyeniye
defend, to	защища́ть	zashishchat'
event	собы́тие (n)	sabytiye
guilty	вино́вный	vinovniy
incident	слу́чай (m)	sluchay
innocent	невино́вный	nivinovniy
judge	судья́ (m)	sud'ya
law	зако́н (m)	zakon
lawyer	юри́ст (m)	yurist
prosecute, to	обвиня́ть	obvinyat'
trial	проце́сс (m)	protsess
valid	действи́тельный	deystvitel'niy

10.5 Police and the social order — Мили́ция и обще́ственный поря́док — Militsiya i abshchestvenniy paryadak

arrest, to	аресто́вывать	aristovyvat'
escape	побе́г (m)	pabyek
jail	тюрьма́ (f)	tyur'ma
kill, to	убива́ть	ubivat'
police	мили́ция (f), поли́ция (f)	militsiya, politsiya
police car	полице́йская маши́на (f)	politseyskaya mashina
police officer	полице́йский (m)	palitsyeyskiy
police station	отделе́ние (n) поли́ции	atdyelyenie politsii
prisoner	заключённый (m)	zaklyuchyonniy
release, to	отпуска́ть	atpuskat'
social order	обще́ственный поря́док (m)	abshchestvenniy paryadak
steal, to	красть	krast'
thief	вор (m)	vor

10.6 The Economy — Эконо́мика — Ekanomika

| bankruptcy | банкро́тство (n) | bankrotstvo |

budget	бюджéт *(m)*	byudzhyet
capital	капитáл *(m)*	kapital
competition	соревновáние *(n)*	sarivnavaniye
develop, to	развивáть	razvivat'
loss	потéря *(f)*	patyerya
plan	план *(m)*	plan
profit	прúбыль *(f)*	pribyl'
spend, to	трáтить	tratit'

10.7 Work	**Рабóта**	**Rabota**
busy	зáнятый	zanyatiy
desk	рабóчий стол *(m)*	rabochiy stol
experience	óпыт *(m)*	opyt
experienced	óпытный	opytniy
hardworking	трудолюбúвый	trudalyubiviy
job	рабóта *(f)*	rabota
lazy	ленúвый	liniviy
look for work, to	искáть рабóту	iskat' rabotu
occupation	заня́тие *(n)*, профéссия *(f)*	zanyatiye, prafessiya
office	кабинéт *(m)*, бюрó *(n)*	kabinyet, byuro
work	рабóта *(f)*	rabota

10.8 Agriculture	**Земледéлие**	**Zimledyeliye**
agriculture	земледéлие *(n)*	zimledyeliye
farm	фéрма *(f)*	fyerma
field	пóле *(n)*	polye
fruit(s)	фрýкты *(pl)*	frukty
grow, to	вырáщивать	vyrashchivat'
land	земля́ *(f)*	zyemlya
milk	молокó *(n)*	malako
milk, to	дойть	dait'
plant, to	сажáть	sazhat'

produce	продýкты *(pl)*	pradukty
produce, to	производи́ть	praizvadit'
vegetables	óвощи *(pl)*	ovashchi
water, to	поливáть	palivat'

10.9 Industry — Промы́шленность — Pramyshlinnost

demonstration	демонстрáция *(f)*	dimanstratsiya
factory	фáбрика *(f)*, завóд *(m)*	fabrika, zavot
industry	промы́шленность *(f)*	promyshlinnost'
machine	маши́на *(f)*	mashina
mine	шáхта *(f)*	shakhta
mining industry	ýгольная промы́шленность *(f)*	ugal'naya pramyshlinnost'
skill	умéние *(n)*, óпыт *(m)*	umyeniye, opyt
trade union	профсоюзы *(pl)*	profsayuzy

10.10 Trade and commerce — Торгóвля и коммéрция — Targovlya i kammyertsiya

bank	банк *(m)*	bank
borrow, to	одолжи́ть *(perf.)*	adalzhit'
commerce	коммéрция *(f)*	kammyertsiya
employee	слýжащий	sluzhashchiy
export, to	экспорти́ровать	ekspartiravat'
foreign trade	междунарóдная торгóвля *(f)*	mezhdunarodnaya targovlya
import, to	импорти́ровать	impartiravat'
lend, to	давáть взаймы́	davat' vzaimy
manager	начáльник *(m)*	nachal'nik
person in charge	отвéтственный	atvyetstvenniy
trade	торгóвля *(f)*	targovlya

10.11 International relations	Междунаро́дные отноше́ния	Mezhdunarodniye atnashyeniya
ambassador	посо́л *(m)*	pasol
army	а́рмия *(f)*	armiya
consulate	ко́нсульство *(n)*	konsul'stva
diplomacy	диплома́тия *(f)*	diplamatiya
diplomat	диплома́т *(m)*	diplamat
embassy	посо́льство *(n)*	pasol'stva
international	междунаро́дный	mezhdunarodniy
military	вое́нный	vayenniy
navy	вое́нно-морски́е си́лы *(pl)*	vayenna-marskiye sily
peace	мир *(m)*	mir
United Nations	Организа́ция *(f)* Объединённых На́ций	Arganizatsiya Ab"yedinyonykh Natsiy
war	война́ *(f)*	vayna

11. Culture and the Arts

11.1 Culture	Культу́ра	Kul'tura
cultural	культу́рный	kul'turniy
culture	культу́ра (f)	kul'tura
custom	обы́чай (m)	abychai
famous	изве́стный	izvyestniy
tradition	тради́ция (f)	traditsiya
traditional	традицио́нный	traditsionniy

11.2 Books	Кни́ги	Knigi
American literature	америка́нская литерату́ра (f)	amyerikanskaya litiratura
book	кни́га (f)	kniga
bookstore	кни́жный магази́н (m)	knizhniy magazin
colon	двоето́чие (n)	dvayetochiye
comma	запята́я (f)	zapitaya
dash	тире́ (n)	tire
dictionary	слова́рь (m)	slavar'
English-Russian dictionary	а́нгло-ру́сский слова́рь (n)	anglo-russkiy slavar'
essay	сочине́ние (n)	sachinyeniye
exclamation point	восклица́тельный знак (m)	vasklitsatil'niy znak
library	библиоте́ка (f)	bibliatyeka
library book	библиоте́чная кни́га (f)	bibliatyechnaya kniga
line	строка́ (f)	straka
literature	литерату́ра (f)	litiratura
modern literature	совреме́нная литерату́ра (f)	savremyennaya lityeratura
novel	рома́н (m)	raman
page	страни́ца (f)	stranitsa
paragraph	пара́граф (m)	paragraf

phrase	фра́за (f)	fraza
poem	стихотворе́ние (n)	stikhatvaryeniye
poetry	поэ́зия (f)	paeziya
punctuation	пунктуа́ция (f)	punktuatsiya
question mark	вопроси́тельный знак (m)	vaprasitil'niy znak
semicolon	то́чка (f) с запято́й	tochka s zapitoy
sentence	предложе́ние (n)	pridlazhyeniye
writer	писа́тель (m)	pisatil'

11.3 The Press	**Пре́сса**	**Pryessa**
article	статья́ (f)	stat'ya
comics	коми́ческие расска́зы (pl)	komichiskiye rasskazy
daily paper	ежедне́вная газе́та (f)	ezhidnyevnaya gazyeta
editor	реда́ктор (m)	ridaktar
evening paper	вече́рняя газе́та (f)	vichyernyaya gazyeta
investigate, to	рассле́довать	raslyedavat'
magazine	журна́л (m)	zhurnal
morning paper	у́тренняя газе́та (f)	utrinnyaya gazyeta
news	но́вости (pl)	novasti
newspaper	газе́та (f)	gazyeta
pictorial	иллюстри́рованный	illyustriravanniy
print, to	печа́тать	pichatat'
reporter	репортёр (m)	ripartyor

11.4 Television and radio	**Телеви́дение и ра́дио**	**Tilividiniye i radio**
broadcast	переда́ча (f)	piridacha
broadcast, to	передава́ть	piridavat'
cassette tape	кассе́та (f)	kassyeta
CD (compact disc)	компа́кт-диск (m)	kampakt-disk
color television	цветно́й телеви́зор (m)	tsvyetnoy tilivizar
give a talk/lecture, to	чита́ть ле́кцию	chitat' lyektsiyu

make a presentation, to	де́лать докла́д	dyelat' daklat
news	но́вости (pl)	novasti
presentation	докла́д (m), презента́ция (f)	daklat; prizintatsiya
program	програ́мма (f)	pragramma
radio	ра́дио (n)	radio
record, to	запи́сывать на магнитофо́н	zapisyvat' na magnitafon
record player	про́йгрыватель (m)	praigryvatel'
station (radio)	програ́мма (f)	pragramma
stereo	сте́рео (n)	styerio
switch off, to	выключа́ть	vyklyuchat'
switch on, to	включа́ть	vklyuchat'
tape	плёнка (f)	plyonka
tape recorder	магнитофо́н (m)	magnitafon
television (set)	телеви́зор (m)	tilivizar
tune in, to	настра́ивать	nastraivat'
TV channel	телевизио́нный кана́л (m)	tilivizionniy kanal
video recorder	ви́деомагнитофо́н (m)	vidiomagnitafon
videotape	ви́деокассе́та (f)	vidiokassyeta

11.5 Science   Нау́ка   Nauka

data	да́нные (pl)	danniye
discover, to	открыва́ть	atkrivat'
discovery	откры́тие (n)	otkritiye
examine, to	иссле́довать	isslyedavat'
experiment	экспериме́нт (m)	ekspirimyent
invent, to	изобрета́ть	izabritat'
invention	изобрете́ние (n)	izabrityeniye
laboratory	лаборато́рия (f)	labaratoriya
method	ме́тод (m)	myetot
science	нау́ка (f)	nauka
scientific	нау́чный	nauchniy
scientist	учёный (m)	uchyoniy

11.6 Religion	Рели́гия	Riligiay
attend church, to	ходи́ть в це́рковь	khadit' f tserkaf'
believe, to	ве́рить	vyerit'
believer	ве́рующий	verayushchiy
Bible	Би́блия *(f)*	Bibliya
Buddhism	будди́зм *(m)*	buddizm
Christianity	христиа́нство *(n)*	khristianstva
Christmas	Рождество́ *(n)*	Razhdistvo
Christmas tree	рожде́ственская ёлка *(f)*	razhdyestvinskaya yolka
church	це́рковь *(f)*	tserkaf'
Easter	Па́сха *(f)*	Paskha
festival	фестива́ль *(m)*	festival'
God	Бог *(m)*	Bok
heaven	рай *(m)*	ray
hell	ад *(m)*	at
Judaism	иудаи́зм *(m)*	iudaizm
monk	мона́х *(m)*	manakh
nun	мона́хиня *(f)*	manakhinya
pray, to	моли́ться	malit'sa
priest	свяще́нник *(m)*	svashchyenik
religion	рели́гия *(f)*	riligiya
Roman Catholic	католи́ческая це́рковь *(f)*	katalichiskaya tserkaf'
Russian Orthodox	правосла́вная це́рковь *(f)*	pravaslavnaya tserkaf'
synagogue	синаго́га *(f)*	sinagoga

11.7 The Arts	Иску́сство	Iskusstva
art	иску́сство *(n)*	iskustva
art gallery	карти́нная галере́я *(f)*	kartinnaya galiryeya
artist	челове́к *(m)* иску́сства	chilavyek iskusstva
canvas	полотно́ *(n)*	palatno
exhibition	вы́ставка *(f)*	vistavka

painter	худо́жник (m)	khudozhnik
painting	карти́на (f)	kartina
sculptor	ску́льптор (m)	skul'ptar
sculpture	скульпту́ра (f)	skul'ptura

11.8 Music — Му́зыка — Muzyka

classical music	класси́ческая му́зыка (f)	klassichiskaya muzyka
concert	конце́рт (m)	kantsert
concert hall	конце́ртный зал (m)	kantsertniy zal
conductor	дирижёр (m)	dirizhor
disco	дискоте́ка (f)	diskatyeka
electronic music	электро́нная му́зыка (f)	eliktronnaya muzyka
folk music	наро́дная му́зыка (f)	narodnaya muzyka
guitar	гита́ра (f)	gitara
music	му́зыка (f)	muzyka
music fan	люби́тель (m) му́зыки	lyubitel' muzyki
music lesson	уро́к (m) му́зыки	urok muzyki
musical instrument	музыка́льный инструме́нт (m)	muzykal'niy instrumyent
musician	музыка́нт (m)	muzykant
opera	о́пера (f)	opyera
orchestra	орке́стр (m)	arkyestr
piano	пиани́но (n)	pianino
play (a musical instrument), to	игра́ть	igrat'
pop music	поп-му́зыка (f)	pop-muzyka
practice, to	практикова́ться	praktikavat'sa
rock music	рок-му́зыка (f)	rok muzyka
sing, to	петь	pyet'
singer	певе́ц (m), певи́ца (f)	pivyets, pivitsa
song	пе́сня (f)	pyesnya
violin	скри́пка (f)	skripka

11.9 Film and drama	Кино́ и дра́ма	Kino i drama
actor	актёр (m)	aktyor
actress	актри́са (f)	aktrisa
comedy	коме́дия (f)	kamyediya
director	дире́ктор (m)	diryektar
documentary	документа́льный фильм (m)	dakumintal'niy fil'm
drama	дра́ма (f)	drama
horror movie	фильм (m) у́жасов	fil'm uzhasov
movie, film	кино́ (n), фильм (m)	kino, fil'm
movie star	кинозвезда́ (f)	kinozvezda
movie theater	кинотеа́тр (m)	kinoteatr
play	пье́са (f), спекта́кль (m)	p'yesa, spektakl'
play, to; act, to	игра́ть	igrat'
science film	нау́чный фильм (m)	nauchniy fil'm
tragedy	траге́дия (f)	tragyediya

12. Education

12.1 Education	Образова́ние	Obrazavaniye
attend school, to	учи́ться в шко́ле	uchit'sa f shkolye
begin, to	начина́ть	nachinat'
education	образова́ние (n)	obrazavaniye
education system	систе́ма (f) образова́ния	sistyema abrazavaniya
exam	экза́мен (m)	ekzamin
graduate, to	ока́нчивать шко́лу	akanchivat' shkolu
graduation	оконча́ние (n) шко́лы	akanchaniye shkoly
holidays	пра́здники (pl)	prazniki
learn, to	учи́ть	uchit'
learning process	уче́бный проце́сс (m)	uchebniy pratses
scholarship	стипе́ндия (f)	stipyendiya
study abroad, to	учи́ться за грани́цей	uchit'sa za granitsey
summer vacation	ле́тние кани́кулы (pl)	lyetniye kanikuly
test	контро́льная рабо́та (f)	kantrol'naya rabota
vacation	кани́кулы (pl)	kanikuly
winter vacation	зи́мние кани́кулы (pl)	zimniye kanikuly

12.2 School	Шко́ла	Shkola
boarding school	шко́ла-интерна́т (f)	shkola-internat
college	колле́дж (m)	kalyedzh
elementary school	нача́льная шко́ла (f)	nachal'naya shkola
institute	институ́т (m)	institut
kindergarten	де́тский сад (m)	dyetskiy sat
school	шко́ла (f)	shkola
study by correspondence	зао́чное обуче́ние (n)	zaochnaye abuchyeniye
technical school	техни́ческая шко́ла (f)	tikhnichiskaya shkola
university	университе́т (m)	universityet

12.3 Teacher and student	Учи́тель и учени́к	Uchitil' i uchinik
assistant principal	за́вуч *(m)*	zavuch
elementary school student	шко́льник, учени́к *(m)*	shkol'nik, uchinik
headmaster	дире́ктор *(m)* ча́стной шко́лы	diryektar chastnoy shkoly
high school student	шко́льник, учени́к *(m)*	shkol'nik, uchinik
lecturer	ле́ктор *(m)*	lyektar
president *(university)*	ре́ктор *(m)* университе́та	ryektar universityeta
principal	дире́ктор *(m)* шко́лы	diryektar shkoly
professor	профе́ссор *(m)*	prafyessar
pupil	учени́к *(m)*	uchinik
student *(university)*	студе́нт *(m)*, студе́нтка *(f)*	studyent, studyentka
teacher	учи́тель *(m)*	uchitel'

12.4 Years of study	Го́ды учёбы	Gody uchyoby
elementary school	нача́льная шко́ла *(f)*	nachal'naya shkola
fifth year	пя́тый год *(m)*	pyatiy got
first year	пе́рвый год *(m)*	pyerviy got
fourth year	четвёртый год *(m)*	chitvyortiy got
high school first year	пе́рвый год *(m)* в шко́ле	perviy got v shkole
second year	второ́й год *(m)*	ftoroy got
sixth year	шесто́й год *(m)*	shistoy got
third year	тре́тий год *(m)*	tretiy got
university first year	пе́рвый год *(m)* университе́та	pyerviy got universityeta

12.5 Subjects	Предме́ты	Pridmyety
accounting	бухга́лтерский учёт *(m)*	bukhgalterskiy uchyot
algebra	а́лгебра *(f)*	algebra
American literature	америка́нская литерату́ра *(f)*	amyerikanskaya litiratura
art	рисова́ние *(n)*; иску́сство *(n)*	risovaniye; iskusstva

biology	биоло́гия (f)	bialogiya
chemistry	хи́мия (f)	khimiya
drafting	черче́ние (n)	chirchyeniye
economics	эконо́мика (f)	ekanomika
English (language)	англи́йский язы́к (m)	anglyskiy yezyk
foreign language	иностра́нный язы́к (m)	inastranniy yezyk
geography	геогра́фия (f)	giagrafiya
geometry	геоме́трия (f)	giamyetriya
gymnastics	гимна́стика (f)	gimnastika
history	исто́рия (f)	istoriya
how many subjects?	ско́лько предме́тов?	skol'ka pridmyetof?
literature	литерату́ра (f)	litiratura
mathematics	матема́тика (f)	matimatika
philosophy	филосо́фия (f)	filasofiya
physics	фи́зика (f)	fizika
politics	поли́тика (f)	palitika
religion	рели́гия (f)	riligiya
Russian grammar	ру́сская грамма́тика (f)	russkaya grammatika
Russian (language)	ру́сский язы́к (m)	russkiy yezyk
Russian literature	ру́сская литерату́ра (f)	russkaya litiratura
social science	обще́ственные нау́ки (pl)	abshchestvyenniye nauki
subject	предме́т (m)	pridmyet
which subject?	како́й предме́т?	kakoy pridmyet?

12.6 School day   Шко́льный день   Shkol'niy dyen'

assembly	собра́ние (n)	sabraniye
attendance	посеща́емость (f)	pasishchaimast'
attention	внима́ние (n)	vnimaniye
blackboard	доска́ (f)	daska
break	переме́на (f)	pirimyena
chalk	мел (m)	myel
classroom	кла́сс (m)	klass

12.7 Study

composition	сочине́ние *(n)*	sachinyeniye
copy	ко́пия *(f)*	kopiya
copy, to	спи́сывать	spisyvat'
detention	наказа́ние *(n)*	nakazaniye
dictation	дикта́нт *(m)*	diktant
end of school day	коне́ц *(m)* шко́льного дня	kanyets shkol'nava dnya
essay	сочине́ние *(n)*, расска́з *(m)*	sachinyeniye, rasskaz
extracurricular activities	дополни́тельные заня́тия *(pl)*	dapalnityel'niye zanyatiya
finish class, to	зако́нчить *(perf.)* уро́к	zakonchit' urok
homework	дома́шняя рабо́та *(f)*	damashnyaya rabota
journal; assignment book	дневни́к *(m)*	dnevnik
lesson	уро́к *(m)*	urok
make a copy, to	сде́лать *(perf.)* ко́пию	sdyelat' kopiyu
notebook	тетра́дь *(f)*	tetrat'
playground	игрова́я площа́дка *(f)*	igravaya plashchatka
schedule	расписа́ние *(n)*	raspisaniye
textbook	уче́бник *(m)*	uchebnik

12.7 Study	Учёба	Uchyoba
drill, to	зубри́ть	zubrit'
forget, to	забыва́ть	zabyvat'
know, to	знать	znat'
knowledge	зна́ние *(n)*	znaniye
learn, to	учи́ть	uchit'
master, to	усоверше́нствоваться *(perf.)*	usavirshyenstvavat'sya
memorize, to	запомина́ть	zapaminat'
mistake	оши́бка *(f)*	ashipka
pay attention, to	уделя́ть внима́ние	udilyat' vnimaniye
read, to	чита́ть	chitat'
research	иссле́дование *(n)*	isslyedovaniye
research, to	иссле́довать	isslyedavat'

review	повторе́ние *(n)*	paftaryeniye
review, to	повторя́ть	paftaryat'
right; correct	пра́вильный, ве́рный	pravil'niy, vyerniy
study *(a subject)*, to	учи́ть *(предме́т)*	uchit' *(predmyet)*
write, to	писа́ть	pisat'
wrong; incorrect	непра́вильный, неве́рный	nepravil'niy, nivyerniy

12.8 Exam Экза́мен Ekzamyen

answer, to	отвеча́ть	atvichat'
ask, to	спра́шивать	sprashivat'
do well *(on an exam)*, to	хорошо́ сдать *(perf.)* экза́мен	kharasho sdat' ekzamin
entrance examination	вступи́тельный экза́мен *(m)*	vstupitel'niy ekzamin
exam	экза́мен *(m)*	ekzamin
examine, to	экзаменова́ть	ekzaminavat'
fail an exam, to	не сдать *(perf.)* экза́мен	ni sdat' ekzamin
pass an exam, to	сдать *(perf.)* экза́мен	sdat' ekzamin
question	вопро́с *(m)*	vapros
result	результа́т *(m)*	risul'tat
test	контро́льная рабо́та *(f)*	kantrol'naya rabota
topic	те́ма *(f)*	tyema

13. Communication

13.1 Language	Язы́к	Yezyk
alphabet	алфави́т *(m)*	alfavit
dialect	диале́кт *(m)*	dialyekt
English (language)	англи́йский язы́к *(m)*	angliyskiy yezyk
expression	выраже́ние *(n)*	vyrazheniye
foreign language	иностра́нный язы́к *(m)*	inastranniy eyzyk
grammar	грамма́тика *(f)*	grammatika
language	язы́к *(m)*	yezyk
letter	бу́ква *(f)*	bukva
meaning	значе́ние *(n)*	znachyeniye
phrase	фра́за *(f)*	fraza
pronunciation	произноше́ние *(n)*	praiznasheniye
sound	звук *(m)*	zvuk
speech	речь *(f)*	ryech
stress	ударе́ние *(n)*	udaryeniye
word	сло́во *(n)*	slova

13.2 Speaking	У́стная речь	Ustnaya ryech'
answer	отве́т *(m)*	atvyet
answer, to	отвеча́ть	atvyechat'
ask, to	спра́шивать	sprashivat'
chat, to	болта́ть	baltat'
conversation	разгово́р *(m)*	razgavor
explain, to	объясня́ть	ab"yesnyat'
explanation	объясне́ние *(n)*	ab"yesnyeniye
hear, to	слы́шать	slyshat'
inform, to	информи́ровать	informirovat'
listen, to	слу́шать	slushat'

loud voice	гро́мкий го́лос *(m)*	gromkiy golas
make a mistake, to	де́лать оши́бку	dyelat' ashipku
make a speech, to	произноси́ть речь	praiznasit' ryech'
request	про́сьба *(f)*	pros'ba
say, to	сказа́ть *(perf.)*	skazat'
soft voice	ти́хий го́лос *(m)*	tikhiy golas
sound	звук *(m)*	zvuk
speak, to	говори́ть	gavarit'
tell, to	расска́зывать	rasskazyvat'
tell a story, to	расска́зывать ска́зки	rasskazyvat' skazki

13.3 Courtesy expressions	Выраже́ния ве́жливости	Vyrazhyeniya vezhlivasti
all right; good	хорошо́	kharasho
fine	прекра́сно	prikrasna
no	нет	nyet
please	пожа́луйста	pazhalsta
thank you	спаси́бо	spasiba
wonderful	прекра́сный	prikrasniy
yes	да	da

13.4 Reading and writing	Чте́ние и письмо́	Chtyeniye i Pis'mo
read, to	чита́ть	chitat'
read aloud, to	чита́ть вслух	chitat' vslukh
read silently, to	чита́ть про себя́	chitat' pro sebya
take notes, to	конспекти́ровать	kanspiktirovat'
write, to	писа́ть	pisat'
write a letter, to	писа́ть письмо́	pisat' pis'mo

13.5 Stationery	Канцеля́рские това́ры	Kantsilyarskiye tavary
ballpoint pen	ша́риковая ру́чка (f)	sharikavaya ruchka
brush	ки́сточка (f)	kistachka
envelope	конве́рт (m)	kanvyert
eraser	ла́стик (m)	lastik
ink	черни́ла (pl)	chirnila
letter paper	бума́га (f) для письма́	bumaga dlya pis'ma
paper	бума́га (f)	bumaga
pen	ру́чка (f)	ruchka
pencil	каранда́ш (m)	karandash
pencil case	пена́л (m)	penal
pencil sharpener	точи́лка (f)	tochilka
ruler	лине́йка (f)	linyeika
typewriter	пи́шущая маши́нка (f)	pishushchaya mashinka

13.6 Mail	По́чта	Pochta
address	а́дрес (m)	adres
airmail	авиапо́чта (f)	aviapochta
contact, to	контакти́ровать	kantaktiravat'
inform, to	информи́ровать	infarmiravat'
letter	письмо́ (n)	pis'mo
mail, to	отправля́ть по по́чте	atpravlyat' pa pochte
mailbox	почто́вый я́щик (m)	pachtoviy yashchik
mailman	почтальо́н (m)	pachtal'yon
parcel	посы́лка (f)	pasylka
packet	паке́т (m), свёрток (m)	pakyet, svyortak
postcard	почто́вая откры́тка (f)	pachtovaya atkrytka
post office	почто́вое отделе́ние (n)	pachtovaye atdelyeniye
post office box	абонеме́нтный я́щик (m)	abanimyentniy yashchik
postage stamp	почто́вая ма́рка (f)	pachtovaya marka
send, to	посыла́ть	pasylat'

stamp	ма́рка *(f)*	marka
stamp collection	колле́кция *(f)* ма́рок	kallyektsiya marak
weigh, to	взве́шивать	vzvyeshivat'
wrap, to	завора́чивать	zavarachivat'

13.7 Telephone and telegrams	**Телефо́н и телегра́мма**	**Tilifon i tiligramma**
answer, to	отвеча́ть	atvichat'
call	звоно́к	zvanok
call, to	звони́ть	zvanit'
cut off, to	обрыва́ть	abryvat'
fax	телефа́кс *(m)*	tilifaks
hello	алё, алло́	alyo, allo
international call	междунаро́дный разгово́р *(m)*	mizhdunarodniy razgavor
long distance call	междугоро́дный разгово́р *(m)*	mizhdugarodniy razgavor
public telephone	телефо́н-автома́т *(m)*	tilifon-aftamat
send a telegram, to	посыла́ть телегра́мму	pasylat' tiligrammu
telegram	телегра́мма *(f)*	tiligramma
telephone	телефо́н *(m)*	tilifon
telephone, to	звони́ть по телефо́ну	zvanit' pa tilifonu
telephone directory (book)	телефо́нная кни́га *(f)*	tilifonnaya kniga
telephone number	но́мер *(m)* телефо́на	nomir tilifona

14. Recreation and Sports

14.1 Friendship	Дру́жба	Druzhba
boyfriend	друг (m)	druk
classmate	однокла́ссник (m)	adnaklassnik
colleague	колле́га (m, f)	kalyega
friend	друг (m)	druk
girlfriend	подру́га (f)	padruga
help, to	помога́ть	pamagat'
helper	помо́щник (m)	pamoshnik
invite, to	приглаша́ть	priglashat'
invitation	приглаше́ние (n)	priglashyeniye
make friends, to	подружи́ться (perf.)	padruzhit'sa
part, to	расстава́ться	rasstavat'sa
pen pals	друзья́ (pl) по перепи́ске	druz'ya pa piripiski
together with	вме́сте с (+ inst.)	vmyeste s

14.2 Parties	Ве́чер, вечери́нка	Vyecher, vyechirinka
accompany, to	сопровожда́ть	sapravazhdat'
arrange, to	организо́вывать	arganizovyvat'
dance, to	танцева́ть	tanzivat'
date	свида́ние (n)	svidaniye
dinner party	зва́ный обе́д (m)	zvaniy abyet
enjoy, to	получа́ть удово́льствие	poluchat' udavol'stviye
greet, to	приве́тствовать	privyetstvavat'
guest	гость (m)	gost'
host, to	принима́ть	prinimat'
introduce, to	представля́ть	pridstavlyat'
may I introduce ...	разреши́те предста́вить ...	razrishitye pridstavit' ...

meet, to	встре́тить (*perf.*)	vstryetit'
play cards, to	игра́ть в ка́рты	igrat' f karty
visit, to	посеща́ть	pasishchat'

14.3 Hobbies	Хо́бби	Khobbi
camera	фотоаппара́т (*m*)	fotaaparat
camping, to go	ходи́ть в похо́д	khadit' f pakhot
cook, to	вари́ть	varit'
dance, to	танцева́ть	tantsivat'
entertainment	развлече́ние (*n*)	razvlichyeniye
fish, to	лови́ть ры́бу	lavit' ribu
garden, to	рабо́тать в саду́	rabotat' f sadu
go to the movies, to	ходи́ть в кино́	khadit' f kino
go on a picnic, to	ходи́ть на пикни́к	khadit' na piknik
go on a trip, to	уе́хать (*perf.*) в путеше́ствие	yekhat' f putishyestviye
go to the opera, to	ходи́ть на о́перу	khadit' na operu
go to the theater, to	ходи́ть в теа́тр	khadit' f tiatr
hiking, to go	ходи́ть пешко́м	khadit' peshkom
hobby	хо́бби (*n*)	khobbi
like, to; I like	нра́виться; мне нра́вится	nravit'sa; mnye nravitsa
interest, to; to be interested in	интересова́ться	intirisavat'sa
listen to the radio, to	слу́шать ра́дио	slushat' radio
listen to records, to	слу́шать пласти́нки	slushat' plastinki
mountain climbing	альпини́зм (*m*)	al'pinizm
photograph, to	фотографи́ровать	fatografiravat'
play checkers, to	игра́ть в ша́шки	igrat' f shashki
play chess, to	игра́ть в ша́хматы	igrat' f shakhmaty
play electronic games, to	игра́ть в электро́нные и́гры	igrat' v iliktronniye igry
play an instrument, to	игра́ть на инструме́нте	igrat' na instrumyente
read a book, to	чита́ть кни́гу	chitat' knigu
read a magazine, to	чита́ть журна́л	chitat' zhurnal
read the newspapers, to	чита́ть газе́ту	chitat' gazyetu

14.4   Sports

rest	о́тдых *(m)*	otdykh
rest, to	отдыха́ть	atdykhat'
sing, to	петь	pyet'
take a walk, to	ходи́ть на прогу́лку	khadit' na pragulku
watch television, to	смотре́ть телеви́зор	smatryet' tilivizar

14.4 Sports	**Спорт**	**Sport**
athlete	спортсме́н *(m)*	sportsmyen
compete, to	соревнова́ться	sarivnavat'sa
competition	соревнова́ние *(n)*	sarivnavaniye
exercise, to	упражня́ться	uprazhnyat'sa
lose, to	проигра́ть; теря́ть	praigrat'; tiryat'
player	игро́к *(m)*	igrok
playing field	игрово́е по́ле *(n)*	igravoye polye
practice, to	практикова́ться	praktikavat'sa
run, to	бе́гать	byegat'
sport(s)	спорт *(m)*	sport
swim, to	пла́вать	plavat'
swimming pool	бассе́йн *(m)*	bassyeyn
swimsuit	купа́льный костю́м *(m)*	kupal'niy kostyum
team	кома́нда *(f)*	kamanda
win, to	вы́играть	vyigrat'

14.5 Kinds of sports	**Ви́ды спо́рта**	**Vidy sporta**
badminton	бадминто́н *(m)*	badminton
baseball	бейсбо́л *(m)*	beysbol
basketball	баскетбо́л *(m)*	basketbol
football	америка́нский футбо́л *(m)*	amirikanskiy futbol
golf	гольф *(m)*	gol'f
high jump	прыжки́ *(pl)* в высоту́	prizhki v vysatu
hockey	хокке́й *(m)*	khakkey

horseback riding	верхова́я езда́ (f)	virkhavaya yezda
horse race	ска́чки (pl)	skachki
ice-skating	ката́ние (n) на конька́х	kataniye na kon'kakh
long distance running	бег (m) на дли́нные диста́нции	beg na dlinniye distantsii
long jump	прыжки́ (pl) в длину́	pryzhki v dlinu
Ping-Pong	пинг-по́нг (m)	pink-ponk
polo	по́ло (n)	pola
pool	билья́рд (m)	bil'yard
rowing	гре́бля (f)	gryeblya
sailboat	па́русная ло́дка (f)	parusnaya lotka
skiing	ката́ние (n) на лы́жах	kataniye na lyzhakh
soccer	футбо́л (m)	futbol
swimming	пла́вание (n)	plavaniye
table tennis	насто́льный те́ннис (m)	nastol'niy tyennis
tennis	те́ннис (m)	tyennis
volleyball	волейбо́л (m)	valeybol
waterskiing	во́дные лы́жи (pl)	vodnye lyzhi

15. Abstract Words

15.1 Relations	Отношéния	Atnashyeniya
able, to be	мочь; быть в состоя́нии	moch'; byt' v sastayaniye
accurate	то́чный	tochniy
become, to	станови́ться	stanavit'sa
change, to	меня́ть	minyat'
do, to; make, to	де́лать	dyelat'
fit, to	подходи́ть	padkhadit'
format	форма́т (m)	farmat
influence	влия́ние (n)	vliyaniye
kind; type	вид (m), тип (m)	vit; tip
opportunity	возмо́жность (f)	vazmozhnast'
own, to	владе́ть	vladyet'
relationships	отношéния (pl)	atnashyeniya
substitute, to	заменя́ть	zaminyat'
suitable	подходя́щий	padkhadyashchiy
there is; there are	вот есть	vot yest
thing	вещь (f)	veshch
useful	ну́жный	nuzhniy

15.2 Comparison	Сравнéние	Sravnyeniye
all kinds (of)	любы́е	lyubiye
as … as …	так же … как и …	tak zhe … kak i …
better than	лу́чше чем	luchshe chem
choose, to	выбира́ть	vibirat'
compare, to	сра́внивать	sravnivat'
comparison	сравнéние (n)	sravnyeniye
entirely	весь	vyes'

even more	да́же бо́льше	dazhi bol'she
most of all	бо́льше всего́	bol'she vsyevo
not as good as	не так хорошо́ как	ni tak kharasho kak
on the contrary	наоборо́т	naoborot
others	други́е	drugiye
representative	представи́тель *(m)*	pridstavitil'
resemble, to	походи́ть на …	pakhadit' na …
same, (the)	тако́й же	takoy zhe
seem as if, to	ка́жется как бу́дто	kazhitsya kak budta
typical	типи́чный	tipichniy

15.3 Intensity — Интенси́вность — Intensivnast'

basic	элемента́рный	elimintarniy
essential	суще́ственный	sushchestvenniy
extremely	о́чень	ochen'
for the most part	в большинстве́ слу́чаев	v bal'shinstvye sluchayev
important	ва́жный	vazhniy
necessary	необходи́мый	niabkhadimiy
need, to	нужда́ться	nuzhdat'sa
nervous	не́рвный	nyervniy
severe	сло́жный	slozhniy
significant	ва́жный	vazhniy
special	специа́льный	spitsial'niy
strength	си́ла *(f)*	sila
strong	си́льный	sil'niy
urgent	сро́чный	srochniy
very	о́чень	ochen'
weak	сла́бый	slabiy

15.4 Giving and taking — Дава́ть и брать — Davat' i brat'

bring along, to	приноси́ть	prinasit'

distribute, to	распределя́ть	raspridilyat'
give, to	дава́ть	davat'
give back, to	возвраща́ть	vazvrashchat'
give a present, to	дари́ть пода́рок *(m)*	darit' padarak
hand over, to	вруча́ть	vruchat'
hold, to	держа́ть	derzhat'
order, to	прика́зывать; зака́зывать	prikazyvat'; zakazyvat'
receive, to	получа́ть	poluchat'
take away, to	забра́ть *(perf.)*	zabrat'

15.5 Reasons	**Причи́ны**	**Prichiny**
aim	цель *(f)*	tsel'
because	потому́	patamu
reason	причи́на *(f)*	prichina
take into account, to	принима́ть во внима́ние	prinimat' va vnimaniye
therefore	поэ́тому	paetomu
why?	почему́?	pachemu?

15.6 Complications	**Тру́дности, сло́жности**	**Trudnasti, slozhnasti**
complicated	сло́жный, тру́дный	slozhniy, trudniy
difficulties	тру́дности *(pl)*	trudnasti
hard	тру́дный	trudniy

15.7 Attractiveness	**Привлека́тельность**	**Privlikatil'nast'**
beautiful	краси́вый	krasiviy
common	обы́чный	abbychniy
cute	симпати́чный	simpatichniy
good-looking	прия́тный	priyatniy
lovable	ми́лый	miliy
popular	популя́рный	papulyarniy
ugly	некраси́вый	nikrasiviy

15.8 Certainty	Уве́ренность	Uvyerinnast'
according to	соотве́тственно с	saatvyetstvina s
although	хотя́	khatya
but	но	no
certain	определённый	apridilyonniy
certainly	определённо	apridilyonna
false	ло́жный, фальши́вый	lozhniy, fal'shiviy
for sure	безусло́вно	bizuslovna
of course	коне́чно	kanyeshna
perhaps	вероя́тно	virayatna
punctually	пунктуа́льно	punktual'na
real; actual	действи́тельный	distvitil'niy
reality	действи́тельность (n)	distvitil'nast'
still	ещё; до сих пор	ishcho; da sikh por

16. Motion and Location

16.1 Movement	Движе́ние	Dvizhyeniye
arrive, to	прибыва́ть	pribyvat'
come, to	приходи́ть	prikhadit'
come back, to	возвраща́ться	vazvrashchat'sa
come down, to	сойти́ (perf.) вниз	sayti vniz
come in, to	войти́ (perf.)	vayti
come out, to	вы́йти (perf.)	viyti
come up, to	подня́ться (perf.)	padnyat'sa
detach, to; separate, to	отделя́ть	atdelyat'
fall down, to	упа́сть (perf.)	upast'
get up, to	встать (perf.)	vstat'
go, to	идти́	idti
leave, to	уходи́ть	ukhadit'
look for, to	иска́ть	iskat'
move, to	дви́гаться; переезжа́ть	dvigat'sa; pereyezhat'
pick up, to	зайти́ (perf.) за (+ acc.)	zayti za
put down, to	опусти́ть (perf.)	apustit'
put into, to	вста́вить (perf.); положи́ть (perf.)	vstavit'; palazhit'
remove, to	устрани́ть (perf.)	ustranit'
send back, to	возвраща́ть	vazvrashchat'
take away, to	забра́ть (perf.)	zabrat'
throw, to	вы́бросить (perf.)	vybrasit'
trip, to; stumble, to	споткну́ться (perf.)	spatykhnut'sa
turn	поворо́т (m)	pavarot
turn, to	поверну́ть (perf.)	pavirnut'
turn left, to	поверну́ть (perf.) нале́во	pavirnut' na lyevo
turn right, to	поверну́ть (perf.) напра́во	pavirnut' na pravo

| unable to find, to be | не мочь найти | ne moch' nayti |
| walk, to | ходить | khadit' |

16.2 This and that   Этот и тот   Etat i Tot

that	тот *(m)*	tot
these	эти *(pl)*	eti
this	этот *(m)*	etot
this kind	этот вид *(m)*	etat vit
this one	вот этот *(m)*	vot etat
this way	так (правильно); сюда	tak (pravil'na); syuda
those	те *(pl)*	tye
which	какой *(m)*	kakoy
which one	который *(m)*	katoriy

16.3 Location   Место-нахождение   Mesto-nakhozhdyeniye

above	над *(+ inst.)*	nat
around	вокруг *(+ gen.)*	vakruk
back	назад	nazat
below	под *(+ acc./inst.)*	pot
between	между *(+ inst.)*	mezhdu
everywhere	везде	vezdye
front	фасад *(m)*	fasat
here	здесь	zdyes'
inside	внутри *(+ gen.)*	vnutri
left	слева	slyeva
neighborhood	соседство *(n)*	sasyetstva
opposite	противоположный	protivopolozhniy
place	место *(n)*	myesta
right	справа	sprava
side	сторона *(f)*	starana
that side	та сторона *(f)*	ta starana

this side	э́та сторона́	eta starana
where	где	gdye

16.4 Direction — Направле́ние — Napravlyeniye

direction	направле́ние	napravlyeniye
east	восто́к (*m*)	vastok
facing	лицо́м к (+ *dat.*)	litsom k
north	се́вер (*m*)	syever
opposite side	противополо́жная сторона́ (*f*)	prativapalozhnaya starana
south	юг (*m*)	yuk
straight	пря́мо	pryama
west	за́пад (*m*)	zapat

16.5 Place — Ме́сто — Myesto

between	ме́жду	myezhdu
beyond	вне; по ту сто́рону	vnye; pa tu storanu
direction	направле́ние (*n*)	napravlyeniye
edge	край (*m*)	kray
front	пере́дняя сторона́ (*f*)	peryednyaya starana
inside	внутри́	vnutri
left	сле́ва	slyeva
lower part	ни́жняя часть (*f*)	nizhnyaya chast'
outside	снару́жи	snaruzhi
part; section	часть (*f*); се́кция (*f*)	chast'; syektsiya
rear	за́дний	zadniy
right	спра́ва	sprava
upper part	ве́рхняя часть (*f*)	vyerkhnyaya chast'
within	внутри́	vnutri

17. Time

17.1 Time	Вре́мя	Vryemya
about (approximately)	приблизи́тельно	priblizitel'na
about (more or less)	о́коло	okala
after	по́сле (+ gen.)	poslye
ago: 5 years ago	наза́д: 5 лет (тому́) наза́д	nazat: 5 lyet (tamu) nazat
all day long	весь день (m)	vyes' den'
already	уже́	uzhye
another time	в друго́е вре́мя	v drugoye vryemya
at last	наконе́ц	nakanyets
at once (immediately)	неме́дленно	nimyedlinna
at that time	в то вре́мя	v to vryemya
beginning	нача́ло (n)	nachala
continue, to	продолжа́ть	pradalzhat'
daylight saving time	ле́тнее вре́мя (n)	lyetniye vryemya
early	ра́но	rana
every time	ка́ждый раз (m)	kazhdiy raz
fast	бы́стро	bystra
for a long time	давно́	davno
half	полови́на (f)	palavina
half a day	полови́на (f) дня	palavina dnya
half a week	полови́на (f) неде́ли	palavina nidyeli
how long?	как до́лго?	kak dolga?
hurry	быстре́е; поспеши́	bystryeye; paspishi
in the future	в бу́дущем	v budushchim
in a moment	че́рез мину́ту	chyeriz minutu
in the past	в про́шлом	v proshlom
in a short time	в коро́ткое вре́мя	v karotkaye vryemya
just	то́лько что	tol'ka chto

17.1 Time

late	по́здно	pozdna
three days later	че́рез три дня	chyeriz tri dnya
later on	пото́м	patom
long time ago, (a)	давно́	davno
new	но́вый	noviy
not yet	ещё нет	ishcho nyet
now	сейча́с	siychas
nowadays	в настоя́щее вре́мя	v nastayashchiye vryemya
office hours	часы́ (pl) приёма	chasy priyoma
old	ста́рый	stariy
once in a while	иногда́	inagda
once upon a time	давны́м-давно́	davnym-davno
previously	пре́жде	pryezhdye
recently	неда́вно	nidavna
right now	сейча́с же	siychas zhe
slow	ме́дленно	myedlinna
sometimes	иногда́	inagda
start, to	начина́ть	nachinat'
stop, to	прекраща́ть	prikrashchat'
subsequently	впосле́дствии	vpaslyetstvii
take your time	не торопи́тесь	ni tarapityes'
these days	э́ти дни (pl)	eti dni
this time	в э́тот раз	v etot raz
time	вре́мя (n)	vryemya
trading hours	поменя́ться часа́ми	paminyat'sa chisami
until now	до настоя́щего вре́мени	da nastayashchiva vryemini
wait a moment	подожди́те мину́тку	padazhditi minutku
when	когда́	kagda
when the time comes	когда́ придёт вре́мя	kagda pridyot vryemya
while (during)	в то вре́мя как	v to vryemya kak

17.2 Beginning and end	Нача́ло и коне́ц	Nachala i kanyets
begin, to	начина́ть	nachinat'
finish, to	зака́нчивать	zakanchivat'
first	пе́рвый	pyerviy
first of all	пре́жде всего́	pryezhdye vsivo
for the first time	в пе́рвый раз	v pyerviy raz
in the beginning	в нача́ле	v nachlye
last one	после́дний	paslyedniy
start	нача́ло (n)	nachala
start, to	начина́ть	nachinat'
stop	остано́вка (f)	astanofka
stop, to	останови́ться (perf.)	astanavit'sa

17.3 Frequency	Частота́	Chastota
always	всегда́	vsigda
first time	пе́рвый раз (m)	pyerviy raz
last time	после́дний раз (m)	paslyedniy raz
next time	сле́дующий раз (m)	slyeduyushchiy raz
often	ча́сто	chasta
once again	ещё раз (m)	ishcho raz
previous time	пре́жде	pryezhdye
seldom	ре́дко	ryetka
sometimes	иногда́	inagda
time	вре́мя (n)	vryemya
usually	обы́чно	abychna

17.4 Speed	Ско́рость	Skorast'
early	ра́но	rana
fast	бы́стро	bystra
gradually	постепе́нно	pastipyenna

hurry up, to	торопи́ться	tarapit'sa
late	по́здно	pozna
slow	ме́дленный	myedlinniy
slowly	ме́дленно	myedlinna
suddenly	вдруг	fdruk

17.5 Year	Год	Got
academic year	академи́ческий год (*m*)	akadimichiskiy got
calendar	календа́рь (*m*)	kalindar'
celebrate the New Year, to	пра́здновать Но́вый год	praznavat' Noviy got
century	век (*m*)	vyek
each year	ка́ждый год (*m*)	kazhdiy got
half year	полови́на го́да	palavina goda
last year	про́шлый год (*m*)	proshliy got
lunar calendar	лу́нный календа́рь	lunniy kalendar'
New Year	Но́вый год (*m*)	Noviy got
next year	сле́дующий год (*m*)	slyeduyushchiy got
solar calendar	со́лнечный календа́рь (*m*)	solnechniy kalendar'
this year	э́тот год (*m*)	etat got
year	год (*m*)	got
year after next (*in 2 years*)	че́рез два го́да	chyeriz dva goda
year before last (*2 years ago*)	два го́да наза́д	dva goda nazat
5 years of age; 5 years old	пять лет	pyat' let

17.6 Seasons	Времена́ го́да	Vryemyena goda
spring	весна́ (*f*)	vesna
summer	ле́то (*n*)	lyeta
autumn; fall	о́сень (*f*)	osyen'
winter	зима́ (*f*)	zima
cold	хо́лодно	kholodna
every month	ка́ждый ме́сяц (*m*)	kazhdiy myesats

half a month	полови́на ме́сяца	palavina myesatsa
last month	после́дний ме́сяц *(m)*	paslyedniy myesats
month	ме́сяц *(m)*	myesats
next month	сле́дующий ме́сяц *(m)*	slyeduyushchiy myesats
one month	оди́н ме́сяц *(m)*	adin myesats
season	вре́мя *(n)* го́да	vryemya goda
warm	тепло́	tiplo

17.7 Months   Ме́сяцы   Myesyatsy

first month	пе́рвый ме́сяц *(m)*	pyerviy myesats
January	янва́рь *(m)*	yanvar'
February	февра́ль *(m)*	fivral'
March	март *(m)*	mart
April	апре́ль *(m)*	apryel'
May	май *(m)*	may
June	ию́нь *(m)*	iyun'
July	ию́ль *(m)*	iyul'
August	а́вгуст *(m)*	avgust
September	сентя́брь *(m)*	sentyabr'
October	октя́брь *(m)*	aktyabr'
November	ноя́брь *(m)*	nayabr'
December	дека́брь *(m)*	dikabr'
twelfth month	двена́дцатый ме́сяц *(m)*	dvinatsatiy myesats

17.8 Days and weeks   Дни и неде́ли   Dni i nidyeli

day after tomorrow	послеза́втра	poslyezaftra
day before yesterday	позавчера́	pozafchera
days	дни *(pl)*	dni
every day	ка́ждый день *(m)*	kazhdiy dyen'
every week	ка́ждая неде́ля *(f)*	kazhdaya nidyelya
last week	после́дняя неде́ля *(f)*	paslyednyaya nidyelya

next week	сле́дующая неде́ля (f)	slyeduyushchaya nidyelya
one day	оди́н день (m)	adin dyen'
other day (the)	друго́й день (m)	drugoy dyen'
these days	э́ти дни	eti dni
thirty-one days	три́дцать оди́н день (m)	tritsat' adin dyen'
this week	э́та неде́ля (f)	eta nidyelya
today	сего́дня	sivodnya
tomorrow	за́втра	zaftra
two days	два дня	dva dnya
week	неде́ля (f)	nidyelya
yesterday	вчера́	fchera

17.9 Days of the week and month	Дни неде́ли и ме́сяца	Dni nidyeli i myesatsa
day	день (m)	dyen'
Monday	понеде́льник (m)	panidyelnik
Tuesday	вто́рник (m)	ftornik
Wednesday	среда́ (f)	sryeda
Thursday	четве́рг (m)	chitvyerk
Friday	пя́тница (f)	pyatnitsa
Saturday	суббо́та (f)	subbota
Sunday	воскресе́нье (n)	voskrisyen'ye
first (day of the month)	пе́рвый	pyerviy
second	второ́й	ftoroy
third	тре́тий	tryetiy
fourth	четвёртый	chitvyortiy
fifth	пя́тый	pyatiy
tenth	деся́тый	disyatiy
thirteenth	трина́дцатый	trinatsatiy
twentieth	двадца́тый	dvatsatiy
thirty-first	три́дцать пе́рвый	tritsat' pyerviy

| week | неде́ля (f) | nidyelya |
| weekend | выходно́й | vikhadnoy |

17.10 Time of day   Вре́мя дня   Vryemya dnya

all day long	весь день (m)	vyes dyen'
daytime	дневно́е вре́мя (n)	dnivnoye vryemya
evening	ве́чер (m)	vyechir
every morning	ка́ждое у́тро (n)	kazhdaye utra
midnight	по́лночь (f)	polnach'
morning	у́тро (n)	utra
noon	по́лдень (m)	poldyen'
this day	э́тот день (m)	etat dyen'
this evening	э́тот ве́чер (m)	etat vyechir
this morning	э́то у́тро (n)	eta utra
whole day, (the)	весь день (m)	vyes' dyen'

17.11 Clock time   Вре́мя   Vryemya

half-an-hour	полчаса́ (m)	polchasa
hour	час (m)	chas
minutes	мину́ты (pl)	minuty
quarter hour	че́тверть (f) ча́са	chyetvert' chasa
seconds	секу́нды (pl)	sikundy
what time is it?	кото́рый час?	katoriy chas?
3:00 A.M.	три часа́ утра́	tri chasa utra
3:00 P.M.	три часа́ дня	tri chasa dnya

18. Quantity

18.1 Size and number	Разме́р и но́мер	Razmyer i nomir
zero	ноль; нуль	nol'; nul'
one	оди́н	adin
two	два	dva
three	три	tri
four	четы́ре	chityre
five	пять	pyat'
six	шесть	shyest'
seven	семь	syem'
eight	во́семь	vosim'
nine	де́вять	dyevat'
ten	де́сять	dyesat'
eleven	оди́ннадцать	adinatsat'
twelve	двена́дцать	dvenatsat'
thirteen	трина́дцать	trinatsat'
fourteen	четы́рнадцать	chityrnatsat'
fifteen	пятна́дцать	pitnatsat'
sixteen	шестна́дцать	shestnatsat'
seventeen	семна́дцать	semnatsat'
eighteen	восемна́дцать	vosemnatsat'
nineteen	девятна́дцать	devatnatsat'
twenty	два́дцать	dvatsat'
twenty-one	два́дцать оди́н	dvatsat' adin
thirty	три́дцать	tritsat'
forty	со́рок	sorak
fifty	пятьдеся́т	pyatdyesyat
sixty	шестьдеся́т	shestdesyat
seventy	се́мьдесят	syem'desat

eighty	восемьдесят	vosem'desat
ninety	девяносто	divanosta
hundred, (one)	сто	sto
thousand, (one)	тысяча *(f)*	tysacha
ten thousand	десять тысяч	dyesat' tysach
add, to	прибавлять	pribavlyat'
broad	широкий	shirokiy
decrease, to	уменьшать	umin'shat'
divide into, to	делить на *(+ acc.)*	dilit' na
fat	толстый	tolstiy
half	половина *(f)*	palavina
increase, to	увеличивать	uvilichivat'
large	большой	bal'shoy
length	длина *(f)*	dlina
lengthen, to	удлинять	udlinyat'
majority	большинство *(n)*	bal'shinstvo
minority	меньшинство *(n)*	men'shinstvo
most	наибольший	naibol'shiy
narrow	узкий	uzkiy
quarter	четверть *(f)*	chyetvert'
several	несколько	nyeskol'ko
share, to	делиться	dilit'sa
size	размер *(m)*	razmyer
small	маленький	malin'kiy
spread out, to	расстилаться	rasstilat'sa
subtract, to	отнимать	atnimat'
thick	толстый	tolstiy
thin	тонкий	tonkiy
wide	широкий	shirokiy

18.2 Length and area	**Длина и площадь**	**Dlina i ploshchat'**
acre	акр *(m)*	akr

18.3   Weight and volume

centimeter	сантиме́тр (*m*)	santimyetr
deep	глубоко́	glubako
foot	фут (*m*)	fut
hectare	гекта́р (*m*)	giktar
height	высота́ (*f*)	vysata
high	высоко́	vysoko
inch	дюйм (*m*)	dyuim
kilometer	киломе́тр (*m*)	kilamyetr
length	длина́ (*f*)	dlina
low	ни́зко	nizka
meter	метр (*m*)	myetr
miles	ми́ли (*pl*)	mili
millimeter	миллиме́тр (*m*)	millimyetr
near	бли́зко	blizka
shallow	ме́лко	myelka
short	коро́ткий	karotkiy

18.3 Weight and volume	Вес и объём	Vyes i ob"yom
gallon	галло́н (*m*)	galon
gram	грамм (*m*)	gramm
heavy	тяжёлый	tizholiy
kilogram	килогра́мм (*m*)	kilagramm
light	лёгкий	lyokhkiy
liter	литр (*m*)	litr
ounce	у́нция (*f*)	untsiya
pound	фунт (*m*)	funt
ton	то́нна (*f*)	tonna
weight	вес (*m*)	vyes

18.4 Estimates	Оце́нки	Otsenki
about	о́коло (*+ gen.*)	okala

approximately	приблизи́тельно	priblizitil'na
generally	вообще́	vaapshche
how long?	как до́лго?	kak dolga?
how many?	ско́лько?	skol'ka?
how much is it?	ско́лько сто́ит?	skol'ka stoit?
less than	ме́ньше чем	myen'she chyem
more than	бо́льше чем	bol'she chyem

18.5 Small quantities — Ма́ленькое коли́чество — Malin'kaye kalichistva

few	немно́го	nimnoga
hardly any	почти́ никто́; почти́ ничего́	pochti nikto; pochti nichivo
little	ма́ло	mala
not much	немно́го	nimnoga
zero; nothing	ноль; ничего́	nol'; nichivo

18.6 Medium amounts — Сре́днее коли́чество — Sryednyeye kalichistva

almost	почти́	pachti
comparatively	сравни́тельно	sravnityel'na
enough	доста́точно	dastatachna
fairly	дово́льно	davol'na
little by little	понемно́гу	panimnogu
sufficient	доста́точно	dastatachna
within	внутри́	vnutri

18.7 Large quantities — Большо́е коли́чество — Bol'shoye kalichistva

all	весь	vyes
completely	по́лностью	polnast'yu
exceedingly	чрезвыча́йно	chrezvychaina

18.8   Measures

excessively	чрезме́рно	chryezmyerna
extremely	о́чень	ochin'
full	по́лный	polniy
many; much	мно́го	mnoga
more than	бо́льше чем	bool'she chem
too much	сли́шком мно́го	slishkam mnoga
very	о́чень	ochin'

18.8 Measures	Измере́ния	Izmeryeniya
bag of	мешо́к (m) с (+ inst.)	mishok s
basket of	корзи́на (f) с (+ inst.)	karzina s
batch (of)	па́чка (f) (+ gen.)	pachka
bottle (of)	буты́лка (f) (+ gen.)	butylka
bowl (of)	ми́ска (f) (+ gen.)	miska
box (of)	коро́бка (f) (+ gen.)	karopka
bunch (of)	пучо́к (m) (+ gen.)	puchok
can of	консе́рвная ба́нка (f) с (+ inst.)	kansyervnaya banka s
carton of	коро́бка (f) с (+ inst.)	karopka s
case of	я́щик (m) с (+ inst.)	yashchik s
course (of food)	блю́до (n) (+ gen.)	blyuda
cup (of)	ча́шка (f) (+ gen.)	chashka
dish (of)	блю́до (n) (+ gen.)	blyuda
dozen	дю́жина (f)	dyuzhina
group of	гру́ппа (f) из (+ gen.)	gruppa iz
kind (of)	вид (m); тип (m)	vid; tip
little (of)	немно́го	nimnoga
meal	еда́ (f)	yeda
packet	паке́т (m) с (+ inst.)	pakyet s
pair (of)	па́ра (f) (+ gen.)	para
pan of	сковорода́ (f) с (+ inst.)	skavarada s
piece (of)	кусо́к (m) (+ gen.)	kusok
pile (of)	па́чка (f) (+ gen.)	pachka

plate (of)	таре́лка *(f) (+ gen.)*	taryelka
pot (of)	кастрю́ля *(f) (+ gen.)*	kastryulya
roll (of)	руло́н *(m) (+ gen.)*	rulon
row (of)	ряд *(m) (+ gen.)*	ryat
section (of)	се́кция *(f) (+ gen.)*	syektsiya
set (of)	набо́р *(m) (+ gen.)*	nabor
slice (of)	кусо́к *(m) (+ gen.)*	kusok
spoon (of)	ло́жка *(f) (+ gen.)*	lozhka
string (of)	нить *(f) (+ gen.)*	nit'
team (of)	кома́нда *(f) (+ gen.)*	kamanda

19. Structural Words

19.1 Auxiliary verbs	Вспомогáтельные глагóлы	Vspamagatil'niye glagoly
be, to	есть	yest'
was	был, былá, бы́ло	byl, byla, byla
were	бы́ли	byli
have, to	имéть	imyet'
had	имéл, имéла, имéло	imyel, imyela, imyela
have	имéли	imyeli

19.2 Question words	Вопросúтельные словá	Vaprasitel'niye slava
how	как	kak
how far	как далекó	kak daliko
how much is it?	скóлько стóит?	skol'ka stoit?
how old	скóлько лет	skol'ka lyet
what	что	shto
when	когдá	kagda
where	где	gdye
which	какóй	kakoy
who	кто	kto
whose	чей	chey
why	почемý	pachimu

19.3 Connecting words	Свя́зки	Svyazki
also	тáкже, тóже	takzhe, tozhe
although	хотя́	khatya
and	и	i

as soon as	как то́лько	kak tol'ka
as well as	та́кже	takzhi
because	потому́	patamu
before	пе́ред, до	pyerit, do
besides	поми́мо	pamima
but	но	no
even	да́же	dazhe
for example	наприме́р	naprimyer
if	е́сли	yesli
in fact	факти́чески	faktichiski
in other words	други́ми слова́ми	drugimi slavami
later on	пото́м	patom
more and more	бо́льше и бо́льше	bol'she i bol'she
(the) more, the better	чем бо́льше тем лу́чше	chem bol'she tyem luchshe
only	то́лько	tol'ka
or	и́ли	ili
otherwise	ина́че	inache
then	пото́м, зате́м	patom, zatyem
therefore	поэ́тому	paetamu

19.4 Prepositions	**Предло́ги**	**Pridlogy**
according (to)	соотве́тственно (+ *dat.*)	saatvyetstvinno
at	на (+ *acc./prep.*)	na
behind	сза́ди (+ *gen.*)	szadi
by	при (+ *prep.*)	pri
compared to	сра́внивая с (+ *instr.*)	sravnivaya s
concerning	относи́тельно (+ *gen.*)	otnasitil'no
down	вниз (+ *gen.*)	vniz
except	кро́ме (+ *gen.*)	kromye
for	за (+ *acc./inst.*)	za
from	от (+ *gen.*)	ot
front, in front	пе́ред (+ *inst.*), спе́реди (+ *gen.*)	pyeret, spyeredi

19.4 Prepositions

in	в *(+ prep.)*	v
out	из *(+ gen.)*	iz
to *(direction)*, into	в *(+ acc.)*	v
together with	вместе с *(+ inst.)*	vmyestye s
toward	по направлéнию к *(+ dat.)*	po napravlyeniyu k
with	с *(+ inst.)*	s

Appendices

Russian-English Glossary

а как вы?	a kak vy?	how about you?	4.1
абрико́с *(m)*	abrikos	apricot	5.5
абонеме́нтный я́щик *(m)*	abanimyentniy yashchik	post office box	13.6
авиапо́чта *(f)*	aviapochta	airmail	13.6
ава́рия *(f)*	avariya	accident	9.5
а́вгуст *(m)*	avgust	August	17.7
авиапо́чта *(f)*	aviapochta	airmail	13.6
Австра́лия *(f)*	Avstraliya	Australia	9.2
авто́бус *(m)*	aftobus	bus	9.5
автомоби́льная ава́рия *(f)*	aftamabil'naya avariya	car accident	9.6
ад *(m)*	at	hell	11.6
а́дрес *(m)*	adres	address	13.6
Азербайджа́н *(m)*	Azirbaidzhan	Azerbaijan	3.4
А́зия *(f)*	Aziya	Asia	9.2
академи́ческий год *(m)*	akadimichiskiy got	academic year	17.5
акр *(m)*	akr	acre	18.2
актёр *(m)*	aktyor	actor	2.14, 11.9
актри́са *(f)*	aktrisa	actress	11.9
а́лгебра *(f)*	algebra	algebra	12.5
алё, алло́	alyo, allo	hello	13.7
Алматы́ *(f)*	Almaty	Almaty (Kazakhstan)	3.4
алфави́т *(m)*	alfavit	alphabet	3.3, 13.1
альпини́зм *(m)*	al'pinizm	mountain climbing	14.3
Аме́рика *(f)*	Amyerika	America	9.2
америка́нец *(m)*, америка́нка *(f)*	amerikanyets, amerikanka	American	9.2
америка́нская литерату́ра *(f)*	amyerikanskaya litiratura	American literature	11.2, 12.5
америка́нский футбо́л *(m)*	amirikanskiy futbol	football	14.5
анана́с *(m)*	ananas	pineapple	5.5
англи́йский язы́к *(m)*	angliyskiy yezyk	English (language)	12.5, 13.1

англича́нин (*m*), англича́нка (*f*)	anglichanin, anglichanka	Englishman, Englishwoman	9.2
А́нглия (*f*)	Angliya	England	9.2
а́нгло-ру́сский слова́рь (*m*)	anglo-russkiy slavar'	English-Russian dictionary	11.2
Антаркти́ческий океа́н (*m*)	Antarktichiskiy akian	Antarctic Ocean	9.4
антиква́рные това́ры (*pl*)	antikvarniye tavary	antiques; antique store	7.1
апельси́н (*m*)	apil'sin	orange	5.5
апельси́новый напи́ток (*m*)	apil'sinaviy napitak	orange drink	5.9
апельси́новый сок (*m*)	apil'sinaviy sok	orange juice	5.9
апре́ль (*m*)	apryel'	April	17.7
апте́ка (*f*)	aptyeka	pharmacy; drugstore	2.7, 7.1
арбу́з (*m*)	arbuz	watermelon	5.5
Аргенти́на (*f*)	Argentina	Argentina	9.2
аресто́вывать	aristovyvat'	arrest, to	10.5
Арме́ния (*f*)	Armyeniya	Armenia	3.4
а́рмия (*f*)	armiya	army	10.11
арома́тный	aramatniy	aromatic	5.8
архите́ктор (*m*)	arkhityektar	architect	2.14
ателье́ (*n*)	atel'ye	tailor	7.1
Атланти́ческий океа́н (*m*)	Atlantichiskiy akian	Atlantic Ocean	9.4
А́фрика (*f*)	Afrika	Africa	9.2
Ашхаба́д (*m*)	Ashkhabat	Ashkhabad (Turkmenistan)	3.4
аэропо́рт (*m*)	aeraport	airport	9.5, 9.8
ба́бушка (*f*)	babushka	grandmother	2.15
бага́ж (*m*)	bagazh	luggage	9.7
бадминто́н (*m*)	badminton	badminton	14.5
баклажа́н (*m*)	baklazhan	eggplant	5.6
Баку́ (*m*)	Baku	Baku (Azerbaijan)	3.4
бале́т (*m*)	balyet	ballet	3.2
балко́н (*m*)	balkon	balcony	8.5
Балти́йское мо́ре (*n*)	Baltiyskaye morye	Baltic Sea	3.4, 9.4
бана́н (*m*)	banan	banana	5.5
банк (*m*)	bank	bank	7.1, 9.8, 10.10
банкро́тство (*n*)	bankrotstvo	bankruptcy	10.6
бар (*m*)	bar	bar	5.3
бара́нина (*f*)	baranina	lamb	5.4
ба́рхат (*m*)	barkhat	velvet	6.4
баскетбо́л (*m*)	basketbol	basketball	14.5
бассе́йн (*m*)	bassyeyn	swimming pool	14.4

бег *(m)* на дли́нные диста́нции	beg na dlinniye distantsii	long distance running	14.5
бе́гать	byegat'	run, to	14.4
бе́дный	byedniy	poor	10.2
бедро́ *(n)*	bidro	thigh	2.2
бе́дствие *(n)*	byetstviye	disaster	1.5
бежа́ть	bizhat'	run, to	1.8
бе́жевый	bezhiviy	beige	6.5
беззабо́тный	bizzabotniy	careless	2.11
безопа́сность *(f)*	bezapasnost'	safety	9.6
безрабо́тный *(m)*	bezrabotniy	unemployed	2.14
безусло́вно	bizuslovna	for sure	15.8
бейсбо́л *(m)*	beysbol	baseball	14.5
Белару́сь *(f)*	Bilarus'	Belarus	3.4
бе́лый	beliy	white	6.5
бельё *(n)*	bel'yo	underwear	6.2
бе́рег *(m)*	berik	shore	1.3
беспоко́иться	bispakoitsa	worry, to	2.8
библиоте́ка *(f)*	bibliatyeka	library	9.8, 11.2
библиоте́карь *(m)*, библиоте́карша *(f)*	bibliatyekar', bibliatyekarsha	librarian	2.14
библиоте́чная кни́га *(f)*	bibliatyechnaya kniga	library book	11.2
Би́блия *(f)*	Bibliya	Bible	11.6
бизнесме́н *(m)*	biznismyen	businessman	2.14
билья́рд *(m)*	bil'yard	pool	14.5
билья́рдная *(f)*	bil'yardnaya	pool room	8.2
биоло́гия *(f)*	bialogiya	biology	12.5
Бишке́к *(m)*	Bishkyek	Bishkek (Kyrgyzstan)	3.4
благодари́ть	blagadarit'	thank, to	4.3
благода́рность *(f)*	blagadarnast'	thanks *(gratitude)*	4.3
бли́зко	blizka	near	18.2
близнецы́ *(pl)*	bliznitsy	twins	2.12
блу́зка *(f)*	bluzka	blouse	6.2
блю́до *(n)* *(+ gen.)*	blyuda	dish, course *(of food)*	5.1, 18.8
блю́дце *(n)*	blyutse	sauce	5.11
Бог *(m)*	Bok	God	11.6
бога́тый	bagatiy	rich	10.2
боле́знь *(f)*	balyezn'	sickness; illness	2.6
боли́т го́рло *(n)*	balit gorla	sore throat, to have a	2.6
болта́ть	baltat'	chat, to	13.2
боль *(f)*	bol'	pain	2.6
больни́ца *(f)*	bol'nitsa	hospital	2.7, 9.8
бо́льно	bol'na	painfully	2.6

бо́льше всего́	bol'she vsyevo	most of all	15.2
бо́льше и бо́льше	bol'she i bol'she	more and more	19.3
бо́льше нет	bol'she nyet	no more	4.2
бо́льше чем	bol'she chyem	more than	18.4, 18.7
большинство́ (n)	bal'shinstvo	majority	18.1
большо́е спаси́бо	bal'shoye spasiba	thank you very much	4.2
большо́й	bal'shoy	large	18.1
Большо́й теа́тр (m)	Bol'shoi tiatr	Bolshoi Theater	3.2
борода́ (f)	barada	beard	2.2
борщ (m)	borshch	borshch	5.7
ботани́ческий сад (m)	batanichiskiy sat	botanical garden	1.7, 9.8
Брази́лия (f)	Braziliya	Brazil	9.2
брасле́т (m)	braslyet	bracelet	6.3
брат (m)	brat	brother	2.12
бре́нди (n)	bryendi	brandy	5.9
бри́ться	britsa	shave, to	2.5
бровь (f)	brov'	eyebrow	2.2
брю́ки (pl)	bryuki	trousers	6.2
будди́зм (m)	budizm	Buddhism	11.6
буди́ть	budit'	wake up, to	2.4
бу́ква (f)	bukva	letter (of alphabet)	3.3, 13.1
бу́лочная (f)	bulachnaya	bakery (bread)	7.1
бума́га (f)	bumaga	paper	13.5
бума́га (f) для письма́	bumaga dlya pis'ma	letter paper	13.5
бума́жник (m)	bumazhnik	wallet	6.3
бума́жные де́ньги (pl)	bumazhniye dyen'gi	paper money	7.3
бутербро́д (m)	buterbrot	sandwich	5.4
буты́лка (f) (+ gen.)	butylka	bottle (of)	18.8
бухга́лтерский учёт (m)	bukhgalterskiy uchyot	accounting	12.5
был, была́, бы́ло	byl, byla, byla	was	19.1
бы́ли	byli	were	19.1
быстре́е; поспеши́	bystryeye; paspishi	hurry	17.1
бы́стро	bystra	fast	17.1, 17.4
быть больны́м	byt' bol'nym	sick, to be	2.6
быть хозя́йкой	byt' khazyaykay	host, to be a	5.1
бюдже́т (m)	byudzhyet	budget	10.6
бюро́ (n)	byuro	office	9.8, 10.7
в (+ acc.)	v	to (direction), into	19.4
в (+ prep.)	v	in	19.4
в большинстве́ слу́чаев	v bal'shinstvye sluchayev	for the most part	15.3
в бу́дущем	v budushchim	in the future	17.1
в друго́е вре́мя	v drugoye vryemya	another time	17.1
в коро́ткое вре́мя	v karotkaye vryemya	in a short time	17.1
в настоя́щее вре́мя	v nastayashchiye vryemya	nowadays	17.1

в нача́ле	v nachlye	in the beginning	17.2
в пе́рвый раз	v pyerviy raz	for the first time	17.2
в про́шлом	v proshlom	in the past	17.1
в то вре́мя	v to vryemya	at that time	17.1
в то вре́мя как	v to vryemya kak	while (during)	17.1
в э́тот раз	v etot raz	this time	17.1
ва́жный	vazhniy	important, significant	2.9, 2.11, 15.3
ва́за (f)	vaza	vase	8.5
валю́та (f)	valyuta	currency	7.3
ва́нна (f)	vanna	bathtub	8.5
ва́нная (f)	vannaya	bathroom	8.2
вари́ть	varit'	cook, to	8.4, 14.3
вари́ть ко́фе	varit' kofe	make coffee, to	5.9
вари́ть на пару́	varit' na paru	steam, to	5.10
вдруг	fdruk	suddenly	17.4
веди́те маши́ну осторо́жно	viditye mashinu astarozhna	drive safely	4.5
ведро́ (n)	vidro	bucket	8.7
ве́жливо	vyezhliva	polite	4.3
ве́жливость (f)	vyezhlivast'	politeness	4.3
везде́	vezdye	everywhere	16.3
век (m)	vyek	century	17.5
Вели́кая Оте́чественная война́ (f)	Velikaya Atechistvinnaya voina	Great Patriotic War	3.5
великоле́пный	vilikalyepniy	terrific	2.9
велосипе́д (m)	vilasipyed	bicycle	9.5
вера́нда (f)	veranda	veranda	8.5
ве́рить	vyerit'	believe, to	11.6
ве́рный	vyerniy	right; correct	12.7
вероя́тно	virayatna	perhaps	15.8
ве́рующий	verayushchiy	believer	11.6
верфь (f)	vyerf'	wharf	9.5
ве́рхняя часть (f)	vyerkhnyaya chast'	upper part	16.5
верхова́я езда́ (f)	virkhavaya yezda	horseback riding	14.5
вес (m)	vyes	weight	18.3
весна́ (f)	vesna	spring	1.6, 17.6
вести́ маши́ну	visti mashinu	drive, to	9.6
весь	vyes'	entirely; all	15.2, 18.7
весь день (m)	vyes' dyen'	whole day, (the); all day long	17.1, 17.10
ве́тер (m)	vyetir	wind	1.5
ве́тки (pl)	vyetki	branches	1.7
ветчина́ (f)	vichina	ham	5.4

Russian	Transliteration	English	Reference
ве́чер *(m)*	vyechir	evening; party	14.2, 17.10
вечери́нка *(f)*	vyechirinka	party	14.2
вече́рнее пла́тье *(n)*	vichyerniye plat'ye	evening gown	6.2
вече́рняя газета *(f)*	vichyernyaya gazyeta	evening paper	11.3
ве́шать	vyesht'	hang, to	8.4
ве́шать бельё	vyeshat' bil'yo	hang out the laundry, to	8.7
вещь *(f)*	veshch	thing	15.1
взве́шивать	vzvyeshivat'	weigh, to	13.6
взро́слый	vzrosliy	adult	2.1
вид *(m)*, тип *(m)*	vit; tip	kind; type	15.1, 18.8
видеокассе́та *(f)*	vidiokassyeta	videotape	11.4
ви́деомагнитофо́н *(m)*	vidiomagnitafon	video recorder	11.4
ви́деть	vidit'	see, to	2.10
ви́лка *(f)*	vilka	fork	5.11
Ви́льнюс *(m)*	Vil'nyus	Vilnius (Lithuania)	3.4
вино́ *(n)*:	vino:	wine:	5.9
кра́сное вино́,	krasnaye vino,	red wine,	
бе́лое вино́	byelaye vino	white wine	
вино́вный	vinovniy	guilty	10.4
виногра́д *(m)*	vinagrat	grapes	5.5
ви́ски *(n)*	viski	whiskey	5.9
виско́за *(f)*	viskoza	rayon	6.4
включа́ть	vklyuchat'	switch on, to	8.4, 11.4
вку́сно	fkusna	tasty, it's	5.1
вку́сный	fkusniy	tasty; delicious	5.8
владе́лец *(m)* до́ма	vladyelets doma	home owner	8.4
владе́ть	vladyet'	own, to	15.1
влия́ние *(n)*	vliyaniye	influence	15.1
вме́сте с *(+ inst.)*	vmyeste s	together with	14.1, 19.4
вне; по ту сто́рону	vnye; pa tu storanu	beyond	16.5
вниз *(+ gen.)*	vniz	down	19.4
внизу́	vnizu	downstairs	8.5
внима́ние *(n)*	vnimaniye	attention	12.6
внук *(m)*	vnuk	grandson	2.12
вну́тренний	vnutriniy	internal	2.7
внутри́	vnutri	within, inside	16.3, 16.5, 18.6
вну́чка *(f)*	vnuchka	granddaughter	2.12
вода́ *(f)*	vada	water	1.3, 5.9
води́тель *(m)*	vaditil'	driver	9.6
во́дные лы́жи *(pl)*	vodnye lyzhi	waterskiing	14.5
вое́нно-морски́е си́лы *(pl)*	vayenna-marskiye sily	navy	10.11
вое́нный	vayenniy	military	10.11
возбужда́ть	vazbuzhdat'	excite, to	2.8

возвраща́ть	vazvrashchat'	give back, to	15.4,
		send back, to	16.1
возвраща́ться	vazvrashchat'sa	come back, to	16.1
во́здух *(m)*	vozdukh	air	1.1
возмо́жность *(f)*	vazmozhnast'	opportunity	15.1
возража́ть	vazrazhat'	oppose, to	10.3
война́ *(f)*	vayna	war	10.11
войти́	vayti	come in, to	16.1
вокру́г *(+ gen.)*	vakruk	around	16.3
волейбо́л *(m)*	valeybol	volleyball	14.5
волна́ *(f)*	valna	wave	1.3
во́лосы *(pl)*	volosy	hair	2.2
вообще́	vaapshche	generally	18.4
вопро́с *(m)*	vapros	question	12.8
вопроси́тельный знак *(m)*	vaprasitil'niy znak	question mark	11.2
вор *(m)*	vor	thief	10.5
воротни́к *(m)*	varatnik	collar	6.1
восемна́дцать	vosemnatsat'	eighteen	18.1
во́семь	vosim'	eight	18.1
во́семьдесят	vosem'desat	eighty	18.1
восклица́тельный знак *(m)*	vasklitsatil'niy znak	exclamation point	11.2
воскресе́нье *(n)*	voskrisyen'ye	Sunday	17.9
восста́ние *(n)*	vasstaniye	revolt	3.5
восста́ние *(n)* декабри́стов	vasstaniye dikabristof	Decembrist Revolt	3.5
восто́к *(m)*	vastok	east	16.4
восхища́ться	vaskhishchat'sa	admire, to	2.8
вот есть	vot yest	there is; there are	15.1
вот э́тот *(m)*	vot etat	this one	16.2
впосле́дствии	vpaslyetstvii	subsequently	17.1
врач *(m)*	vrach	doctor	2.14
времена́ *(pl)* го́да	vrimina goda	seasons	1.6
вре́мя *(n)*	vryemya	time	17.1, 17.3
вре́мя *(n)* глаго́ла	vryemya glagola	verb tense	3.3
вре́мя *(n)* го́да	vryemye goda	season	1.6, 17.6
вре́мя *(n)* прибы́тия	vryemye pribytiya	arrival time	9.7
вре́мя *(n)* отъе́зда	vryemye at"yezda	departure time	9.7
вруча́ть	vruchat'	hand over, to	15.4
всё в поря́дке	vsyo v paryatki	all right; that's all right;	2.9
всегда́	vsigda	always	17.3
встава́ть	vstavat'	get up, to	2.4

вста́вить *(perf.)*; положи́ть *(perf.)*	vstavit'; palazhit'	put into, to	16.1
встать *(perf.)*	vstat'	get up, to	16.1
встре́тить *(perf.)*	vstryetit'	meet, to	14.2
вступи́тельный экза́мен *(m)*	vstupitel'niy ekzamin	entrance examination	12.8
Втора́я мирова́я война́ *(f)*	Vtaraya miravaya vaina	World War II	3.5
вто́рник *(m)*	ftornik	Tuesday	17.9
второ́й	ftoroy	second	17.9
второ́й год *(m)*	ftoroy got	second year	12.4
вход *(m)*	vkhot	entrance	8.5
входи́ть	vkhadit'	enter, to; get on, to	8.4, 9.6
вчера́	fchera	yesterday	17.8
вы о́чень добры́	vy ochin' dabry	you are too kind	4.3
Вы, Вас, Вам	vy, vas, vam	you *(polite)*, you, (to) you	2.13
вы, вас, вам	vy, vas, vam	you *(plural)*, you, (to) you	2.13
выбира́ть	vibirat'	elect, to; choose, to	10.3, 15.2
вы́боры *(pl)*	vybary	election(s)	10.3
вы́бросить *(perf.)*	vybrasit'	throw, to	16.1
вы́играть *(perf.)*	vyigrat'	win, to	14.4
вы́йти *(perf.)*	viyti	come out, to	16.1
выключа́тель *(m)*	vyklyuchatel'	switch	8.5
выключа́ть	vyklyuchat'	switch off, to	8.4, 11.4
выноси́ть му́сор	vynasit' musar	put the garbage out, to	8.7
выраже́ние *(n)*	vyrazheniye	expression	13.1
выра́щивать	vyrashchivat'	grow, to	10.8
выра́щивать живо́тных	vyrashchivat' zhivotnykh	raise animals, to	1.8
высо́кий	vysokiy	tall	2.2
высоко́	vysoko	high	18.2
высокоме́рный	vysakomyerniy	arrogant	2.11
высота́ *(f)*	vysata	height	18.2
вы́ставка *(f)*	vistavka	exhibition	11.7
вытира́ть	vytirat'	wipe, to	8.7
вытира́ть пыль	vitirat' pyl'	dust, to	8.7
выходи́ть	vykhadit'	get off, to	9.6
выходно́й	vikhadnoy	weekend	17.9
газ *(m)*	gaz	gas	8.6
газе́та *(f)*	gazyeta	newspaper	11.3
газо́н *(m)*	gazon	lawn	1.7, 8.4
галло́н *(m)*	galon	gallon	18.3
га́лстук *(m)*	galstuk	tie	6.3

гара́ж (m)	garazh	garage	8.1
гастроно́м (m)	gastranom	grocery store	7.1
гвоздь (m)	gvozd'	nail (metal)	8.8
где	gdye	where	16.3, 19.2
гекта́р (m)	giktar	hectare	18.2
геогра́фия (f)	giagrafiya	geography	3.4, 12.5
геоме́трия (f)	giamyetriya	geometry	12.5
Герма́ния (f)	Germaniya	Germany	9.2
гигие́на (f)	gigiyena	hygiene	2.5
гид (m)	git	tour guide; guide	2.14, 9.7
гимна́стика (f)	gimnastika	gymnastics	12.5
гита́ра (f)	gitara	guitar	11.8
гла́дить	gladit'	iron (clothes), to	8.7
глаз (m)	glaz	eye	2.2
гла́сный звук (m):	glasniy zvuk:	vowel:	3.3
уда́рный,	udarniy,	stressed,	
безуда́рный	bezudarniy	unstressed	
глубоко́	glubako	deep	18.2
глу́пый	glupiy	stupid	2.11
говори́ть	gavarit'	speak, to	13.2
говя́дина (f)	govyadina	beef	5.4
год (m)	got	year	17.5
головна́я боль (f)	galavnaya bol'	headache	2.6
голо́дный	galodniy	hungry	5.1
голубо́й	galuboy	blue	6.5
голубцы́ (pl)	golubtsy	golubtsi (stuffed cabbage)	5.7
гольф (m)	gol'f	golf	14.5
Гонко́нг (m)	Gankonk	Hong Kong	9.2
гора́ (f)	gora	mountain	1.2
горе́ть	garyet'	burn, to	1.5
го́рло (n)	gorla	throat	2.2
го́род (m)	gorat	city	3.1, 9.2
го́рький	gor'kiy	bitter	5.8
горя́чая вода́ (f)	garyachaya vada	hot water	2.5
горя́чий	garyachiy	hot (boiling)	5.8
горя́чий чай (m)	garyachiy chay	hot tea	5.9
господи́н (m)	gaspadin	Mr.	2.15
госпожа́ (f)	gaspazha	Mrs.	2.15
гости́ная (f)	gastinaya	living room	8.2
гости́ница (f)	gastinitsa	hotel	9.7, 9.8
гость (m)	gost'	guest	14.2
град (m)	grat	hail	1.4
грамм (m)	gramm	gram	18.3

грамма́тика *(f)*	grammatika	grammar	13.1
гра́фство *(n)*	grafstva	county	9.2
гре́бля *(f)*	gryeblya	rowing	14.5
Гре́ция *(f)*	Gryetsiya	Greece	9.2
грибы́ *(pl)*	griby	mushrooms	5.6, 5.7
грипп *(m)*	gripp	influenza	2.6
гром *(m)*	grom	thunder	1.4
гро́мкий го́лос *(m)*	gromkiy golas	loud voice	13.2
грудна́я кле́тка *(f)*	grudnaya klyetka	chest	2.2
грудь *(f)*	grud'	breast	2.2
Гру́зия *(f)*	Gruziya	Georgia	3.4
гру́ппа *(f)* из (+ *gen.*)	gruppa iz	group of	18.8
гру́ппа *(f)* славя́нских языков	gruppa slavyanskikh yezykov	Slavic language family	3.3
гру́стный	grustniy	sad	2.8
гру́ша *(f)*	grusha	pear	5.5
гря́зно	gryazna	dirty	8.7
гря́зный	gryazniy	dirty	6.1
гуля́ш *(m)*	gulyash	goulash	5.7
да	da	yes	4.2, 13.3
дава́ть	davat'	give, to	15.4
дава́ть взаймы́	davat' vzaimy	lend, to	10.10
давле́ние *(n)*	davlyeniye	blood pressure	2.6
давно́	davno	long time ago, (a) for a long time	17.1
давны́м-давно́	davnym-davno	once upon a time	17.1
да́же	dazhe	even	19.3
да́же бо́льше	dazhi bol'she	even more	15.2
да́нные *(pl)*	danniye	data	11.5
дари́ть пода́рок	darit' padarak	give a present, to	15.4
два	dva	two	18.1
два го́да наза́д	dva goda nazat	year before last (*2 years ago*)	17.5
два дня	dva dnya	two days	17.8
двадца́тый	dvatsatiy	twentieth	17.9
два́дцать	dvatsat'	twenty	18.1
два́дцать оди́н	dvatsat' adin	twenty-one	18.1
двена́дцатый ме́сяц *(m)*	dvinatsatiy myesats	twelfth month	17.7
двена́дцать	dvenatsat'	twelve	18.1
дверно́й звоно́к *(m)*	dvernoy zvanok	doorbell	8.5
дверь *(f)*	dvyer'	door	8.5
дви́гаться; переезжа́ть	dvigat'sa; pereyezhat'	move, to	16.1
движе́ние *(n)*	dvizhyeniye	traffic; movement	9.6, 16.1
двор *(m)*	dvor	backyard	8.4

Дворе́ц (*m*) съе́здов	Dvaryets s"yezdof	Palace of Congresses	3.2
дворяни́н (*m*)	dvarinin	nobleman	3.5
де́вочка (*f*); де́вушка (*f*)	dyevachka; dyevushka	girl	2.1
де́вочки (*pl*)	dyevachki	girls	2.15
де́вушка (*f*)	dyevushka	Miss	2.15
девяно́сто	divanosta	ninety	18.1
девятна́дцать	devatnatsat'	nineteen	18.1
де́вять	dyevat'	nine	18.1
дед (*m*)	dyed	grandpa	2.12
де́душка (*m*)	dyedushka	grandfather	2.12, 2.15
действи́тельность (*f*)	distvitil'nast'	reality	15.8
действи́тельный	deystvitel'niy	valid; real; actual	10.4, 15.8
дека́брь (*m*)	dikabr'	December	17.7
де́лать	dyelat'	do, to; make, to	15.1
де́лать докла́д	dyelat' daklat	make a presentation, to	11.4
де́лать оши́бку	dyelat' ashipku	make a mistake, to	13.2
деликате́сы (*pl*)	dilikatyesy	delicacies	5.1
дели́ть на (+ *acc.*)	dilit' na	divide into, to	18.1
дели́ться	dilit'sa	share, to	18.1
демокра́тия (*f*)	dimakratiya	democracy	3.5, 10.3
демонстра́ция (*f*)	dimanstratsiya	demonstration	10.9
день (*m*)	dyen'	day	1.1, 2.4, 17.9
день (*m*) рожде́ния	dyen' razhdyeniye	birthday	2.3
День (*m*) Труда́	Den' Truda	Labor Day	3.1
День Октя́брьской Револю́ции	Den' Oktyabr'skoy Revolyutsie	October Revolution Day	3.1
де́ньги (*pl*)	dyen'gi	money	7.3
дере́вня (*f*)	deryevnya	village	3.1, 9.2
де́рево (*n*)	dyereva	tree; wood	1.7, 8.8
держа́ть	derzhat'	hold, to	15.4
деся́тый	disyatiy	tenth	17.9
де́сять	dyesat'	ten	18.1
де́сять ты́сяч	dyesat' tysach	ten thousand	18.1
де́тский сад (*m*)	dyetskiy sat	kindergarten	12.2
джи́нсы (*pl*)	dzhinsy	jeans	6.2
диале́кт (*m*)	dialyekt	dialect	13.1
ди́кие живо́тные (*pl*)	dikiye zhivotniye	wild animals	1.8
дикта́нт (*m*)	diktant	dictation	12.6
диктату́ра (*f*)	diktatura	dictatorship	3.5
дина́стия (*f*)	dinastiya	dynasty	3.5
дина́стия (*f*) Рома́новых	dinastiya Romanavykh	Romanov dynasty	3.5
диплома́т (*m*)	diplamat	diplomat	2.14, 10.11
диплома́тия (*f*)	diplamatiya	diplomacy	10.11
дире́ктор (*m*)	diryektar	director	11.9

дире́ктор *(m)* шко́лы	diryektar shkoly	principal	12.3
дире́ктор *(m)* ча́стной шко́лы	diryektar chastnoy shkoly	headmaster	12.3
дирижёр *(m)*	dirizhyor	conductor *(of orchestra/band)*	2.14, 11.8
дискоте́ка *(f)*	diskatyeka	disco	9.8, 11.8
длина́ *(f)*	dlina	length	18.1, 18.2
дли́нный	dlinniy	long	6.1
дневни́к *(m)*	dnevnik	journal; assignment book	12.6
дневно́е вре́мя *(n)*	dnivnoye vryemya	daytime	17.10
дни *(pl)*	dni	days	17.8
до	do	before	19.3
до за́втра	da zaftra	see you tomorrow	4.5
до настоя́щего вре́мени	da nastayashchiva vryemini	until now	17.1
до свида́ния	da svidaniya	good-bye	4.5
до сих пор	da sikh por	still	15.8
до ско́рого	da skorava	see you soon	4.5
добро́ пожа́ловать	dabro pazhalavat'	welcome	4.4
до́брое у́тро *(n)*	dobraye utra	good morning	4.1
добросерде́чный	dabrasirdyechniy	warmhearted	2.11
до́брый	dobriy	kind	2.11
до́брый ве́чер *(m)*	dobriy vyecher	good evening	4.1
до́брый день *(m)*	dobriy dyen'	good afternoon	4.1
дово́льно	davol'na	fairly	18.6
дово́льный	davol'niy	comfortable; contented	2.9
дождли́вый	dazhdliviy	rainy	1.4
дождли́вый сезо́н *(m)*	dazhdliviy sizon	rainy season	1.4
дождь *(m)*	dozhd'	rain	1.4
дои́ть	dait'	milk, to	10.8
докла́д *(m)*, презента́ция *(f)*	daklat; prizintatsiya	presentation	11.4
до́ктор *(m)*	doktr	doctor; physician	2.7
документа́льный фильм *(m)*	dakumintal'niy fil'm	documentary	11.9
до́ллар *(m)*	dollar	dollar	7.3
дом *(m)*	dom	house	8.1
дома́шнее живо́тное *(n)*	damashniye zhivotnaye	pet	1.8
дома́шняя рабо́та *(f)*	damashnyaya rabota	homework	12.6
домохозя́йка *(f)*	damakhazyaika	housewife	2.14
дополни́тельные заня́тия *(pl)*	dapalnityel'niye zanyatiya	extracurricular activities	12.6
доро́га *(f)*	daroga	road	9.3
дороги́е друзья́ *(pl)*	daragiye druz'ya	dear friends	2.15

дорогóй	daragoy	expensive	7.3
дорóжка (f)	darozhka	footpath	9.3
доскá (f)	daska	blackboard	12.6
доставля́ть	dastavlyat'	deliver	7.2
достáточно	dastatachna	sufficient; enough	18.6
достопримечáтельности (pl)	dastaprimichatel'nasti	places of interest	9.7
дочь (f)	doch	daughter	2.12
дрáма (f)	drama	drama	11.9
друг (m)	druk	friend; boyfriend	14.1
другúе	drugiye	others	15.2
другúми словáми	drugimi slavami	in other words	19.3
другóй день	drugoy dyen'	other day, the	17.8
дрýжба (f)	druzhba	friendship	14.1
дружелю́бный	druzhilyubniy	friendly	2.11
друзья́ (pl) по перепúске	druz'ya pa piripiski	pen pals	14.1
Дýма (f)	Duma	Duma (parliament)	3.1
дýмать	dumat'	think, to	2.10
дуть	dut'	blow, to	1.4
душ (m)	dush	shower	8.5
Душанбé (m)	Dushanbe	Dushanbe (Tajikistan)	3.4
дýшный	dushniy	sultry	1.4
дым (m)	dym	smoke	5.12
ды́ня (f)	dynya	melon	5.5
дю́жина (f)	dyuzhina	dozen	18.8
дюйм (m)	dyuim	inch	18.2
дя́дя (m)	dyadya	uncle	2.12
Еврóпа (f)	Yevropa	Europe	9.2
едá (f)	yeda	food; meal	5.1, 18.8
едúнственное числó (n)	yedinstvinnoye chislo	singular	3.3
ежеднéвная газéта (f)	ezhidnyevnaya gazyeta	daily paper	11.3
éздить	yezdit'	ride, to	9.5
Еревáн (m)	Yerivan	Yerevan (Armenia)	3.4
éсли	yesli	if	19.3
есть	yest'	eat; be, to	5.1, 19.1
ещё нет	ishcho nyet	not yet	17.1
ещё раз	ishcho raz	once again	17.3
ещё; до сих пор	ishcho; da sikh por	still	15.8
жар (m)	zhar	fever	2.6
жáрить	zharit'	fry, to	5.10
жáрко	zharka	hot	1.4, 8.6
жвáчка (f)	zhvachka	chewing gum	5.4
желéзо (n)	zhilyeza	iron (element)	8.8
желýдок (m)	zhiludak	stomach	2.2

Russian	Transliteration	English	Reference
жена́ (f)	zhina	wife	2.12
жени́ться	zhinit'sa	marry, to	2.3
же́нщина (f)	zhenshchina	woman	2.1
Жёлтое мо́ре (n)	Zhyoltaye morye	Yellow Sea	9.4
жёлтый	zhyoltiy	yellow	6.5
живо́й	zhivoy	alive; lively	1.7, 2.3, 2.11
живо́т (m)	zhivot	abdomen	2.2
живо́тное (n)	zhivotnoye	animal	1.8
жизнь (f)	zhizn'	life	2.3
жи́рный	zhirniy	oily	5.8
жить	zhit'	live, to	8.4
журна́л (m)	zhurnal	magazine	11.3
журна́льный стол (m)	zhurnal'niy stol	coffee table	8.3
за (+ acc./inst.)	za	for	19.4
забо́р (m)	zabor	fence	8.5
забо́титься	zabotitsa	take care of, to	2.8
забра́ть (perf.)	zabrat'	take away, to	15.4, 16.1
забыва́ть	zabyvat'	forget, to	12.7
завёртывать	zavyortyvat'	wrap, to	7.2
заво́д (m)	zavot	factory	10.9
заво́рачивать	zavarachivat'	wrap, to	13.6
за́втра	zaftra	tomorrow	17.8
за́втрак (m)	zaftrak	breakfast	5.2
за́вуч (m)	zavuch	assistant principal	12.3
завяза́ть (perf.)	zavyazat'	tie, to	6.3
загоре́ться (perf.)	zagaryet'sa	catch fire, to	1.5
за́дний	zadniy	rear	16.5
зажéчь (perf.) огонь	zazhyech agon'	light a fire, to	8.6
зажига́лка (f)	zazhigalka	lighter	5.12
зайти́ за (+ acc.)	zayti za	pick up, to	16.1
заказа́ть (perf.)	zakazat'	order, to	7.2
заказа́ть (perf.) еду́	zakazat' yedu	order food, to	5.3
заказа́ть (perf.) ко́мнату (в гости́нице)	zakazat' komnatu (v gastinitse)	reserve a room (in a hotel)	9.7
зака́нчивать	zakanchivat'	finish, to	17.2
заключённый (m)	zaklyuchyonniy	prisoner	10.5
зако́н (m)	zakon	law	10.4
зако́нчен	zakonchin	completed	8.9
зако́нчить (perf.) уро́к (m)	zakonchit' urok	finish class, to	12.6
закры́ть	zakrit'	close, to	8.4
заку́сочная (f)	zakusochnaya	snackbar	9.8
зали́в (m)	zalif	bay	1.2
заменя́ть	zaminyat'	substitute, to	15.1

замо́к *(m)*	zamok	lock	8.5
заморо́женный	zamarozhenniy	frozen	5.4
за́навес *(m)*	zanavyes	curtain	8.5
заня́тие *(n)*, профе́ссия *(f)*	zanyatiye, prafessiya	occupation	10.7
за́нятый	zanyatiy	busy	10.7
зао́чное обуче́ние *(n)*	zaochnaye abuchyeniye	study by correspondence	12.2
за́пад *(m)*	zapat	west	16.4
за́падная медици́на *(f)*	zapadnaya miditsina	Western medicine	2.7
запасно́й вход *(m)*	zapasnoy vkhot	back entrance	8.5
запира́ть дверь	zapirat' dvyer'	lock the door, to	8.4
записа́ть *(perf.)*	zapisat'	make a list, to	7.2
запи́сывать на магнитофо́н	zapisyvat' na magnitafon	record, to	11.4
запомина́ть	zapaminat'	memorize, to	12.7
за́понки *(pl)*	zapanki	cufflinks	6.3
запра́вочная ста́нция *(f)*	zapravachnaya stantsiya	gas station	9.5
запреща́ть	zaprishchat'	prohibit, to	10.2
запята́я *(f)*	zapitaya	comma	11.2
застёгивать	zastyogivat'	button, to	6.1
застёжка *(f)*	zastyozhka	snap	8.9
засыпа́ть	zasypat'	go to sleep, to	2.4
зате́м	zatyem	then	19.3
защища́ть	zashishchat'	defend, to	10.4
зва́ный обе́д *(m)*	zvaniy abyet	dinner party	14.2
звезда́ *(f)*	zvyezda	star	1.1
звони́ть	zvanit'	call, to	13.7
звони́ть в дверь	zvanit' v dvyer'	ring the doorbell, to	8.4
звони́ть по телефо́ну	zvanit' pa tilifonu	telephone, to	13.7
звоно́к	zvanok	call	13.7
звук *(m)*	zvuk	sound	3.3, 13.1, 13.2
зда́ние *(n)*	zdaniye	building	8.1
здесь	zdyes'	here	16.3
здоро́вый	zdaroviy	healthy	2.6
здоро́вье *(n)*	zdarov'ye	health	2.6
здра́вствуйте	zdrastvuite	hello	4.1
зелёный	zilyoniy	green	6.5
зелёный горо́шек *(m)*	zilyoniy garoshik	green peas	5.6
земледе́лие *(n)*	zimledyeliye	agriculture	10.8
землетрясе́ние *(n)*	zimlitrisyeniye	earthquake	1.5
земля́ *(f)*	zimlya	earth: land; land	1.2, 10.8
зе́ркало *(n)*	zyerkala	mirror	8.5
зима́ *(f)*	zima	winter	1.6, 17.6

Зимба́бве (n)	Zimbabve	Zimbabwe	9.2
зи́мние кани́кулы (pl)	zimniye kanikuly	winter vacation	12.1
Зи́мный дворе́ц (m)	Zimniy dvaryets	Winter Palace	3.2
зло́бный	zlobniy	wicked	2.11
зна́ние (n)	znaniye	knowledge	12.7
знать	znat'	know, to	2.10, 12.7
значе́ние (n)	znachyeniye	meaning	13.1
Золото́е кольцо́ (n)	Zalatoye kal'tso	Golden Ring	3.2
золото́й	zalatoy	golden	6.5
зонт (m)	zont	umbrella	6.3
зоопа́рк (m)	zaapark	zoo	1.8, 9.8
зубна́я па́ста (f)	zubnaya pasta	toothpaste	2.5
зубна́я щётка (f)	zubnaya shchyotka	toothbrush	2.5
зубно́й врач (m)	zubnoy vrach	dentist	2.7, 2.14
зубри́ть	zubrit'	drill, to	12.7
зу́бы (pl)	zuby	teeth	2.2
и	i	and	19.3
игла́ (f)	igla	needle	6.1
игра́ть	igrat'	play (a musical instrument), to; play, to; act, to	11.8, 11.9
игра́ть в ка́рты	igrat' f karty	play cards, to	14.2
игра́ть в ша́хматы	igrat' f shakhmaty	play chess, to	14.3
игра́ть в ша́шки	igrat' f shashki	play checkers, to	14.3
игра́ть в электро́нные и́гры	igrat' v iliktronniye igry	play electronic games, to	14.3
игра́ть на инструме́нте	igrat' na instrumyente	play an instrument, to	14.3
игрова́я площа́дка (f)	igravaya plashchatka	playground	12.6
игрово́е по́ле (n)	igravoye polye	playing field	14.4
игро́к (m)	igrok	player	14.4
игру́шки (pl)	igrushki	toy store	7.1
идеа́льный	idial'niy	ideal	10.2
идти́	idti	go, to	16.1
идти́ в туале́т	iti f tualyet	go to the bathroom, to	2.5
идти́ к врачу́	iti k vrachu	go to the doctor, to	2.6
из (+ gen.)	iz	out	19.4
избало́ванный	izbalovanniy	spoiled	2.11
изве́стный	izvyestniy	famous	11.1
извини́те	izvinitye	excuse me	4.2
изда́тель (m)	izdatil'	publisher	2.14
измене́ния (pl)	izmenyeniya	change	10.2
изобрета́ть	izabritat'	invent, to	11.5
изобрете́ние (n)	izabrityeniye	invention	11.5
и́ли	ili	or	19.3

иллюстри́рованный	illyustriravanniy	pictorial	11.3
име́л, име́ла, име́ло	imyel, imyela, imyela	had	19.1
име́ли	imyeli	have	19.1
име́ть	imyet'	have, to	19.1
импера́тор *(m)*	impiratar	emperor	3.5
импорти́ровать	impartiravat'	import, to	10.10
и́мя *(n)*	imya	first name	2.12
ина́че	inache	otherwise	19.3
Инди́йский океа́н *(m)*	Indiyskiy akian	Indian Ocean	9.4
Индоне́зия *(f)*	Indanyeziya	Indonesia	9.2
инжене́р *(m)*	inzhinyer	engineer	2.14
инжене́р-строи́тель *(m)*	inzhinyer-straityel'	civil engineer	2.14
иногда́	inagda	sometimes; once in a while	17.1, 17.3
иностра́нец *(m)*, иностра́нка *(f)*	inastranyets, inastranka	foreigner	9.1
иностра́нный язы́к *(m)*	inastranniy eyzyk	foreign language	12.5, 13.1
институ́т *(m)*	institut	college; institute	9.8, 12.2
инструме́нт *(m)*	instrumyent	tool	8.8
интеллектуа́л *(m)*	intiliktual	intellectual	2.14
интере́сный	intiryesniy	interesting	2.9
интересова́ться	intirisavat'sa	interest, to; to be interested in	14.3
информи́ровать	infarmiravat'	inform, to	13.2, 13.6
Ирла́ндия *(f)*	Irlandiya	Ireland	9.2
иска́ть	iskat'	look for, to	16.1
иска́ть рабо́ту	iskat' rabotu	look for work, to	10.7
иску́сство *(n)*	iskustva	art	11.7
Испа́ния *(f)*	Ispaniya	Spain	9.2
испо́льзовать	ispol'zavat'	use, to	8.9
иссле́дование *(n)*	isslyedovaniye	research	12.7
иссле́дователь *(m)*	isslyedavatil'	researcher	2.14
иссле́довать	isslyedavat'	examine, to; research, to	11.5, 12.7
истори́ческий пери́од *(m)*	istarichiskiy piriot	historical period	3.5
исто́рия *(f)*	istoriya	history	12.5
истоща́ть	istashchat'	exhaust, to	2.8
Ита́лия *(f)*	Italiya	Italy	9.2
иудаи́зм *(m)*	iudaizm	Judaism	11.6
ию́ль *(m)*	iyul'	July	17.7
ию́нь *(m)*	iyun'	June	17.7
кабине́т *(m)*	kabinet	study	8.2
кабине́т *(m)*, бюро́ *(n)*	kabinyet, byuro	office	9.8, 10.7
Кавка́зские го́ры *(pl)*	Kavkazskiye gory	Caucasus Mountains	3.4

ка́ждая неде́ля (f)	kazhdaya nidyelya	every week	17.8
ка́ждое у́тро (n)	kazhdaye utra	every morning	17.10
ка́ждый	kazhdiy	everyone	2.13
ка́ждый год (m)	kazhdiy got	each year	17.5
ка́ждый день (m)	kazhdiy dyen'	every day	17.8
ка́ждый ме́сяц (m)	kazhdiy myesats	every month	17.6
ка́ждый раз (m)	kazhdiy raz	every time	17.1
ка́жется как бу́дто	kazhitsya kak budta	seem as if, to	15.2
Казахста́н (m)	Kazakhstan	Kazakhstan	3.4
как	kak	how	19.2
как вам подхо́дит	kak vam padkhodit	suit yourself	4.2
как вас зову́т?	kak vas zavut?	what is your name?	4.4
как вы пожива́ете?	kak vy pazhivaite?	how are you?	4.4
как далеко́	kak daliko	how far	19.2
как дела́?	kak dela?	how are things?	4.1
как до́лго?	kak dolga?	how long?	17.1, 18.4
как пожива́ете? А вы?	kak pazhivaite? A vy?	how are you? And you?	4.1
как то́лько	kak tol'ka	as soon as	19.3
как ужа́сно	kak uzhasna	how terrible	2.9
как хоти́те	kak khatite	as you wish	4.2
како́й	kakoy	which	16.2, 19.2
како́й предме́т?	kakoy pridmyet?	which subject?	12.5
календа́рь (m)	kalindar'	calendar	17.5
ка́менщик (m)	kamin'shchik	bricklayer	2.14
ка́мень (m)	kamin'	stone	1.2
Кана́да (f)	Kanada	Canada	9.2
кана́дец (m), кана́дка (f)	kanadyets, kanadka	Canadian	9.2
кани́кулы (pl)	kanikuly	vacation	12.1
канцеля́рские това́ры (pl)	kantsilyarskiye tavary	stationery shop	7.1
капита́л (m)	kapital	capital	10.6
капитали́зм (m)	kapitalizm	capitalism	10.3
капу́ста (f)	kapusta	cabbage	5.6
каранда́ш (m)	karandash	pencil	13.5
карма́н (m)	karman	pocket	6.1
ка́рта (f)	karta	map	9.1
карти́на (f)	kartina	picture; painting	8.5, 11.7
карти́нная галере́я (f)	kartinnaya galiryeya	art gallery	9.8, 11.7
карто́шка (f)	kartoshka	potato	5.4, 5.6
Каспи́йское мо́ре (n)	Kaspiyskaya morye	Caspian Sea	9.4
кассе́та (f)	kassyeta	cassette tape	11.4
касси́р (m), касси́рша (f)	kasir, kasirsha	cashier	2.14, 7.2
кастрю́ля (f) (+ gen.)	kastryulya	pot (of)	18.8
ката́ние (n) на конька́х	kataniye na kon'kakh	ice-skating	14.5
ката́ние (n) на лы́жах	kataniye na lyzhakh	skiing	14.5

католи́ческая це́рковь *(f)*	katalichiskaya tserkaf'	Roman Catholic	11.6
кафе́ *(n)*	kafye	café	5.3
кафете́рий *(m)*	kafityeriy	cafeteria	5.3
ка́шлять	kashlyat'	cough, to	2.6
кварти́ра *(f)*	kvartira	apartment	8.1
квита́нция *(f)*	kvitantsiya	receipt	7.2
кéды *(pl)*	kyedy	tennis shoes	6.3
Ки́ев *(m)*	Kiyef	Kiev (Ukraine)	3.4
Ки́евская Русь *(f)*	Kiyevskaya Rus'	Kievan Rus	3.5
килогра́мм *(m)*	kilagramm	kilogram	18.3
киломе́тр *(m)*	kilamyetr	kilometer	18.2
кино́ *(n)*, фильм *(m)*	kino, fil'm	movie, film	11.9
кинозвезда́ *(f)*	kinozvezda	movie star	11.9
кинотеа́тр *(m)*	kinatiatr	movie theater	9.8, 11.9
кипячёная вода́ *(f)*	kipachyonaya vada	boiled water	5.9
кирпи́ч *(m)*	kirpich	brick	8.8
ки́слый	kisliy	sour	5.8
ки́сточка *(f)*	kistachka	brush	13.5
Кита́й *(m)*	Kitay	China	9.2
Кишинёв *(m)*	Kishinyov	Kishinev (Moldova)	3.4
класси́ческая му́зыка *(f)*	klassichiskaya muzyka	classical music	11.8
кла́сс *(m)*	klass	classroom	12.6
клей *(m)*	klyey	glue	8.9
кли́мат *(m)*	klimat	climate	1.4
клубни́ка *(f)*	klubnika	strawberry	5.5
ключи́ *(pl)*	klyuchi	keys	8.5
кни́га *(f)*	kniga	book	11.2
кни́жная по́лка *(f)*	knizhnaya polka	bookshelf	8.5
кни́жный магази́н *(m)*	knizhniy magazin	bookstore	7.1, 9.8, 11.2
кни́жный шкаф *(m)*	knizhniy shkaf	bookcase	8.3
ковёр *(m)*	kavyor	carpet	8.5
когда́	kagda	when	17.1, 19.2
когда́ придёт вре́мя	kagda pridyot vryemya	when the time comes	17.1
ко́жа *(f)*	kozha	skin; leather	1.8, 2.2, 6.4
ко́ка-ко́ла *(f)*	koka-kola	Coca-Cola®	5.9
коли́чество *(n)*	kalichistva	quantity	18.5
колле́га *(m, f)*	kalyega	colleague	14.1
колле́дж *(m)*	kalyedzh	college	12.2
колле́кция *(f)* ма́рок	kallyektsiya marak	stamp collection	13.6
кольцо́ *(n)*	kal'tso	ring	6.3
кома́нда *(f)* (+ *gen.*)	kamanda	team; team (of)	14.4, 18.8
коме́дия *(f)*	kamyediya	comedy	11.9
коми́ческие расска́зы *(pl)*	komichiskiye rasskazy	comics	11.3
комме́рция *(f)*	kammyertsiya	commerce	10.10

коммуни́зм (m)	kammunizm	communism	10.3
ко́мната (f)	komnata	room (in a house)	8.2
ко́мната (f) для госте́й	komnata dlya gostey	guest room	8.2
компа́кт-диск (m)	kampakt-disk	CD (compact disc)	11.4
конве́рт (m)	kanvyert	envelop	13.5
конди́терская (f)	kanditerskaya	bakery (sweets)	5.3
кондиционе́р (m)	kanditsianyer	air conditioner	8.6
кондициони́рованный во́здух (m)	kanditsianiravanniy vozdukh	air conditioning	8.6
конду́ктор (m), конду́кторша (f)	kanduktar, kanduktarsha	conductor (ticket seller)	2.14
коне́ц (m)	kanyets	end	17.2
коне́ц (m) шко́льного дня	kanyets shkol'nava dnya	end of school day	12.6
коне́чно	kanyeshna	of course	15.8
консе́рвная ба́нка (f) с (+ inst.)	kansyervnaya banka s	can of	18.8
конспекти́ровать	kanspiktirovat'	take notes, to	13.4
ко́нсульство (n)	konsul'stva	consulate	10.11
контакти́ровать	kantaktiravat'	contact, to	13.6
контине́нт (m)	kantinyent	continent	1.2
контро́льная рабо́та (f)	kantrol'naya rabota	test	12.1, 12.8
конфе́та (f)	kanfyeta	candy	5.4
конце́рт (m)	kantsert	concert	11.8
конце́ртный зал (m)	kantsyertniy zal	concert hall	9.8, 11.8
Конце́ртный зал (m) и́мени Чайко́вского	Kantsertniy zal imini Chaikovskava	Tchaikovsky Concert Hall	3.2
ко́пия (f)	kopiya	copy	12.6
кора́бль (m)	karabl'	ship	9.5
ко́рень (m)	koren'	root	1.7
Коре́я (f)	Koryeya	Korea	9.2
корзи́на (f) с (+ inst.)	karzina s	basket of	18.8
коридо́р (m)	karidor	corridor	8.2
кори́чневый	karichniviy	brown	6.5
коро́бка (f) (+ inst.)	karopka	box (of); carton (of)	18.8
коро́ва (f)	karova	cow	1.9
коро́ль (m)	karol'	king	10.3
коро́ткий, ма́ленький	karotkiy, malin'kiy	short	2.2, 6.1, 18.2
коси́лка (f) для травы́	kasilka dlya travy	lawnmower	8.8
кость (f)	kost'	bone	2.2
костю́м (m)	kastyum	suit	6.2
кото́рый	katoriy	which one	16.2
кото́рый час?	katoriy chas?	what time is it?	17.11
ко́шка (f)	koshka	cat	1.9

край (*m*)	kray	edge	16.5
краси́вый	krasiviy	beautiful	15.7
кра́сная икра́ (*f*) с блина́ми	krasnaya ikra s blinami	red caviar with blinis	5.7
Кра́сное мо́ре (*n*)	Krasnaye morye	Red Sea	9.4
кра́сный	krasniy	red	6.5
красть	krast'	steal, to	10.5
креди́тная ка́рточка (*f*)	kriditnaya kartochka	credit card	7.3
крем (*m*)	kryem	cream	5.4
крем (*m*) для боти́нок	kryem dlya batinak	shoe polish	6.3
Кремль (*m*)	Kreml'	Kremlin	3.2
кре́мовый	kryemaviy	cream	6.5
кре́пкий	krepkiy	strong	5.8
крепостно́е пра́во (*n*)	kripastnoye prava	serfdom	3.5
кре́сло (*n*)	kryesla	armchair	8.3
крестья́нин (*m*), крестья́нка (*f*)	krist'yanin, krist'yanka	peasant	2.14
крича́ть; пла́кать	krichat'; plakat'	cry, to	2.8
крова́ть (*f*)	kravat'	bed	8.3
кровь (*f*)	krov'	blood	2.2
кро́ме (+ *gen.*)	kromye	except	19.4
кро́ткий	krotkiy	gentle	2.11
кру́жево (*n*)	kruzhivo	lace	6.4
кры́ша (*f*)	krysha	roof	8.5
кто	kto	who	19.2
кто, кого́, кому́	kto, kavo, kamu	who, whom, (to) whom	2.13
Ку́ба (*f*)	Kuba	Cuba	9.2
кукуру́за (*f*)	kukuruza	corn	5.6
кулебя́ка (*f*)	kulibyaka	kulibyaka (*cabbage bread*)	5.7
культу́ра (*f*)	kul'tura	culture	10.1, 11.1
культу́рный	kul'turniy	cultural	11.1
купа́льный костю́м (*m*)	kupal'niy kostyum	swimsuit	14.4
кури́ть	kurit'	smoke, to	5.12
ку́рица (*f*)	kuritsa	chicken	1.9, 5.4
куса́ть	kusat'	bite, to	1.8
кусо́к (*m*) (+ *gen.*)	kusok	piece (of); slice (of)	18.8
куст (*m*)	kust	bush	1.7
ку́хня (*f*)	kukhnya	cuisine; kitchen	5.7, 8.2
Кыргызста́н (*m*)	Kyrgystan	Kyrgyzstan	3.4
лаборато́рия (*f*)	labaratoriya	laboratory	11.5
ла́стик (*m*)	lastik	eraser	13.5
Ла́твия (*f*)	Latviya	Latvia	3.4
Лати́нская Аме́рика (*f*)	Latinskaya Amyerika	Latin America	9.2
ла́ять	layet'	bark, to	1.8

ле́ктор *(m)*	lyektar	lecturer	2.14, 12.3
лени́вый	liniviy	lazy	2.11, 10.7
лес *(m)*	lyes	forest	1.7
ле́стница *(f)*	lyesnitsa	stairs	8.5
лета́ть	litat'	fly	1.8
ле́тнее вре́мя *(n)*	lyetniye vryemya	daylight saving time	17.1
ле́тние кани́кулы *(pl)*	lyetniye kanikuly	summer vacation	12.1
Ле́тний дворе́ц *(m)*	Letniy dvaryets	Summer Palace	3.2
ле́то *(n)*	lyeta	summer	1.6, 17.6
лёгкие *(pl)*	lyokiye	lungs	2.2
лёгкий	lyokhkiy	light	18.3
лёд *(m)*	lyot	ice	5.9
лён *(m)*	lyon	linen	6.4
либерали́зм *(m)*	libiralizm	liberalism	10.3
лимо́н *(m)*	limon	lemon	5.5
лимона́д *(m)*	limanat	lemonade	5.9
лине́йка *(f)*	linyeika	ruler	13.5
лист *(m)*	list	leaf	1.7
Литва́ *(f)*	Litva	Lithuania	3.4
литерату́ра *(f)*	litiratura	literature	11.2, 12.5
литр *(m)*	litr	liter	18.3
лифт *(m)*	lift	elevator	8.5
лицо́ *(n)*	litso	face	2.2
лицо́м к *(+ dat.)*	litsom k	facing	16.4
лови́ть ры́бу	lavit' ribu	fish, to	14.3
ло́дка *(f)*	lotka	boat	9.5
ложи́ться	lazhitsa	lie down, to	2.4
ложи́ться спать	lazhit'sa spat'	go to bed, to	2.4
ло́жка *(f) (+ gen.)*	lozhka	spoon; spoon (of)	5.11, 18.8
ло́жный, фальши́вый	lozhniy, fal'shiviy	false	15.8
лома́ть	lamat'	break, to	8.9
лук *(m)*	luk	onion	5.6
луна́ *(f)*	luna	moon	1.1
лу́нный календа́рь *(m)*	lunniy kalendar'	lunar calendar	17.5
лу́чше чем	luchshe chem	better than	15.2
льстить	l'stit'	flatter, to	2.9
люби́тель *(m)* му́зыки	lyubitel' muzyki	music fan	11.8
люби́ть	lyubit'	love, to	2.9
любо́вь *(f)*	lyubov'	love	2.9
любы́е	lyubiye	all kinds (of)	15.2
лю́ди *(pl)*	lyudi	people	2.1
Мавзоле́й *(m)* Ле́нина	Mavzalyei Lenina	Lenin's tomb	3.2
магази́н *(m)*	magazin	shop; store	7.2, 9.8
магнитофо́н *(m)*	magnitafon	tape recorder	11.4

мада́м (f)	madam	madam	2.15
май (m)	may	May	17.7
ма́йка (f)	mayka	T-shirt; undershirt	6.2
ма́ленький	malin'kiy	small	18.1
мали́на (f)	malina	raspberry	5.5
ма́ло	mala	little	18.5
Ма́лый теа́тр (m)	Maliy tiatr	Maly Theater	3.2
ма́льчик (m)	mal'chik	boy	2.1
ма́льчики (pl)	mal'chiki	boys	2.15
ма́ма (f)	mama	mom	2.12
ма́нго (n)	manga	mango	5.5
мандари́н (m)	mandarin	mandarin (orange)	5.5
ма́рка (f)	marka	stamp	13.6
март (m)	mart	March	17.7
ма́сло (n)	masla	butter	5.4
матема́тика (f)	matimatika	mathematics	12.5
материа́л (m)	matirial	fabric; material	6.4, 8.8
матери́к (m)	matirik	mainland	1.2
матро́с (m)	matros	sailor	2.14
мать (f)	mat'	mother	2.12
ма́чеха (f)	machikha	stepmother	2.12
маши́на (f)	mashina	car; machine	9.5, 10.9
мгла (f)	mgla	mist	1.4
ме́бель (f)	myebil'	furniture	8.3
ме́бельный магази́н (m)	myebil'niy magazin	furniture store	7.1
медве́дь (m)	midvyet'	bear	1.9
медици́на (f)	miditsina	medicine	2.7
ме́дленно	myedlinna	slow; slowly	17.1, 17.4
ме́дленный	myedliniy	slow	17.4
медсестра́ (f)	medsistra	nurse	2.7, 2.14
ме́жду (+ inst.)	mezhdu	between	16.3, 16.5
междунаро́дная торго́вля (f)	mezhdunarodnaya targovlya	foreign trade	10.10
междунаро́дный	mezhdunarodniy	international	10.11
Междунаро́дный же́нский день	Mezhdunarodniy zhenskiy dyen'	International Woman's Day	3.1
междунаро́дный разгово́р (m)	mizhdunarodniy razgavor	international call	13.7
Ме́ксика (f)	Myeksika	Mexico	9.2
мел (m)	myel	chalk	12.6
ме́лко	myelka	shallow	18.2
ме́лочь (f); сда́ча (f)	myeloch; sdacha	change	7.3
ме́ньше чем	myen'she chyem	less than	18.4
меньшинство́ (n)	men'shinstvo	minority	18.1

меню́ (n)	minyu	menu	5.3
меня́ зову́т …	minya zavut …	my name is …	4.4
меня́ть	minyat'	exchange, to; change, to	7.2, 15.1
ме́стные жи́тели (pl)	myestniye zhitili	local residents	9.1
ме́сто (n)	myesta	place	16.3
ме́сяц (m)	myesats	month	17.6
метла́ (f)	mitla	broom	8.7
ме́тод (m)	myetot	method	11.5
методи́чный	mitadichniy	methodical	2.11
метр (m)	myetr	meter	18.2
метро́ (n)	metro	metro; subway	3.1, 9.5
меха́ник (m)	mikhanik	mechanic	2.14
мечта́ть	michtat'	dream, to	2.4
мешо́к (m) с (+ inst.)	mishok s	bag of	18.8
мёртвый	myortviy	dead; dead, to be	1.7, 2.3
ми́кроволно́вая печь (f)	mikravalnovaya pech	microwave oven	5.11
ми́ли (pl)	mili	miles	18.2
милиционе́р (m)	militsianyer	policeman	2.14
мили́ция (f)	militsiya	police station	9.8
мили́ция (f), поли́ция (f)	militsiya, politsiya	police	10.5
миллиме́тр (m)	millimyetr	millimeter	18.2
ми́лый	miliy	nice; lovable	2.9, 2.11, 15.7
минера́льная вода́ (f)	miniral'naya vada	mineral water	5.9
Министе́рство (n) иностра́нных дел	Ministyerstva inastrannykh dyel	Department of Foreign Affairs	10.3
Министе́рство (n) образова́ния	Ministyerstva abrazavaniya	Department of Education	10.3
Минск (m)	Minsk	Minsk (Belarus)	3.4
мину́ты (pl)	minuty	minutes	17.11
мир (m)	mir	world; peace	9.1, 10.11
ми́ска (f) (+ gen.)	miska	bowl; bowl (of)	5.11, 18.8
младе́нец (m)	mladyenits	baby	2.1
мне́ние (n)	mnyeniye	opinion	10.3
мно́го	mnoga	many; much	18.7
мно́жественное число́ (n)	mnozhistvennoye chislo	plural	3.3
мо́дный	modniy	fashionable	6.1
мо́жно вас побеспоко́ить?	mozhna vas pabispakoit'?	may I trouble you?	4.2
мозг (m)	mozg	brain	2.2
мо́крый	mokriy	wet	1.4
Молдо́ва (f)	Maldova	Moldova	3.4
моли́ться	malit'sa	pray, to	11.6
мо́лния (f)	molniya	lightning	1.4

Russian	Transliteration	English	Ref
молодо́й	maladoy	young	2.3
молодо́й челове́к (m)	maladoy chilavyek	young person	2.1
молоко́ (n)	malako	milk	5.9, 10.8
молото́к (m)	malatok	hammer	8.8
мона́х (m)	manakh	monk	11.6
мона́хиня (f)	manakhinya	nun	11.6
мо́ре (n)	morye	sea	9.4
морко́вь (f)	morkov'	carrots	5.6
моро́женое (n)	marozhinaye	ice cream	5.4
моро́сящий дождь (m)	marasyashchiy dozhd'	drizzle	1.4
Москва́ (f)	Maskva	Moscow (Russia)	3.1, 3.4
Москва́-река́ (f)	Maskva-rika	Moskva River	3.4
Моско́вский университе́т (m)	Maskofskiy univirsityet	Moscow University	3.2
мост (m)	most	bridge	9.3
мотоци́кл (m)	matatsikl	motorcycle	9.5
мочь; быть в состоя́нии	moch'; byt' v sastayaniye	able, to be	15.1
муж (m)	muzh	husband	2.12
мужчи́на (m)	muzhchina	man	2.1
музе́й (m)	muzyey	museum	9.8
музе́й (m) Пу́шкина	muzey Pushkina	Pushkin Museum	3.2
музе́й-уса́дьба (m) Ясная Поля́на	muzey-usat'ba Yasnaya Palyana	Yasnaya Polyana Estate Museum	3.2
му́зыка (f)	muzyka	music	11.8
музыка́льный инструме́нт (m)	muzykal'niy instrumyent	musical instrument	11.8
музыка́нт (m)	muzykant	musician	2.14, 11.8
мураве́й (m)	muravyei	ant	1.9
му́скул (m)	muskl	muscle	2.2
му́сорное ведро́ (n)	musarnaye vidro	trash can	8.5
мы, нас, нам	my, nas, nam	we, us, (to) us	2.13
мы́ло (n)	myla	soap	2.5, 8.7
мыть го́лову	myt' golavu	shampoo one's hair, to	2.5
мыть лицо́	myt' litso	wash one's face, to	2.5
мыть маши́ну	myt' mashinu	wash the car, to	8.4
мыть посу́ду	myt' pasudu	wash dishes, to	8.7
мыть; стира́ть	myt'; stirat'	wash, to	8.7
мя́гкий	myakhkiy	tender; soft	5.8, 8.8
мя́гкий знак (m)	myakhkiy znak	soft sign	3.3
мя́гкий; кро́ткий	myakhkiy; krotkiy	gentle	2.11
мясно́й магази́н (m)	myasnoy magazin	butcher shop	7.1
мясно́й сала́т (m)	misnoy salat	meat salad	5.7
мя́со (n)	myasa	meat	5.4
на (+ acc./prep.)	na	at	19.4

на здоро́вье!	na zdarov'ye!	cheers!	4.2
набо́р *(m)* *(+ gen.)*	nabor	set (of)	18.8
наверху́	naverkhu	upstairs	8.5
наводне́ние *(n)*	navadnyeniye	flood	1.5
над *(+ inst.)*	nat	above	16.3
наде́яться	nadyeyatsa	hope, to	2.8
надёжный	nadyozhniy	reliable	2.11
наза́д	nazat	back	16.3
наза́д: 5 лет (тому́) наза́д	nazat: 5 lyet (tamu) nazat	ago: 5 years ago	17.1
наибо́льший	naibol'shiy	most	18.1
наказа́ние *(n)*	nakazaniye	detention	12.6
наконе́ц	nakanyets	at last	17.1
накрыва́ть на стол	nakryvat' na stol	set the table, to	5.1
нали́чные де́ньги *(pl)*	nalichniye dyen'gi	cash	7.3
наме́рение *(n)*	namyereniye	intention	2.8
наоборо́т	naoborot	on the contrary	15.2
напи́тки *(pl)*	napitki	drinks	5.9
направле́ние *(n)*	napravlyeniye	direction	16.4, 16.5
наприме́р	naprimyer	for example	19.3
наро́дная му́зыка *(f)*	narodnaya muzyka	folk music	11.8
населе́ние *(n)*	nasilyeniye	population	9.1, 10.2
насто́льная ла́мпа *(f)*	nastol'naya lampa	desk lamp	8.5
насто́льный те́ннис *(m)*	nastol'niy tyennis	table tennis	14.5
настра́ивать	nastraivat'	tune in, to	11.4
нау́ка *(f)*	nauka	science	11.5
нау́чный	nauchniy	scientific	11.5
нау́чный фильм *(m)*	nauchniy fil'm	science film	11.9
нача́ло *(n)*	nachala	beginning; start	17.1, 17.2
нача́льная шко́ла *(f)*	nachal'naya shkola	elementary school	12.2, 12.4
нача́льник *(m)*	nachal'nik	manager	10.10
начина́ть	nachinat'	begin, to; start, to	12.1, 17.1, 17.2
не мочь найти́	ne moch' nayti	be unable to find, to	16.1
не рабо́тает	ni rabotayet	broken *(out of order)*	8.9
не сдать *(perf.)* экза́мен	ni sdat' ekzamin	fail an exam, to	12.8
не так хорошо́ как	ni tak kharasho kak	not as good as	15.2
не торопи́тесь	ni tarapityes'	take your time	17.1
не́бо *(n)*	nyeba	sky	1.1
небоскрёб *(m)*	nibaskryop	skyscraper	8.1
Нева́ *(f)*	Neva	Neva (river)	3.4
нева́жный	nivazhniy	unimportant	2.9
невино́вный	nivinovniy	innocent	10.4
неда́вно	nidavna	recently	17.1
неде́ля *(f)*	nidyelya	week	17.8, 17.9

нейло́н *(m)*	neilon	nylon	6.4
некраси́вый	nikrasiviy	ugly	6.1, 15.7
неме́дленно	nimyedlinna	at once *(immediately)*	17.1
немно́го	nimnoga	few; little (of); not much	18.5, 18.8
ненадёжный	ninadyozhniy	untrustworthy	2.11
необходи́мый	niabkhadimiy	necessary	15.3
неожи́данный	niazhidanniy	unexpected	1.5, 2.8
непра́вильный, неве́рный	nepravil'niy, nivyerniy	wrong; incorrect	12.7
неприя́тности *(pl)*	nipriyatnasti	trouble	2.9
не́рвный	nyervniy	nervous	2.8, 15.3
не́рвы *(pl)*	nyervy	nerves	2.2
не́сколько	nyeskol'ko	several	18.1
не сто́ит благода́рности	ni stoit blagadarnasti	don't mention it	4.3
нет	nyet	no	4.2, 13.3
нет пробле́м	nyet prablyem	no problem	4.2
неуда́ча *(f)*	niudacha	bad luck	2.9
неуда́чный	niudachniy	unsuccessful	2.9
неумоли́мый	niumalimiy	stern	2.11
ни́жняя часть *(f)*	nizhnyaya chast'	lower part	16.5
ни́зко	nizka	low	18.2
ни́тка *(f)*	nitka	thread	6.1
нить *(f)* *(+ gen.)*	nit'	string (of)	18.8
ничего́	nichivo	never mind, that's all right	4.2
но	no	but	15.8, 19.3
Но́вая Зела́ндия *(f)*	Novaya Zilandiya	New Zealand	9.2
но́вости *(pl)*	novasti	news	11.3, 11.4
но́вый	noviy	new	17.1
Но́вый год *(m)*	Noviy got	New Year('s)	17.5
нога́ *(f)*	naga	foot; leg	2.2
но́готь *(m)*	nogat'	nail *(finger/toe)*	2.2
нож *(m)*	nozh	knife	5.11
но́жницы *(pl)*	nozhnitsy	scissors	6.1, 8.8
ноль; нуль; ничего́	nol'; nul'; nichivo	zero; nothing	18.1, 18.5
но́мер *(m)*	nomir	room *(in a hotel)*; number *(house)*; number	8.2, 9.3, 18.1
но́мер *(m)* на двои́х	nomir na dvoikh	double room *(in a hotel)*	8.2
но́мер *(m)* телефо́на	nomir tilifona	telephone number	13.7
но́мер *(m)* на одного́	nomir na adnovo	single room *(in a hotel)*	8.2
нос *(m)*	nos	nose	2.2
носи́ть	nasit'	wear, to	6.1
носки́ *(pl)*	naski	socks	6.2
носово́й плато́к *(m)*	nasavoy platok	handkerchief	6.3

ноя́брь *(m)*	nayabr'	November	17.7
нра́виться; мне нра́вится	nravit'sa; mnye nravitsa	like, to; I like	2.9, 14.3
нужда́ться	nuzhdat'sa	need, to	15.3
ну́жный	nuzhniy	useful	15.1
обвиня́ть	obvinyat'	prosecute, to	10.4
обе́д *(m)*	abyet	dinner	5.2
о́блако *(n)*	oblaka	cloud	1.4
о́блачно	oblachna	cloudy	1.4
облегча́ть	ablikhchat'	relieve, to	2.8
обме́н *(m)*	abmyen	exchange	7.3
обме́н де́нег	abmyen dyenig	money exchange	7.3
образова́ние *(n)*	obrazavaniye	education	12.1
обрыва́ть	abryvat'	cut off, to	13.7
обставля́ть	apstavlyat'	decorate, to	8.4
о́бувь *(f)*	obuv'	shoe shop	7.1
обще́ственные нау́ки *(pl)*	obshchestveniye nauki	social science	12.5
обще́ственный поря́док *(m)*	obshchestveniy paryadak	social order	10.5
о́бщество *(n)*	opshistva	society	10.1
общи́на *(f)*	abshchina	community	9.2
объём *(m)*	ob"yom	volume	18.3
объясне́ние *(n)*	ab"yesnyeniye	explanation	13.2
объясня́ть	ab"yesnyat'	explain, to	13.2
обы́чай *(m)*	abychay	custom	10.1, 11.1
обы́чно	abychna	usually	17.3
обы́чный	abbychniy	common	15.7
обя́занность *(f)*	abyazannast'	duty; responsibility	10.1
о́вощи *(pl)*	ovashchi	vegetables	5.6, 10.8
овощно́е блю́до *(n)*	avoshchnoye blyuda	vegetable dish	5.6
огуре́ц *(m)*	aguryets	cucumber	5.6
оде́жда *(f)*	adyezhda	clothes; clothing	6.1
одея́ло *(n)*	adiyala	blanket	8.3
оди́н	adin	one	18.1
оди́н день	adin dyen'	one day	17.8
оди́н ме́сяц	adin myesats	one month	17.6
оди́ннадцать	adinatsat'	eleven	18.1
одино́кий	adinokiy	lonely	2.8
однокла́ссник *(m)*	adnaklassnik	classmate	14.1
одолжи́ть	adalzhit'	borrow, to	7.2, 10.10
о́зеро *(n)*	ozira	lake	1.3
О́зеро *(n)* Байка́л	Ozero Baikal	Lake Baikal	3.4
озорно́й	azarnoy	mischievous	2.11
ока́нчивать шко́лу	akanchivat' shkolu	graduate, to	12.1
океа́н *(m)*	akian	ocean	1.3, 9.4

оккупáция *(f)*	akupatsiya	occupation	3.5
окнó *(n)*	akno	window	8.5
óколо *(+ gen.)*	okala	about *(more or less)*	17.1, 18.4
оконча́ние *(n)*	akanchaniye	ending	3.3
оконча́ние *(n)* шко́лы	akanchaniye shkoly	graduation	12.1
октя́брь *(m)*	aktyabr'	October	17.7
Октя́брьская револю́ция *(f)*	Aktyabr'skaya rivalutsiya	October Revolution	3.5
оле́нь *(m)*	alyen'	deer	1.9
он, его́, ему́	on, yevo, yemu	he, him, (to) him	2.13
она́, её, ей	ana, yeyo, yey	she, her, (to) her	2.13
они́, их, им	ani, ikh, im	they, them, (to) them	2.13
опа́сность *(f)*	apasnast'	danger	1.5, 9.6
óпера *(f)*	opira	opera	3.2, 11.8
опера́тор *(m)*	apiratr	operator	2.14
опера́ция *(f)*	apiratsiya	operation; surgery	2.7
определённо	apridilyonna	certainly	15.8
определённый	apridilyonniy	certain	15.8
опусти́ть *(perf.)*	apustit'	put down, to	16.1
óпыт *(m)*	opyt	experience; skill	10.7, 10.9
óпытный	opytniy	experienced	10.7
ора́нжевый	aranzhiviy	orange	6.5
Организа́ция *(f)* Объединённых На́ций	Arganizatsiya Ab"yedinyonykh Natsiy	United Nations	10.11
организо́вывать	arganizovyvat'	arrange, to	14.2
оре́хи *(pl)*	aryekhi	nuts	5.4
орке́стр *(m)*	arkyestr	orchestra	11.8
освобожде́ние *(n)*	asvabazhdyeniye	liberation	3.5
óсень *(f)*	osen'	fall, autumn	1.6, 17.6
осознава́ть	asaznavat'	realize, to	2.10
оставля́ть маши́ну	astavlyat' mashinu	park, to	9.5
оставля́ть; уходи́ть	astavlyat'; ukhadit'	leave, to	8.4
остана́вливаться	astanavlivat'sya	stop, to	9.5
останови́ться *(perf.)*	astanavit'sa	stop, to	17.2
остано́вка *(f)*	ostanofka	stop *(bus, trolley, etc.)*	9.5, 17.2
осторо́жно	astarozhna	careful; carefully	9.6
осторо́жный	astarozhniy	careful	2.8, 2.11
óстров *(m)*	ostraf	island	1.2
óстрый	ostriy	hot *(spicy)*; sharp	5.8, 8.8
от *(+ gen.)*	ot	from	19.4
отве́т *(m)*	atvyet	answer	13.2
отве́тственный	atvyetstvenniy	person in charge	10.10
отвеча́ть	atvichat'	answer, to	12.8, 13.2, 13.7

Russian	Transliteration	English	Ref
отвёртка (f)	atvyortka	screwdriver	8.8
отвёртывать	atvyortyvat'	unscrew, to	8.9
отделение (n) полиции	atdyelyenie politsii	police station	10.5
отделять	atdelyat'	detach, to; separate, to	16.1
отдых (m)	otdykh	rest	14.3
отдыхать	atdykhat'	rest, to	14.3
отец (m)	atyets	father	2.12
открывать	atkrivat'	open, to; discover, to	8.4, 11.5
открытие (n)	otkritiye	discovery	11.5
откуда вы?	atkuda vy?	where are you from?	4.1
отнимать	atnimat'	subtract, to	18.1
относительно (+ gen.)	otnasitil'no	concerning	19.4
отношения (pl)	atnashyeniya	attitudes; relationships	2.9, 15.1
отопительный прибор (m)	atapityel'niy pribor	heater	8.6
отопление (n)	ataplyeniye	heating	8.6
отправлять по почте	atpravlyat' pa pochte	mail, to	13.6
отпускать	atpuskat'	release, to	10.5
отчим (m)	ochim	stepfather	2.12
отъезд (m)	at"yezd	departure	9.7
отъезжать	at"yezhat'	depart, to	9.7
официант (m)	afitsiant	waiter	5.3
очень	ochen'	extremely; very	15.3, 18.7
очень плохо	ochin' plokha	very bad	2.9
очки (pl)	achki	glasses	6.3
очки (pl) от солнца	achki at sontsa	sunglasses	6.3
ошибка (f)	ashipka	mistake	12.7
падеж (m)	padyezh	case	3.3
пакет (m), свёрток (m)	pakyet, svyortak	packet	13.6, 18.8
пальто (n)	pal'to	coat	6.2
памятник (m) жёртвам войны	pamyatnik zhertvam voyny	war memorial	9.8
папа (m)	papa	dad	2.12
пара (f) (+ gen.)	para	pair; pair (of)	6.3, 18.8
параграф (m)	paragraf	paragraph	11.2
парадный вход (m)	paradniy vkhot	front entrance	8.5
парикмахер (m)	parikmakher	hairdresser; barber	2.14
парикмахерская (f)	parikmakherskaya	barber shop	7.1
парк (m)	park	park	9.8
парламент (m)	parlament	parliament	10.3
парусная лодка (f)	parusnaya lotka	sailboat	14.5
Пасха (f)	Paskha	Easter	11.6
пахнуть	pakhnut'	smell, to	5.8

пациент *(m)*, пациентка *(f)*	patsiyent, patsiyentka	patient *(noun)*	2.7
пачка *(f) (+ gen.)*	pachka	batch (of); pile (of)	18.8
певец *(m)*, певица *(f)*	pivyets, pivitsa	singer	2.14, 11.8
пельмени *(pl)*	pil'myeni	pelmeni *(ravioli)*	5.7
пенал *(m)*	penal	pencil case	13.5
пенсионер *(m)*	pinsianyer	retiree	2.14
пепельница *(f)*	pyepil'nitsa	ashtray	5.12
Первая мировая война *(f)*	Pervaya miravaya vaina	World War I	3.5
первый	pyerviy	first	17.2, 17.9
первый год *(m)*	pyerviy got	first year	12.4
первый год *(m)* в школе	perviy got v shkole	high school first year	12.4
первый год *(m)* университета	pyerviy got universityeta	university first year	12.4
первый месяц *(m)*	pyerviy myesats	first month	17.7
первый раз *(m)*	pyerviy raz	first time	17.3
перед *(+ inst.)*, спереди *(+ gen.)*	pyeret, spyeredi	front, in front	19.4
перед, до	pyerit, do	before	19.3
передавать	piridavat'	broadcast, to	11.4
передайте привет …	piridaite privyet …	give my regards to …	4.5
передача *(f)*	piridacha	broadcast	11.4
передняя сторона *(f)*	peryednyaya starana	front	16.5
перекрёсток *(m)*	pirikryostak	intersection	9.3
перекусить	pirikusit'	snack, to have a	5.1
перелом *(m)*	pirilom	fracture (of the bone)	2.7
перемена *(f)*	pirimyena	break	12.6
переодеть	piriadyet'	change (clothes), to	6.1
переход *(m)* для пешеходов	pirikhot dlya pishikhodof	pedestrian crossing	9.3
переходить улицу	pikhadit' ulitsu	cross the street, to	9.3
перец *(m)*	pyerits	pepper	5.4
персик *(m)*	persik	peach	5.5
перчатки *(pl)*	pirchatki	gloves	6.3
песня *(f)*	pyesnya	song	11.8
Петродворец *(m)*	Pitradvaryets	Petrodvorets	3.2
петь	pyet'	sing, to	11.8, 14.3
печатать	pichatat'	print, to	11.3
печь	pyech'	bake	5.10
пешеход *(m)*	pishikhot	pedestrian	9.3, 9.6
пианино *(n)*	pianino	piano	11.8
пиво *(n)*	piva	beer	5.9
пижама *(f)*	pizhama	pajamas	6.2

пилóт (*m*)	pilot	pilot	2.14
пинг-пóнг (*m*)	pink-ponk	Ping-Pong	14.5
пирóг (*m*)	pirok	cake	5.4
пирогú (*pl*) с мя́сом	piragi s myasam	pirogi with meat	5.7
пирогú с грибáми	piragi s gribami	pirogi with mushrooms	5.7
пирогú с картóшкой	piragi s kartoshkoy	pirogi with potatoes	5.7
писáтель (*m*), писáтельница (*f*)	pisatel', pisatel'nitsa	writer	2.14, 11.2
писáть	pisat'	write, to	12.7, 13.4
писáть письмó	pisat' pis'mo	write a letter, to	13.4
пи́сьменный стол (*m*)	pis'menniy stol	desk	8.3
письмó (*n*)	pis'mo	letter (*missive*)	13.6
пить за (+ асс.)	pit' za	drink to, to	5.1
пи́шущая маши́нка (*f*)	pishushchaya mashinka	typewriter	13.5
плáвание (*n*)	plavaniye	swimming	14.5
плáвать	plavat'	swim, to	14.4
плáкать	plakat'	cry, to	2.8
план (*m*)	plan	plan	10.6
плáстик (*m*)	plastik	plastic	6.4
плáта (*f*) за кварти́ру	plata za kvartiru	rent	8.4
плати́ть	platit'	pay, to	5.3, 7.2
плáтье (*n*)	plat'ye	dress	6.2
плащ (*m*)	plashch	raincoat	6.2
плечó (*n*)	plicho	shoulder	2.2
плёнка (*f*)	plyonka	tape	11.4
плитá (*f*)	plita	stove	5.11
плоть (*f*)	plot'	flesh	2.2
плохóй	plakhoy	bad	2.9
плóщадь (*f*)	ploshchat'	area	18.2
пляж (*m*)	plyazh	beach	1.3
по направлéнию к (+ *dat.*)	po napravlyeniyu k	toward	19.4
побéг (*m*)	pabyek	escape	10.5
пóвар (*m*)	povar	cook	2.14
повáренная кни́га (*f*)	pavarennaya kniga	cookbook	5.10
поверну́ть (*perf.*)	pavirnut'	turn, to	16.1
поверну́ть (*perf.*) налéво	pavirnut' na lyevo	turn left, to	16.1
поверну́ть (*perf.*) напрáво	pavirnut' na pravo	turn right, to	16.1
пови́дло (*n*)	pavidla	jam	5.4
поворóт (*m*)	pavarot	turn	16.1
повторéние (*n*)	paftaryeniye	review	12.7
повторя́ть	paftaryat'	review, to	12.7
погаси́ть огóнь	pagasit' agon'	put out a fire, to	8.6
погóда (*f*)	pagoda	weather	1.4

Russian	Transliteration	English	Ref
под (+ acc./inst.)	pot	below	16.3
подáрок (m)	padarak	gift; present	4.3
подготóвить (perf.)	padgatovit'	prepare, to	9.7
подзéмный	padzyemniy	underground	9.5
подзéмный перехóд (m)	padzyemniy pirikhot	underpass	9.3
подметáть	padmitat'	sweep, to	8.7
подня́ться (perf.)	padnyat'sa	come up, to	16.1
подожди́те мину́тку	padazhditye minutku	wait a minute	4.2
подру́га (f)	padruga	girlfriend	14.1
подружи́ться (perf.)	padruzhit'sa	make friends, to	14.1
подря́дчик (m)	padryadchik	contractor	2.14
поду́шка (f)	padushka	pillow	8.3
поду́шка (f) для дивáна	padushka dlya divana	cushion	8.5
подходи́ть	padkhadit'	fit, to	15.1
подходя́щий	padkhadyashchiy	suitable	15.1
пóезд (m)	poyezd	train	9.5
пожáлуйста	pazhalsta	please	4.3
пожáлуйста, заходи́те	pazhalsta, zakhaditye	please come in	4.2
пожáр (m)	pazhar	fire	1.5
пожилóй вóзраст (m)	pazhiloy vozrast	old age	2.3
пожилóй человéк (m)	pazhiloy chilavyek	old person	2.1
позавчерá	pozafchera	day before yesterday	17.8
пóздно	pozdna	late	17.1, 17.4
поздравля́ем	pazdravlyayem	congratulations	4.2
пóйти в ресторáн	paiti v ristaran	go to a restaurant, to	5.3
поколéние (n)	pakalyeniye	generation	2.12
покрывáло (n)	pakryvala	bedspread	8.3
покупáтель (m)	pakupatil'	customer	7.2
покупáть	pakupat'	buy, to	7.2
пóлдень (m)	poldyen'	noon	17.10
пóлдник (m)	poldnik	afternoon snack	5.2
пóле (n)	polye	field	10.8
поливáть	palivat'	water, to	10.8
поливáть цветы́	palivat' tsvyety	water the plants, to	8.4
поликли́ника (f)	paliklinika	clinic	2.7
поли́тик (m)	palitik	politician	2.14, 10.3
поли́тика (f)	palitika	politics	10.3, 12.5
полити́ческая пáртия (f)	palitichiskaya partiya	political party	10.3
полицéйская маши́на (f)	politseyskaya mashina	police car	10.5
полицéйский (m)	palitsyeyskiy	police officer	10.5
пóлки (pl)	polki	shelves	8.3
пóлное и́мя (n)	polnaye imya	full name	2.12
пóлностью	polnast'yu	completely	18.7
пóлночь (f)	polnach'	midnight	17.10

полный	polniy	full	18.7
поло (n)	pola	polo	14.5
половина (f)	palavina	half	17.1, 18.1
половина (f) года	palavina goda	half year	17.5
половина (f) дня	palavina dnya	half a day	17.1
половина (f) месяца	palavina myesatsa	half a month	17.6
половина (f) недели	palavina nidyeli	half a week	17.1
положить (perf.)	palazhit'	put into, to	16.1
полоса (f), линия (f)	palasa, liniya	lane (highway)	9.3
полоскать горло	palaskat' gorla	gargle, to	2.5
полотенце (n)	palatyentse	towel	2.5, 8.7
полотно (n)	palatno	canvas	11.7
получать	paluchat'	receive, to	7.2, 15.4
получать удовольствие	poluchat' udavol'stviye	enjoy, to	14.2
полчаса	polchasa	half-an-hour	17.11
Польша (f)	Pol'sha	Poland	9.2
поменяться часами	paminyat'sa chisami	trading hours	17.1
помидор (m)	pamidor	tomato	5.6
помимо	pamima	besides	19.3
помогать	pamagat'	help, to	14.1
помощник (m)	pamoshnik	helper	14.1
понедельник (m)	panidyelnik	Monday	17.9
понемногу	panimnogu	little by little	18.6
понимать	panimat'	understand, to	2.10
понос (m)	panos	diarrhea	2.6
поп-музыка (f)	pop-muzyka	pop music	11.8
поправляться	papravlyat'sa	gain weight, to	2.2
популярный	papulyarniy	popular	15.7
портной (m)	partnoy	tailor	2.14, 6.1
посещаемость (f)	pasishchaimast'	attendance	12.6
посещать	pasishchat'	visit, to	9.7, 14.2
после (+ gen.)	poslye	after	17.1
последний	paslyedniy	last one	17.2
последний месяц (m)	paslyedniy myesats	last month	17.6
последний раз (m)	paslyedniy raz	last time	17.3
последняя неделя (f)	paslyednyaya nidyelya	last week	17.8
послезавтра	poslyezaftra	day after tomorrow	17.8
послушный	paslushniy	obedient	2.11
посол (m)	pasol	ambassador	10.11
посольство (n)	pasol'stva	embassy	10.11
постепенно	pastipyenna	gradually	17.4
посудное полотенце (n)	pasudnaye palatyentse	dishcloth	8.7
посылать	pasylat'	send, to	13.6
посылать телеграмму	pasylat' tiligrammu	send a telegram, to	13.7

посы́лка (f)	pasylka	parcel	13.6
потéря (f)	patyerya	loss	10.6
потолóк (m)	patalok	ceiling	8.5
потóм, затéм	patom, zatyem	later on; then	17.1, 19.3
потомý	patamu	because	15.5, 19.3
походи́ть на …	pakhadit' na …	resemble, to	15.2
пóчва (f)	pochva	soil	1.2
почемý?	pachemu?	why?	15.5, 19.2
пóчта (f)	pochta	post office; mail	7.1, 9.8, 13.6
почтальóн (m)	pachtal'on	mailman	2.14, 13.6
почти́	pachti	almost	18.6
почти́ никтó;	pochti nikto;	hardly any	18.5
почти́ ничегó	pochti nichivo		
почтóвая мáрка (f)	pachtovaya marka	postage stamp	13.6
почтóвая откры́тка (f)	pachtovaya atkrytka	postcard	13.6
почтóвое отделéние (n)	pachtovaye atdelyeniye	post office	13.6
почтóвый я́щик (m)	pachtoviy yashchik	mailbox	13.6
поэ́зия (f)	paeziya	poetry	11.2
поэ́тому	paetomu	therefore	15.5, 19.3
прáвильный, вéрный	pravil'niy, vyerniy	right; correct	12.7
прави́тельство (n)	pravitel'stva	government	3.5, 10.3
прáвить	pravit'	rule, to	3.5
правослáвная цéрковь (f)	pravaslavnaya tserkaf'	Russian Orthodox	11.6
прáздники (pl)	prazniki	holidays	12.1
прáздновать Нóвый год	praznavat' Noviy got	celebrate the New Year, to	17.5
практиковáться	praktikavat'sa	practice, to	11.8, 14.4
прáчечная (f)	prachichnaya	laundry	8.2
прéдки (pl)	pretki	ancestors	2.12
предложéние (n)	pridlazhyeniye	sentence	11.2
предложи́ть (perf.) тост	pridlazhit' tost	make a toast, to	4.2
предмéт (m)	pridmyet	subject	12.5
председáтель (m)	pridsidatel'	chairman	10.3
представи́тель (m)	pridstavitil'	representative	10.3, 15.2
предстáвить (perf.)	pridstavit'	introduce, to	4.4
представля́ть	pridstavlyat'	represent, to;	10.3,
		introduce, to	14.2
прéжде	pryezhdye	previously;	17.1
		previous time	17.3
прéжде всегó	pryezhdye vsivo	first of all	17.2
президéнт (m)	prezidyent	president	3.1, 10.3
презентáция (f)	prizintatsiya	presentation	11.4
прекрáсно	prikrasna	fine	13.3
прекрáсный	prikrasniy	wonderful	2.9, 13.3
прекращáть	prikrashchat'	stop, to	17.1

премье́р-мини́стр *(m)*	prim'yer ministr	prime minister	10.3
пре́сса *(f)*	pryessa	press (the)	11.3
при *(+ prep.)*	pri	by	19.4
прибавля́ть	pribavlyat'	add, to	18.1
приблизи́тельно	priblizitil'na	about;	17.1,
		approximately	18.4
прибо́ры *(pl)*	pribory	utensils	5.11
прибыва́ть	pribyvat'	arrive, to	9.7, 16.1
при́быль *(f)*	pribyl'	profit	10.6
прибы́тие *(n)*	pribitiye	arrival	4.4, 9.7
приве́тствовать	privyetstvavat'	greet, to	14.2
привы́кнуть *(perf.)*	privyknut'	get used to, to	2.11
привя́зывать	privyazivat'	tie, to	8.9
пригласи́ть *(perf.)* на обе́д	priglasit' na abyet	invite to dinner, to	5.1
приглаша́ть	priglashat'	invite, to	14.1
приглаше́ние *(n)*	priglashyeniye	invitation	14.1
при́город *(m)*	prigarat	suburb	9.2
пригото́вить *(perf.)* еду́	prigatovit' yedu	cook a meal, to	5.10
пригото́вить *(perf.)* чай	prigatovit' chay	make tea, to	5.9
прика́зывать; зака́зывать	prikazyvat'; zakazyvat'	order, to	15.4
прикрепля́ть	prikreplyat'	fasten, to	8.9
приле́жный	prilyezhniy	studious	2.11
приме́рочная *(f)*	primyerachnaya	fitting room	7.2
принима́ть	prinimat'	host, to	14.2
принима́ть ва́нну	prinimat' vannu	take a bath, to	2.5
принима́ть во внима́ние	prinimat' va vnimaniye	take into account, to	15.5
принима́ть душ	prinimat' dush	shower, to	2.5
принима́ть лека́рство	prinimat' likarstva	take medicine, to	2.7
принима́ть уча́стие	prinimat' uchastiye	participate, to	10.1
приноси́ть	prinasit'	bring along, to	15.4
приро́дный	prirodniy	natural	1.5
приско́рбный	priskorbniy	regrettable	2.8
пристёгивать(ся)	pristyogivat'(sya)	buckle up, to	9.5
приходи́ть	prikhadit'	come, to	16.1
причёсывать во́лосы	prichyosyvat' volasy	comb one's hair, to	2.5
причи́на *(f)*	prichina	reason	15.5
прия́тно познако́миться	priyatna paznakomit'sa	pleased to meet you	4.4
прия́тный	priyatniy	good-looking	15.7
пробле́ма *(f)*	prablyema	problem	10.2
прови́нция *(f)*, о́бласть *(f)*	pravintsiya, oblast'	province	9.2
проводи́ть собра́ние	pravadit' sabraniye	hold a meeting, to	10.1
провожа́ть	pravazhat'	see someone off, to	9.7

прогрáмма (f)	pragramma	station (radio); program	11.4
прогрéсс (m)	pragress	progress	10.2
прогрессúвный	pragressivniy	progressive	10.2
прогýливать собáку	pragulivat' sabaku	walk the dog, to	1.8
продавáть	pradavat'	sell, to	7.2
продавéц (m)	pradavyets	salesperson	7.2
продавéц (m), продавщúца (f)	pradavyets, pradavshchitsa	salesclerk	2.14
продолжáть	pradalzhat'	continue, to	17.1
продýкты (pl)	pradukty	produce	10.8
проигрáть (perf.); терáть	praigrat'; tiryat'	lose, to	14.4
прóигрыватель (m)	praigryvatel'	record player	11.4
производúть	praizvadit'	produce, to	10.8
произносúть речь	praiznasit' ryech'	make a speech, to	13.2
произношéние (n)	praiznasheniye	pronunciation	13.1
промы́шленность (f)	promyshlinnost'	industry	10.9
проницáтельный	pranitsatel'niy	sharp	2.11
простúте	prastite	sorry	4.3
простудúться (perf.)	prastudit'sa	catch a cold, to	2.6
прóсьба (f)	pros'ba	request	13.2
противополóжная сторонá (f)	prativapalozhnaya starana	opposite side	16.4
противополóжный	protivopolozhniy	opposite	16.3
профéссия (f)	prafyessiya	profession; occupation	2.14, 10.7
профéссор (m)	prafyessar	professor	12.3
профсою́зы (pl)	profsayuzy	trade union	10.9
процéсс (m)	protsess	trial	10.4
… процéнтов скúдка (f)	… pratsyentaf skitka	… percent off	7.2
прóшлый год	proshliy got	last year	17.5
прощáть	prashchat'	forgive, to	2.9
пруд (m)	prut	pond	1.3
прыжкú (pl) в высотý	prizhki v vysatu	high jump	14.5
прыжкú (pl) в длинý	pryzhki v dlinu	long jump	14.5
прáжка (f)	pryazhka	buckle	6.1
прáмо	pryama	straight	16.4
прямóй	primoi	straightforward	2.11
птúца (f)	ptitsa	bird	1.9
пýговица (f)	pugavitsa	button	6.1
пулóвер (m)	pulovyer	pullover	6.2
пунктуáльно	punktual'na	punctually	15.8
пунктуáция (f)	punktuatsiya	punctuation	11.2
пусты́ня (f)	pustynye	desert	1.2
путешéственник (m)	putishyestvinik	traveler	9.7

путешéствия (pl)	putishyestviya	travel	9.7
путешéствовать	putishyestvavat'	travel, to	9.7
пучóк (m) (+ gen.)	puchok	bunch (of)	18.8
пчелá (f)	pchila	bee	1.9
пылесóс (m)	pylisos	vacuum cleaner	8.7
пыль (f)	pyl'	dust	8.7
пьéса (f), спектáкль (m)	p'yesa, spektakl'	play	11.9
пьяный	p'yaniy	drunk; tipsy	5.9
пятнáдцать	pitnatsat'	fifteen	18.1
пятница (f)	pyatnitsa	Friday	17.9
пятый	pyatiy	fifth (day of the month)	17.9
пятый год (m)	pyatiy got	fifth year	12.4
пять	pyat'	five	18.1
пятьдесят	pyatdyesyat	fifty	18.1
рабóта (f)	rabota	work; job	10.7
рабóтать в садý	rabotat' f sadu	garden, to	14.3
рабóчий (m)	rabochiy	worker	2.14
рабóчий стол (m)	rabochiy stol	desk	10.7
рад вас видеть	Rat vas vidit'	I'm glad to see you	4.2
радиáтор (m)	radiatar	radiator	8.6
рáдио (n)	radio	radio	11.4
разбитый на кусóчки	razbitiy na kusochki	broken into pieces	8.9
развивáть	razvivat'	develop, to	2.2, 10.6
развлечéние (n)	razvlichyeniye	entertainment	14.3
разводиться	razvodit'sa	divorce, to	2.3
разговóр	razgavor	conversation	13.2
раздевáть	razdivat'	take off (undress), to	6.1
раздражáть	razdrazhat'	annoy, to	2.8
размéр (m)	razmyer	size	6.1, 18.1
разóрванный	razorvanniy	torn	8.9
разорвáть (perf.)	razarvat'	tear, to	8.9
разочаровáть (perf.)	razachiravat'	disappoint, to	2.8
разрешите вам помóчь	razrishiti vam pamoch	let me help you	4.2
разрешите вам представить …	razrishiti vam pridstavit' …	may I introduce (to you) …	4.4
разрешите представить …?	razrishiti pridstavit' …?	may I introduce …?	14.2
разýмный	razumniy	reasonable	2.11
рай (m)	ray	heaven	11.6
райóн (m)	rayon	region	9.2
рак (m) лёгких	rak lyokhkikh	lung cancer	5.12
рáковина (f)	rakovina	sink	8.5
рáненый	raniniy	injured	1.5
рáнить; повредить (perf.)	ranit'; pavridit'	injure, to	2.6

ра́но	rana	early	17.1, 17.4
расписа́ние (n)	raspisaniye	schedule	9.7, 12.6
распределя́ть	raspridilyat'	distribute, to	15.4
распрода́жа (f)	raspradazha	sale	7.2
распро́дан	rasprodan	sold out	7.2
расска́з (m)	rasskaz	composition	11.2, 12.6
расска́зывать	rasskazyvat'	tell, to	13.2
расска́зывать ска́зки	rasskazyvat' skazki	tell a story, to	13.2
рассле́довать	raslyedavat'	investigate	11.3
расстава́ться	rasstavat'sa	part, to	14.1
расстила́ться	rasstilat'sa	spread out, to	18.1
расте́ние (n)	rastyeniye	plant	1.7
расти́	rasti	grow, to	2.2
расти́тельное ма́сло (n)	rastitel'naye masla	oil (cooking)	5.4
ребёнок (m)	rebyonak	child	2.1
ребя́та (pl)	ribyata	guys; kids	2.15
ревни́вый	rivniviy	jealous	2.8
револю́ция (f)	rivalutsiya	revolution	3.5
реда́ктор (m)	ridaktar	editor	11.3
ре́дко	ryetka	seldom	17.3
ре́зать	ryezat'	cut, to	8.9
результа́т (m)	risul'tat	result	12.8
река́ (f)	rika	river	1.3
река́ Во́лга (f)	rika Volga	Volga River	3.4
ре́ктор (m) университе́та	ryektar universiteta	president (University)	12.3
рели́гия (f)	riligiya	religion	11.6, 12.5
реме́нь (m)	rimyen'	seat belt	9.5
ремо́нт (m)	remont	repairs	8.9
рентге́н (m)	rentgen	X ray	2.7
ре́па (f)	ryepa	turnip	5.6
репортёр (m)	ripartyor	reporter	2.14, 11.3
респу́блика (f)	rispublika	republic	3.5
рестора́н (m)	ristaran	restaurant	5.3, 9.8
реце́пт (m)	ritsept	prescription	2.6
речь (f)	ryech	speech	13.1
реша́ть	rishat'	decide, to	10.4
реше́ние (n)	rishyeniye	decision	10.4
Ри́га (f)	Riga	Riga (Latvia)	3.4
рисова́ние (n); иску́сство (n)	risovaniye; iskusstva	art	12.5
ро́бкий	robkiy	timid; shy	2.11
род (m): мужско́й, же́нский, сре́дний	rot: muzhskoi, zhenskiy, sredniy	gender: masculine, feminine, neuter	3.3
роди́тели (pl)	raditili	parents	2.12

родúться	radit'sa	born, to be	2.3
рóдственник *(m)*	rotstvennik	relative; relation	2.12
рождéственская ёлка *(f)*	razhdyestvinskaya yolka	Christmas tree	11.6
Рождествó *(n)*	Razhdistvo	Christmas	11.6
розéтка *(f)*	razyetka	plug	8.5
рóзовый	rozaviy	pink	6.5
рок-мýзыка *(f)*	rok-muzyka	rock music	11.8
ромáн *(m)*	raman	novel	11.2
Россúя *(f)*	Rassiya	Russia	3.4, 9.2
рот *(m)*	rot	mouth	2.2
рубáшка *(f)*	rubashka	shirt	6.2
рубль *(m)*	rubl'	ruble	7.3
рукá *(f)*	ruka	hand; arm	2.2
рукáв *(m)*	rukaf	sleeve	6.1
рулóн *(m) (+ gen.)*	rulon	roll (of)	18.8
рýсская валюта *(f)*	russkaya valyuta	Russian currency	7.3
рýсская граммáтика *(f)*	russkaya grammatika	Russian grammar	12.5
рýсская литератýра *(f)*	russkaya litiratura	Russian literature	12.5
рýсский *(m)*, рýсская *(f)*	russkiy, russkaya	Russian	9.2
рýсский язы́к *(m)*	russkiy yezyk	Russian (language)	3.3, 12.5
ручéй *(m)*	ruchyei	creek	1.3
рýчка *(f)*	ruchka	pen	13.5
ры́ба *(f)*	ryba	fish	1.9, 5.4
рыбáк *(m)*	rybak	fisherman	2.14
ры́бный магазúн *(m)*	ribniy magazin	fish shop	7.1
ры́бный суп *(m)*	ribniy sup	fish soup	5.7
ры́нок *(m)*	rinak	market	7.1
ряд *(m) (+ gen.)*	ryat	row (of)	18.8
ря́дом	ryadom	close	8.4
с *(+ inst.)*	s	with	19.4
сад *(m)*	sat	garden	1.7, 8.4
садúтесь, пожáлуйста	saditis', pazhalsta	take a seat, please	4.2
садóвник *(m)*	sadovnik	gardener	2.14
Садóвое кольцó *(n)*	Sadovaye kal'tso	Boulevard Ring	3.2
сажáть	sazhat'	plant, to	10.8
салáт *(m)*	salat	salad; lettuce	5.4, 5.6
салáт *(m)* из огурцóв	salat iz agurtsof	cucumber salad	5.7
салáт *(m)* из помидóр	salat iz pamidor	tomato salad	5.7
салфéтка *(f)*	salfyetka	napkin	5.11
самолёт *(m)*	samalyot	airplane	9.5
сандáлии *(pl)*	sandalii	sandals	6.3
сантимéтр *(m)*	santimyetr	centimeter	18.2
сапогú *(pl)*	sapagi	boots	6.3
сатúн *(m)*	satin	satin	6.4

са́хар *(m)*	sakhar	sugar	5.4
свет *(m)*	svyet	light	1.1, 8.5
свети́ть	svitit'	shine, to	1.1
све́тлый	svetliy	light	6.5
светофо́р *(m)*	svitafor	traffic light	9.3
свида́ние *(n)*	svidaniye	date	14.2
свини́на *(f)*	svinina	pork	5.4
свобо́да *(f)*	svaboda	freedom	10.2, 10.3
свобо́дная ко́мната *(f)*	svabodnaya komnata	spare room	8.2
свобо́дный	svabodniy	loose	6.1
сво́дка *(f)* пого́ды	svotka pagody	weather report	1.4
свяще́нник *(m)*	svishchyennik	minister; priest	10.3, 11.6
сгиба́ть	sgibat'	bend, to	8.9
сдава́ть	sdavat'	rent, to	8.4
сдать *(perf.)* экза́мен	sdat' ekzamin	pass an exam, to	12.8
сда́ча *(f)*	sdacha	change	7.3
сде́ланный из … *(+ gen.)*	sdelanniy iz …	made of …	6.1
сде́лать *(perf.)* ко́пию	sdyelat' kopiyu	make a copy, to	12.6
се́вер *(m)*	syever	north	16.4
Се́верное мо́ре *(n)*	Syevernoye morye	North Sea	9.4
Се́верный Ледови́тый океа́н *(m)*	Syeverniy Lidavitiy akian	Arctic Ocean	9.4
сего́дня	sivodnya	today	17.8
сейча́с	siychas	now	17.1
сейча́с же	siychas zhe	right now	17.1
секрета́рь *(m)*, секрета́рша *(f)*	sikritar', sikritarsha	secretary	2.14
секу́нды *(pl)*	sikundy	seconds	17.11
се́кция *(f) (+ gen.)*	syektsiya	section of	18.8
сельдере́й *(m)*	sildiryey	celery	5.6
се́льская ме́стность *(f)*	syel'skaya myestnost'	countryside	9.2
семена́ *(pl)*	simina	seeds	1.7
семна́дцать	semnatsat'	seventeen	18.1
семь	syem'	seven	18.1
се́мьдесят	syem'desat	seventy	18.1
семья́ *(f)*	sem'ya	family	2.12
сентя́брь *(m)*	sentyabr'	September	17.7
серди́тый	serditiy	angry	2.8
се́рдце *(n)*	sertse	heart	2.2
сере́бряный	siryebriniy	silver	6.5
се́рый	syeriy	gray	6.5
се́рьги *(pl)*	syer'gi	earrings	6.3
сестра́ *(f)*	sistra	sister	2.12
сза́ди *(+ gen.)*	szadi	behind	19.4

Сиби́рь (f)	Sibir'	Siberia	3.4
сигаре́ты (pl)	sigaryety	cigarettes	5.12
сига́ры (pl)	sigary	cigars	5.12
си́ла (f)	sila	strength	15.3
си́льный	sil'niy	strong	15.3
си́льный ве́тер (m)	sil'niy vyetir	strong wind	1.5
си́льный; убеди́тельный	sil'niy; ubiditel'niy	forceful	2.11
симпати́чный	simpatichniy	cute	15.7
синаго́га (f)	sinagoga	synagogue	11.6
Сингапу́р (m)	Singapur	Singapore	9.2
синте́тика (f)	sintyetika	synthetic	6.4
систе́ма (f)	sistyema	system	10.1
систе́ма (f) образова́ния	sistyema abrazavaniya	education system	12.1
сказа́ть (perf.)	skazat'	say, to	13.2
ска́чки (pl)	skachki	horse race	14.5
ски́дка (f)	skitka	discount	7.2
сковорода́ (f)	skavarada	pan	18.8
ско́лько?	skol'ka?	how many?	18.4
ско́лько лет?	skol'ka lyet?	how old?	19.2
ско́лько предме́тов?	skol'ka pridmyetof?	how many subjects?	12.5
ско́лько сто́ит?	skol'ka stoit?	how much is it?	7.3, 18.4, 19.2
ско́рость (f)	skorast'	speed	17.4
скри́пка (f)	skripka	violin	11.8
скро́мный	skromniy	modest	2.11
ску́льптор (m)	skul'ptar	sculptor	11.7
скульпту́ра (f)	skul'ptura	sculpture	11.7
ску́чный	skuchniy	boring	2.8
сла́бый	slabiy	weak (of a drink); weak	5.8, 15.3
сла́дкий	slatkiy	sweet	5.8
сла́дости (pl)	sladasti	sweets	5.4
сле́ва	slyeva	left	16.3, 16.5
сле́дующая неде́ля (f)	slyeduyushchaya nidyelya	next week	17.8
сле́дующий год (m)	slyeduyushchiy got	next year	17.5
сле́дующий ме́сяц (m)	slyeduyushchiy myesats	next month	17.6
сле́дующий раз (m)	slyeduyushchiy raz	next time	17.3
сли́ва (f)	sliva	plum	5.5
сли́шком мно́го	slishkam mnoga	too much	18.7
слова́рь (m)	slavar'	dictionary	11.2
сло́во (n)	slova	word	13.1
слог (m)	slok	syllable	3.3
сло́жный	slozhniy	severe	15.3
сло́жный, тру́дный	slozhniy, trudniy	complicated	15.6
сло́манный	slomanniy	broken (damaged)	8.9

Russian	Transliteration	English	Reference
сломáть(ся)	slomat'(sa)	break down, to	9.5
слон (*m*)	slon	elephant	1.9
слýжащий	sluzhashchiy	employee	10.10
слýчай (*m*)	sluchay	incident	10.4
случáться	sluchat'sa	happen, to	1.5
слýшать	slushat'	listen, to	2.10, 13.2
слýшать пластúнки	slushat' plastinki	listen to records, to	14.3
слýшать рáдио	slushat' radio	listen to the radio, to	14.3
слы́шать	slyshat'	hear, to	2.10, 13.2
смешнóй	smishnoy	funny	2.8
смея́ться	smiyatsa	laugh, to	2.8
смотрéть достоприме-чáтельности	smatryet' dastaprimichatyel'nasti	sightsee, to	9.7
смотрéть телевúзор	smatryet' tilivizar	watch television, to	14.3
смущáть	smushchat'	embarrass, to	2.8
снарýжи	snaruzhi	outside	16.5
снег (*m*)	snyek	snow	1.4
снéжный обвáл (*m*)	snyezhniy abval	avalanche	1.5
снотвóрное (*n*)	snatvornaye	sleeping pill	2.7
собрáние (*n*)	sabraniye	meeting	10.1
собы́тие (*n*)	sabytiye	event	10.4
Совéтский Сою́з (*m*)	Savetskii Sayuz	Soviet Union	3.4
совремéнная литератýра (*f*)	savremyennaya lityeratura	modern literature	11.2
соглáсный звук (*m*): твёрдый, мя́гкий, звóнкий, глухóй	saglasniy zvuk: tvyordiy, myakhkiy, zvonkiy, glukhoy	consonant: hard, soft, voiced, unvoiced	3.3
соглашáться	saglashat'sa	agree, to	10.3
сóдовая водá (*f*)	sodavaya vada	soda water	5.9
Содрýжество (*n*) Независúмых Госудáрств (СНГ)	Sadruzhistva Nizavisimykh Gasudarstf (SNG)	Commonwealth of Independent States (CIS)	3.1, 3.4
сожалéть	sazhalyet'	regret, to	2.8
сознáтельный	saznatel'niy	conscientious	2.11
сойтú (*perf.*) вниз	sayti vniz	come down, to	16.1
солдáт (*m*)	saldat	soldier	2.14
солёный	salyoniy	salty	5.8
сóлнечный календáрь (*m*)	solnechniy kalendar'	solar calendar	17.5
сóлнечный свет (*m*)	solnichniy svyet	sunlight	1.1
сóлнце (*n*)	sontse	sun	1.1
соль (*f*)	sol'	salt	5.4
сóнный	sonniy	sleepy	2.4
соотвéтственно (+ *dat.*)	saatvyetstvinno	according to	15.8, 19.4

сопровождáть	sapravazhdat'	accompany, to	14.2
соревновáние *(n)*	sarivnavaniye	competition	10.6, 14.4
соревновáться	sarivnavat'sa	compete, to	14.4
сóрок	sorak	forty	18.1
сосéди *(pl)*	sasyedi	neighbors	8.4
сосéдство *(n)*	sasyetstva	neighborhood	16.3
софá *(f)*; дивáн *(m)*	safa; divan	sofa	8.3
социалúзм *(m)*	satsializm	socialism	10.3
сочинéние *(n)*, рассквáз *(m)*	sachinyeniye, rasskaz	essay; composition	11.2, 12.6
спáльня *(f)*	spal'nya	bedroom	8.2
спáржа *(f)*	sparzha	asparagus	5.6
спасúбо	spasiba	thank you	4.2
спасúбо за гостеприúмство	spasiba za gastipriimstva	thank you for your hospitality	4.5
спать	spat'	asleep, to be; sleep, to	2.4
спектáкль *(m)*	spektakl'	play	11.9
специалúст *(m)* по компьютерам	spitsialist pa kamp'uteram	computer specialist	2.14
специáльно	spitsial'na	especially	2.11
специáльный	spitsial'niy	special	15.3
спúсывать	spisyvat'	copy, to	12.6
спúчки *(pl)*	spichki	matches	5.12
спокóйной нóчи	spakoynoy nochi	good night	4.1
спорт *(m)*	sport	sport	14.4
спортúвные товáры *(pl)*	spartivniye tavary	sporting goods store	7.1
спортúвный костюм *(m)*	spartivniy kastyum	sweat suit	6.2
спортсмéн *(m)*	sportsmyen	athlete	14.4
спосóбный	spasobniy	capable	2.11
споткнýться *(perf.)*	spatykhnut'sa	trip, to; stumble, to	16.1
спрáва	sprava	right	16.3, 16.5
спрáшивать	sprashivat'	ask, to	12.8, 13.2
спускáться	spuskat'sa	descend to; come down, to	8.4
сравнéние *(n)*	sravnyeniye	comparison	15.2
срáвнивать	sravnivat'	compare, to	15.2
срáвнивая с (+ instr.)	sravnivaya s	compared to	19.4
сравнúтельно	sravnityel'na	comparatively	18.6
средá *(f)*	sryeda	Wednesday	17.9
Средизéмное мóре *(n)*	Sridizyemnaya morye	Mediterranean Sea	9.4
срéдний	sryednii	medium	18.6
срóчный	srochniy	urgent	15.3
стáвить заплáту	stavit' zaplatu	patch, to	8.9
стакáн *(m)*	stakan	glass *(tumbler)*	5.11

становиться	stanavit'sa	become, to	15.1
старый	stariy	old	17.1
статья (f)	stat'ya	article	11.3
стекло (n)	stiklo	glass (material)	8.8
стена (f)	styena	wall	8.5
стерео (n)	styerio	stereo	11.4
стипендия (f)	stipyendiya	scholarship	12.1
стиральная машина (f)	stiral'naya mashina	washing machine	8.7
стиральный порошок (m)	stiral'niy parashok	laundry detergent	8.7
стирать	stirat'	wash, to; launder, to	6.1, 8.7
стирка (f)	stirka	washing	8.7
стихотворение (n)	stikhatvaryeniye	poem	11.2
сто	sto	hundred	18.1
стол (m)	stol	table	8.3
столица (f)	stalitsa	capital (city)	3.4
столовая (f) (в школе)	stalovaya (f shkole)	dining hall (in a school)	5.3
столовая (дома)	stalovaya (doma)	dining room (in a home)	5.3, 8.2
сторона (f)	starana	side	16.3
страдать	stradat'	suffer, to	1.5
страна (f)	strana	country	9.1
страница (f)	stranitsa	page	11.2
строгий	strogiy	strict	2.11
строительная площадка (f)	straitel'naya plashchatka	construction site	8.1
строить	stroit'	build, to	8.1
строка (f)	straka	line	11.2
студент (m), студентка (f)	studyent, studyentka	student (University)	12.3
стул (m)	stul	chair	8.3
стучать	stuchat'	knock, to	8.4
суббота (f)	subbota	Saturday	17.9
сувенир (m)	suvinir	souvenir	4.3
сувениры (pl)	suviniry	souvenir shop	7.1
судья (m)	sud'ya	judge	2.14, 10.4
сумка (f)	sumka	bag; handbag; purse	6.3, 7.2
суп (m)	sup	soup	5.4
супермаркет (m)	supermarkit	supermarket	7.1
сухо	sukha	dry	1.4
сухой	sukhoy	dry	5.8
сушить на солнце	sushit' na sontse	dry in the sun, to	8.7
сушка (f)	sushka	dryer	8.7
существенный	sushchestvenniy	essential	15.3

счастли́вого пути́!	schastlivava puti!	bon voyage!; have a good trip!	4.5
счастли́вый	schastliviy	happy	2.8
счёт *(m)*	schyot	check; bill	5.3, 7.2
США *(pl)*	SShA	USA	9.2
сын *(m)*	syn	son	2.12
сыр *(m)*	syr	cheese	5.4
сюда́	syuda	this way	16.2
таба́к *(m)*	tabak	tobacco	5.12
таба́чная ла́вка *(f)*	tabachnaya lavka	tobacco shop	7.1
табуре́тка *(f)*	taburyetka	stool	8.3
Таджикиста́н *(m)*	Tazhikistan	Tajikistan	3.4
тайга́ *(f)*	taiga	taiga	3.4
так (пра́вильно); сюда́	tak (pravil'na); syuda	this way	16.2
так же … как и …	tak zhe … kak i …	as … as …	15.2
так себе́	tak sibye	so-so	4.2
та́кже, то́же	takzhe, tozhe	as well as; also	19.3
тако́й же	takoy zhe	same, (the)	15.2
такси́ *(n)*	taksi	taxi	9.5
та́лия *(f)*	taliya	waist	2.2
Та́ллин *(m)*	Tallin	Tallinn (Estonia)	3.4
Танза́ния *(f)*	Tanzaniya	Tanzania	9.2
танцева́льный зал *(m)*	tantsival'niy zal	dance hall	9.8
танцева́ть	tanzivat'	dance, to	14.2, 14.3
та́почки *(pl)*	tapachki	slippers	6.3
таре́лка *(f)*	taryelka	plate	5.11, 18.8
Ташке́нт *(m)*	Tashkyent	Tashkent (Uzbekistan)	3.4
Тбили́си *(m)*	Tbilisi	Tbilisi (Georgia)	3.4
твёрдый	tvyordiy	tough; hard, firm	5.8, 8.8
твёрдый знак *(m)*	tvyordiy znak	hard sign	3.3
те *(pl)*	tye	those	16.2
теа́тр *(m)*	tiatr	theater	9.8
телеви́дение *(n)*	tilividiniye	television	11.4
телевизио́нный кана́л *(m)*	tilivizionniy kanal	TV channel	11.4
телеви́зор *(m)*	tilivizar	television (set)	11.4
телегра́мма *(f)*	tiligramma	telegram	13.7
телефа́кс *(m)*	tilifaks	fax	13.7
телефо́н *(m)*	tilifon	telephone	13.7
телефо́н-автома́т *(m)*	tilifon-avtamat	public telephone	9.8, 13.7
телефо́нная бу́дка *(f)*	tilifonnaya butka	telephone booth	9.8
телефо́нная кни́га *(f)*	tilifonnaya kniga	telephone directory *(book)*	13.7
те́ло *(n)*	tyela	body	2.2
те́ма *(f)*	tyema	topic	12.8
темпера́мент *(m)*	temperament	temperament	2.8

температу́ра (f)	timpiratura	temperature	1.4, 2.6
те́ннис (m)	tyennis	tennis	14.5
тепло́	tiplo	warm	1.4, 8.6, 17.6
термо́метр (m)	termometr	thermometer	1.4
те́рмос (m)	tyermos	thermos	5.11
терпели́вый	tirpiliviy	patient (adj.)	2.11
теря́ть	tiryat'	lose, to	2.8, 14.4
тетра́дь (f)	tetrat'	notebook	12.6
те́хник (m)	tyekhnik	technician	2.14
техни́ческая шко́ла (f)	tikhnichiskaya shkola	technical school	12.2
течь	tyech'	flow, to	1.3
тёмный	tyomniy	dark	1.1, 6.5
тёплая вода́ (f)	tyoplaya vada	warm water	2.5
тётя (f)	tyotya	aunt	2.12
типи́чный	tipichniy	typical	15.2
тире́ (n)	tire	dash	11.2
ти́хий го́лос (m)	tikhiy golas	soft voice	13.2
Ти́хий океа́н (m)	Tichiy akian	Pacific Ocean	9.4
ткань (f)	tkan'	cloth; fabric	6.4
то́же, та́кже	tozhe	as well as; also	19.3
толка́ть	talkat'	push, to	8.9
то́лстый	tolstiy	fat; thick	2.2, 18.1
то́лько	tol'ka	only	19.3
то́лько что	tol'ka chto	just	17.1
тома́тный сок (m)	tamatniy sok	tomato juice	5.7
то́нкий	tonkiy	thin	18.1
то́нна (f)	tonna	ton	18.3
торгова́ться	targavat'sa	bargain, to	7.2
торго́вля (f)	targovlya	trade	10.10
торопи́ться	tarapit'sa	hurry up, to	17.4
торт (m)	tort	torte	5.4
тоскова́ть	taskavat'	long for, to	2.8
тост (m)	tost	toast	5.4
тот (m)	tot	that	16.2
точи́лка (f)	tochilka	pencil sharpener	13.5
то́чка (f) с запято́й	tochka s zapitoy	semicolon	11.2
то́чный	tochniy	accurate	15.1
трава́ (f)	trava	grass	1.7
траге́дия (f)	tragyediya	tragedy	11.9
традицио́нный	traditsionniy	traditional	11.1
тради́ция (f)	traditsiya	tradition	10.1, 11.1
трамва́й (m)	tramvay	streetcar; tram	9.5
тра́нспорт (m)	transport	transport; transportation	9.5

тра́тить	tratit'	spend, to	10.6
тре́тий	tryetiy	third	17.9
тре́тий год *(m)*	tretiy got	third year	12.4
Третьяко́вская галере́я *(f)*	Tret'yakofskaya galeryeya	Tretyekov Art Gallery	3.2
три	tri	three	18.1
три часа́ дня	tri chasa dnya	3:00 P.M.	17.11
три часа́ утра́	tri chasa utra	3:00 A.M.	17.11
три́дцать	tritsat'	thirty	18.1
три́дцать оди́н день *(m)*	tritsat' adin dyen'	thirty-one days	17.8
три́дцать пе́рвый	tritsat' pyerviy	thirty-first	17.9
трина́дцатый	trinatsatiy	thirteenth	17.9
трина́дцать	trinatsat'	thirteen	18.1
тролле́йбус *(m)*	traleybus	trolley	9.5
тропи́нка *(f)*	trapinka	path	8.4
тру́бка *(f)*	trupka	pipe	5.12
тру́дности *(pl)*	trudnasti	difficulties	15.6
тру́дный	trudniy	hard, difficult	15.6
трудолюби́вый	trudalyubiviy	hardworking	2.11, 10.7
трусы́ *(pl)*	trusy	underpants	6.2
туале́т *(m)*	tualyet	toilet	8.2, 8.5
туале́тная бума́га *(f)*	tualyetnaya bumaga	toilet paper	2.5, 8.5
туале́ты *(pl)*	tualyety	public toilets; restrooms	9.8
тума́н *(m)*	tuman	fog	1.4
ту́ндра *(f)*	tundra	tundra	3.4
тупо́й	tupoy	blunt	8.8
тури́зм *(m)*	turizm	tourism	3.2
тури́стская гру́ппа *(f)*	turiskaya grupa	tour group	9.7
тури́стский авто́бус *(m)*	turistkiy avtobus	tour bus	9.7
Туркмениста́н *(m)*	Turkministan	Turkmenistan	3.4
туши́ть	tushit'	simmer, to	5.10
ты, тебя́, тебе́	ty, tibya, tibye	you *(singular)*, you, (to) you	2.13
ты́ква *(f)*	tykva	pumpkin	5.6
ты́сяча *(f)*	tysacha	thousand	18.1
тюрьма́ *(f)*	tyur'ma	jail	10.5
тяжёлый	tizholiy	heavy	18.3
тяну́ть	tanut'	pull, to	8.9
убива́ть	ubivat'	kill, to	10.5
убира́ть	ubirat'	clean, to	8.7
убира́ть крова́ть	ubirat' kravat'	make the bed, to	8.4
убо́рка *(f)*	uborka	cleaning	8.7
увели́чивать	uvilichivat'	increase, to	18.1
у́гол *(m)*	ugal	corner	9.3

у́гольная промы́шленность *(f)*	ugal'naya pramyshlinnost'	mining industry	10.9
угоща́йтесь	ugashchaytes'	help yourself	5.1
ударе́ние *(n)*	udaryeniye	stress	3.3, 13.1
уда́ча *(f)*	udacha	(good luck); success	2.9
уделя́ть внима́ние	udilyat' vnimaniye	pay attention, to	12.7
удлиня́ть	udlinyat'	lengthen, to	18.1
уезжа́ть	uyezhat'	leave, to	9.7
уе́хать *(perf.)* в путеше́ствие	yekhat' f putishyestviye	go on a trip, to	14.3
ужа́лить *(perf.)*	uzhalit'	sting, to	1.8
ужа́сный	uzhasniy	terrible	2.8
уже́	uzhye	already	17.1
у́жин *(m)*	uzhin	supper	5.2
Узбекиста́н *(m)*	Uzbekistan	Uzbekistan	3.4
у́зкий	uzkiy	narrow	18.1
Украи́на *(f)*	Ukraina	Ukraine	3.4
у́ксус *(m)*	uksus	vinegar	5.4
у́лица *(f)*	ulitsa	street	9.3
уме́ние *(n)*, о́пыт *(m)*	umyeniye, opyt	skill	10.9
уменьша́ть	umin'shat'	decrease, to	18.1
умере́ть *(perf.)*	umiryet'	die, to	2.3
у́мный	umniy	clever; intelligent	2.11
умыва́ться; мыть лицо́	umyvat'sya; myt' litso	wash one's face, to	2.5
универса́льный магази́н	universal'niy magazin	department store	7.1, 9.8
университе́т *(m)*	universityet	university	9.8, 12.2
у́нция *(f)*	untsiya	ounce	18.3
упако́вывать	upakovyvat'	pack, to	9.7
упа́сть *(perf.)*	upast'	fall down, to	16.1
упражня́ться	uprazhnyat'sa	exercise, to	14.4
урага́н *(m)*	uragan	hurricane	1.5
Ура́льские го́ры *(pl)*	Ural'skiye gory	Ural Mountains	3.4
уро́к *(m)*	urok	lesson	12.6
уро́к *(m)* му́зыки	urok muzyki	music lesson	11.8
усоверше́нствоваться	usavirshyenstvavat'sya	master, to	12.7
уста́лый	ustaliy	tired	2.4
устрани́ть	ustranit'	remove, to	16.1
у́тка *(f)*	utka	duck	1.9
у́тренняя газе́та *(f)*	utrinnyaya gazyeta	morning paper	11.3
у́тро *(n)*	utra	morning	17.10
утю́г *(m)*	utyuk	iron *(for clothes)*	8.7
у́хо *(n)*	ukha	ear	2.2
уходи́ть	ukhadit'	leave, to	16.1

Russian	Transliteration	English	Reference
учёба *(f)*	uchyoba	studies	12.4
учéбник *(m)*	uchebnik	textbook	12.6
учéбный процéсс *(m)*	uchebniy pratses	learning process	12.1
ученúк *(m)*	uchinik	pupil	12.3
учёный *(m)*	uchyoniy	scientist	2.14, 11.5
учúтель *(m)*, учúтельница *(f)*	uchitil', uchitil'nitsa	teacher	2.14, 12.3
учúтывать	uchityvat'	consider, to	2.10
учúть	uchit'	learn, to	12.1, 12.7
учúть *(предмéт)*	uchit' *(predmyet)*	study *(a subject)*, to	12.7
учúться в шкóле	uchit'sa f shkolye	attend school, to	12.1
учúться за granúцей	uchit'sa za granitsey	study abroad, to	12.1
фáбрика *(f)*, завóд *(m)*	fabrika, zavot	factory	10.9
фактúчески	faktichiski	in fact	19.3
фамúлия *(f)*	familiye	last name	2.12
фасáд *(m)*	fasat	front	16.3
феврáль *(m)*	fivral'	February	17.7
фéрма *(f)*	fyerma	farm	10.8
фéрмер *(m)*	fyermer	farmer	2.14
фестивáль *(m)*	festival'	festival	11.6
фúзика *(f)*	fizika	physics	12.5
физиотерапúя *(f)*	fizioterapiya	physical therapy	2.7
Филиппúны *(pl)*	Filippiny	Philippines	9.2
филосóфия *(f)*	filasofiya	philosophy	12.5
фильм *(m)*	fil'm	movie, film	11.9
фильм *(m)* ýжасов	fil'm uzhasov	horror movie	11.9
фиолéтовый	fialyetaviy	purple	6.5
фóрма *(f)*	forma	uniform	6.1
формáт *(m)*	farmat	format	15.1
фототовáры *(pl)*	fotatavary	photo shop	7.1
фотоаппарáт *(m)*	fotaaparat	camera	14.3
фотóграф *(m)*	fatograf	photographer	2.14
фотографúровать	fatografiravat'	photograph, to	14.3
фрáза *(f)*	fraza	phrase	11.2, 13.1
Фрáнция *(f)*	Frantsiya	France	9.2
фруктóвый напúток *(m)*	fruktoviy napitak	fruit drink	5.9
фруктóвый сад *(m)*	fruktoviy sat	orchard	1.7
фрýкты *(pl)*	frukty	fruit(s)	5.5, 10.8
фунт *(m)*	funt	pound	18.3
фут *(m)*	fut	foot	18.2
футбóл *(m)*	futbol	soccer	14.5
харáктер *(m)*	kharakter	character	2.11
хвалúть	khvalit'	praise, to; commend, to	2.9
хвáстаться	khvastatsa	boast, to	2.9

хи́мия (f)	khimiya	chemistry	12.5
химчи́стка (f)	khimchistka	dry cleaner's;	7.1,
		dry cleaning	6.1
хиру́рг (m)	khirurk	surgeon	2.14
хи́трый	khitriy	shrewd	2.11
хлеб (m)	khlep	bread	5.4
хло́пок (m)	khlopak	cotton	6.4
хо́бби (n)	khobbi	hobby	14.3
ходи́ть	khadit'	walk, to	16.1
ходи́ть в кино́	khadit' f kino	go to the movies, to	14.3
ходи́ть в похо́д	khadit' f pakhot	camping, to go	14.3
ходи́ть в теа́тр	khadit' f tiatr	go to the theater, to	14.3
ходи́ть в це́рковь	khadit' f tserkaf'	attend church, to	11.6
ходи́ть на о́перу	khadit' na operu	go to the opera, to	14.3
ходи́ть на пикни́к	khadit' na piknik	go on a picnic, to	14.3
ходи́ть на прогу́лку	khadit' na pragulku	take a walk, to	14.3
ходи́ть пешко́м	khadit' peshkom	hiking, to go	14.3
хозя́йственный магази́н (m)	khazyaistvenniy magazin	hardware store	7.1
хокке́й (m)	khakkey	hockey	14.5
холм (m)	kholm	hill	1.2
холо́дная вода́ (f)	khalodnaya vada	cold water	2.5
хо́лодно	kholadna	cold	1.4, 8.6, 17.6
холо́дное блю́до (n)	khalodnaye blyuda	cold dish	5.1
холо́дные заку́ски (pl)	khalodnye zakuski	cold appetizers	5.1, 5.7
холо́дный напи́ток (m)	khalodniy napitak	cold drink	5.9
хоро́шее настрое́ние (n)	kharoshiye nastrayeniye	good spirits/mood	2.6
хоро́ший	kharoshiy	good	2.9
хорошо́	kharasho	good; all right; O.K.	4.2, 13.3
хорошо́ па́хнуть	kharasho pakhnut'	it smells good	5.8
хорошо́ сдать (perf.) экза́мен	kharasho sdat' ekzamin	do well (on an exam), to	12.8
хорошо́ сиде́ть	kharasho sidyet'	fit, to	6.1
хоте́ть пить	khatyet' pit'	thirsty, to be	5.1, 5.9
хотя́	khatya	although	15.8, 19.3
христиа́нство (n)	khristianstva	Christianity	11.6
худе́ть	khudyet'	lose weight, to	2.2
худо́жник (m)	khudozhnik	artist; painter	2.14, 11.7
худо́й	khudoy	thin	2.2
цари́ца (f)	tsaritsa	tsarina	3.5
царь (m)	tsar'	tsar	3.5
Царь-Ко́локол	Tsar'-kolakal	Tsar Bell	3.2
Царь-Пу́шка	Tsar'-pushka	Tsar Cannon	3.2
цвет (m)	tsvet	color	6.1, 6.5

цветной телевизор *(m)*	tsvyetnoy tilivizar	color television	11.4
цветок *(m)*	tsvitok	flower	1.7
цель *(f)*	tsel'	aim	15.5
цемент *(m)*	tsimyent	cement	8.8
цена *(f)*	tsina	price	7.3
цент *(m)*	tsyent	cent	7.3
центр *(m)*	tsyentr	downtown	3.1
центральное отопление *(n)*	tsentral'naye ataplyeniye	central heating	8.6
Центральный театр *(m)* кукол	Tsintral'niy tiatr kukal	Central Puppet Theater	3.2
цепочка *(f)*	tsipochka	necklace	6.3
церковь *(f)*	tserkaf'	church	9.8, 11.6
чаевые *(pl)*	chayeviye	tip	5.3, 7.2
чай *(m)*	chay	tea	5.9
чай со льдом	chay so l'dom	iced tea	5.9
чайник *(m)*	chaynik	teapot; kettle	5.9, 5.11
час *(m)*	chas	hour	17.11
части *(pl)* тела	chasti tyela	parts of the body	2.2
часто	chasta	often	17.3
часть *(f)*; секция *(f)*	chast'; syektsiya	part; section	16.5
часы *(pl)*	chasy	watch; watches	6.3, 7.1
часы *(pl)* приёма	chasy priyoma	office hours	17.1
чашка *(f)*	chashka	teacup; cup	5.11, 18.8
чей	chey	whose	19.2
чек *(m)*	chyek	check	7.3
человек *(m)*	chilavyek	person	2.1
человек *(m)* искусства	chilavyek iskusstva	artist	11.7
человек *(m)* среднего возраста	chilavyek sryedneva vozrasta	middle-aged person	2.1
чем больше тем лучше	chem bol'she tyem luchshe	(the) more, the better	19.3
через два года	chyeriz dva goda	year after next *(in 2 years)*	17.5
через минуту	chyeriz minutu	in a moment	17.1
через три дня	chyeriz tri dnya	three days later	17.1
чернила *(pl)*	chirnila	ink	13.5
черчение *(n)*	chirchyeniye	drafting	12.5
чеснок *(m)*	chisnok	garlic	5.4
честный	chyestniy	honest	2.11
четверг *(m)*	chitvyerk	Thursday	17.9
четверть *(f)*	chyetvert'	quarter	18.1
четверть *(f)* часа	chyetvert' chasa	quarter hour	17.11
четвёртый	chitvyortiy	fourth	17.9
четвёртый год *(m)*	chitvyortiy got	fourth year	12.4

четы́ре	chityre	four	18.1
четы́ре вре́мени го́да	chityri vryemini goda	four seasons	1.6
четы́рнадцать	chityrnatsat'	fourteen	18.1
чёрная икра́ (f) с блина́ми	chyornaya ikra s blinami	black caviar with blinis	5.7
Чёрное мо́ре (n)	Chyornoye morye	Black Sea	3.4, 9.4
чёрный	chyorniy	black	6.5
Чи́ли (n)	Chili	Chile	9.2
чини́ть	chinit'	fix, to; repair, to	8.9
чи́стить зу́бы	chistit' zuby	brush one's teeth, to	2.5
чи́сто	chista	clean	8.7
чи́стый	chistiy	clean	6.1
чита́ть	chitat'	read, to	12.7, 13.4
чита́ть вслух	chitat' vslukh	read aloud, to	13.4
чита́ть газе́ту	chitat' gazyetu	read the newspapers, to	14.3
чита́ть журна́л	chitat' zhurnal	read a magazine, to	14.3
чита́ть кни́гу	chitat' knigu	read a book, to	14.3
чита́ть ле́кцию	chitat' lyektsiyu	give a talk/lecture, to	11.4
чита́ть про себя́	chitat' pro sebya	read silently, to	13.4
чрезвыча́йно	chrezvychaina	exceedingly	18.7
чрезме́рно	chryezmyerna	excessively	18.7
чте́ние	chtyeniye	reading	13.4
что	shto	what	19.2
что случи́лось?	shto sluchilas'?	what happened?	4.2
чу́вствовать	chustvavat'	feel, to	2.6, 2.8
чу́вствовать себя́ хорошо́	chustvavat' sebya kharasho	well, to be/feel	2.6
чулки́ (pl)	chulki	stockings	6.2
шампу́нь (m)	shampun'	shampoo	8.7
ша́риковая ру́чка (f)	sharikavaya ruchka	ballpoint pen	13.5
шарф (m)	sharf	scarf	6.3
ша́хта (f)	shakhta	mine	10.9
шахтёр (m)	shakhtyor	miner	2.14
шве́дский стол (m)	shvetskiy stol	buffet	5.1
шве́йная маши́на (f)	shveynaya mashina	sewing machine	6.1
шерсть (f)	sherst'	wool	6.4
шестна́дцать	shestnatsat'	sixteen	18.1
шесто́й год (m)	shistoy got	sixth year	12.4
шесть	shyest'	six	18.1
шестьдеся́т	shestdesyat	sixty	18.1
шёлк (m)	shyolk	silk	6.4
широ́кий	shirokiy	wide; broad	18.1
шить	shit'	sew, to	6.1
шкаф (m)	shkaf	closet	8.3

шко́ла *(f)*	shkola	school	9.8, 12.2
шко́ла-интерна́т *(m)*	shkola-internat	boarding school	12.2
шко́льник *(m)*	shkol'nik	elementary school student; high school student	12.3
шко́льный день *(m)*	shkol'niy dyen'	school day	12.6
шку́ра *(f)*	shkura	hide	1.8
шнурки́ *(pl)*	shnurki	shoelaces	6.3
шокола́д *(m)*	shikalat	chocolate	5.4
шо́рты *(pl)*	shorty	shorts	6.2
шоссе́ *(n)*	shasse	freeway	9.3
Шотла́ндия *(f)*	Shatlandiya	Scotland	9.2
шпина́т *(m)*	shpinat	spinach	5.6
штат *(m)*	shtat	state	9.2
шторм *(m)*	shtorm	storm	1.5
щётка *(f)*	shchyotka	scrubbing brush	8.7
щи *(pl)*	shchi	shchi *(fish soup)*	5.7
эвакуа́ция *(f)*	evakuatsiya	evacuation	3.5
экза́мен *(m)*	ekzamin	exam	12.1, 12.8
экзаменова́ть	ekzaminavat'	examine, to	12.8
эконо́мика *(f)*	ekanomika	economics; economy	12.5, 10.6
экспериме́нт *(m)*	ekspirimyent	experiment	11.5
экспорти́ровать	ekspartiravat'	export, to	10.10
эле́ктрик *(m)*	elyektrik	electrician	2.14
электри́ческий вентиля́тор *(m)*	eliktrichiskiy vintilyatr	electric fan	8.6
электро́нная му́зыка *(f)*	eliktronnaya muzyka	electronic music	11.8
элемента́рный	elimintarniy	basic	15.3
эмо́ции *(pl)*	imotsii	emotions	2.8
энтузиа́зм *(m)*	entuziazm	enthusiasm	2.9
Эрмита́ж *(m)*	Ermitazh	Hermitage Museum	3.2
эскала́тор *(m)*	eskalatar	escalator	8.5
Эсто́ния *(f)*	Estoniya	Estonia	3.4
э́та неде́ля *(f)*	eta nidyelya	this week	17.8
э́та сторона́ *(f)*	eta starana	this side	16.3
эта́ж *(m)*	etazh	floor; story	8.1
э́ти *(pl)*	eti	these	16.2
э́ти дни	eti dni	these day(s)	17.1, 17.8
э́то у́тро *(n)*	eta utra	this morning	17.10
э́то хорошо́?	eta kharasho?	is it all right?	4.2
э́тот *(m)*	etot	this	16.2
э́тот ве́чер *(m)*	etat vyechir	this evening	17.10
э́тот вид *(m)*	etat vit	this kind	16.2

э́тот год *(m)*	etat got	this year	17.5
э́тот день *(m)*	etat dyen'	this day	17.10
ю́бка *(f)*	yupka	skirt	6.2
ювели́рные изде́лия *(pl)*	yuvilirnye izdyeliya	jewelry	6.3
ювели́рный магази́н *(m)*	yuvelirniy magazin	jewelry shop	7.1
юг *(m)*	yuk	south	16.4
Ю́жная А́фрика *(f)*	Yuzhnaya Afrika	South Africa	9.2
юри́ст *(m)*	yurist	lawyer	2.14, 10.4
я вас сто лет не ви́дел	ya vas sto lyet ni vidil	haven't seen you for ages	4.1
я заплачу́	ya zaplachu	let me pay	7.2
я э́того не заслу́живаю	ya etova ni zasluzhivayu	I don't deserve it	4.2
я, меня́, мне	ya, minya, mnye	I, me, (to) me	2.13
я́блоко *(n)*	yablaka	apple	5.5
я́годицы *(f)*	yagaditsy	buttocks	2.2
язы́к *(m)*	yezyk	language; tongue	13.1, 2.2
яи́чница *(f)*	yaichnitsa	fried eggs	5.4
яйцо́ *(n)*	yaitso	egg	5.4
яйцо́ вкруту́ю	yaitso vkrutuyu	hard-boiled egg	5.4
янва́рь *(m)*	yanvar'	January	17.7
Япо́ния *(f)*	Yaponiya	Japan	9.2
я́ркий	yarkiy	bright	1.1
я́сно	yasna	clear	1.4
я́сный	yasniy	clear	2.10
я́щик *(m)*	yashchik	drawer	8.5
я́щик *(m)* с *(+ inst.)*	yashchik s	case of	18.8

English-Russian Glossary

abdomen	живо́т *(m)*	zhivot	2.2
able, to be	мочь; быть в состоя́нии	moch'; byt' v sastayaniye	15.1
about	о́коло *(+ gen.)*	okala	18.4
about *(approximately)*	приблизи́тельно	priblizitel'na	17.1
about *(more or less)*	о́коло	okala	17.1
above	над *(+ inst.)*	nat	16.3
academic year	академи́ческий год *(m)*	akadimichiskiy got	17.5
accessories *(clothing)*	предме́ты *(pl)* туале́та	pridmyety tualeta	6.3
accident	ава́рия *(f)*	avariya	9.5
accompany, to	сопровожда́ть	sapravazhdat'	14.2
according to	соотве́тственно с; соотве́тственно *(+ dat.)*	saatvyetstvina s; saatvyetstvinno	15.8, 19.4
accounting	бухга́лтерский учёт *(m)*	bukhgalterskiy uchyot	12.5
accurate	то́чный	tochniy	15.1
acre	акр *(m)*	akr	18.2
actor	актёр *(m)*	aktyor	2.14, 11.9
actress	актри́са *(f)*	aktrisa	11.9
add, to	прибавля́ть	pribavlyat'	18.1
address	а́дрес *(m)*	adres	13.6
address, forms of	фо́рма *(f)* обраще́ния	forma obrashchyeniya	2.15
admire, to	восхища́ться	vaskhishchat'sa	2.8
adult	взро́слый	vzrosliy	2.1
Africa	А́фрика *(f)*	Afrika	9.2
after	по́сле *(+ gen.)*	poslye	17.1
afternoon snack	по́лдник *(m)*	poldnik	5.2
ago: 5 years ago	наза́д: 5 лет (тому́) наза́д	nazat: 5 lyet (tamu) nazat	17.1
agree, to	соглаша́ться	saglashat'sa	10.3
agriculture	земледе́лие *(n)*	zimledyeliye	10.8
aim	цель *(f)*	tsel'	15.5
air	во́здух *(m)*	vozdukh	1.1
air conditioner	кондиционе́р *(m)*	kanditsianyer	8.6
air conditioning	кондициони́рованный во́здух *(m)*	kanditsianiravanniy vozdukh	8.6
airmail	авиапо́чта *(f)*	aviapochta	13.6
airplane	самолёт *(m)*	samalyot	9.5
airport	аэропо́рт *(m)*	aeroport	9.5, 9.8
algebra	а́лгебра *(f)*	algebra	12.5

alive	живóй	zhivoy	1.7, 2.3
all	весь	vyes	18.7
all day long	весь день *(m)*	vyes' den'	17.1, 17.10
all kinds (of)	любы́е	lyubiye	15.2
all right	хорошó	kharasho	13.3
all right; that's all right	всё в порядке	vsyo v paryatke	2.9
Almaty (Kazakhstan)	Алматы́ *(f)*	Almaty	3.4
almost	почти́	pachti	18.6
alphabet	алфави́т *(m)*	alfavit	3.3, 13.1
already	ужé	uzhye	17.1
also	тáкже, тóже	takzhe, tozhe	19.3
although	хотя́	khatya	15.8, 19.3
always	всегдá	vsigda	17.3
ambassador	посóл *(m)*	pasol	10.11
America	Амéрика *(f)*	Amyerika	9.2
American	америкáнец *(m)*, америкáнка *(f)*	amerikanyets, amerikanka	9.2
American literature	америкáнская литератýра *(f)*	amyerikanskaya litiratura	11.2, 12.5
ancestors	прéдки *(pl)*	pretki	2.12
and	и	i	19.3
angry	серди́тый	serditiy	2.8
animal	живóтное *(n)*	zhivotnoye	1.8
annoy, to	раздражáть	razdrazhat'	2.8
another time	в другóе врéмя	v drugoye vryemya	17.1
answer	отвéт *(m)*	atvyet	13.2
answer, to	отвечáть	atvyechat'	12.8, 13.2, 13.7
ant	муравéй *(m)*	muravyei	1.9
Antarctic Ocean	Антаркти́ческий океáн *(m)*	Antarktichiskiy akian	9.4
antiques; antique store	антиквáрные товáры *(pl)*	antikvarniye tavary	7.1
apartment	кварти́ра *(f)*	kvartira	8.1
apologies	извинéния *(pl)*	izvinyeniya	4.3
apple	я́блоко *(n)*	yablaka	5.5
approximately	приблизи́тельно	priblizitil'na	18.4
apricot	абрикóс *(m)*	abrikos	5.5
April	апрéль *(m)*	apryel'	17.7
architect	архитéктор *(m)*	arkhityektar	2.14
Arctic Ocean	Сéверный Ледови́тый океáн *(m)*	Syeverniy Lidavitiy akian	9.4
area	плóщадь *(f)*	ploshchat'	18.2
Argentina	Аргенти́на *(f)*	Argentina	9.2
arm	рукá *(f)*	ruka	2.2
armchair	крéсло *(n)*	kryesla	8.3

English	Russian	Transliteration	Reference
Armenia	Арме́ния *(f)*	Armyeniya	3.4
army	а́рмия *(f)*	armiya	10.11
aromatic	арома́тный	aramatniy	5.8
around	вокру́г *(+ gen.)*	vakruk	16.3
arrange, to	организо́вывать	arganizovyvat'	14.2
arrest, to	аресто́вывать	aristovyvat'	10.5
arrival	прибы́тие *(n)*	pribitiye	4.4, 9.7
arrival time	вре́мя *(n)* прибы́тия	vryemye pribytiya	9.7
arrive, to	прибыва́ть	pribyvat'	9.7, 16.1
arrogant	высокоме́рный	vysakomyerniy	2.11
art	иску́сство *(n)*;	iskusstva;	11.7,
	рисова́ние *(n)*	risovaniye	12.5
art gallery	карти́нная галере́я *(f)*	kartinnaya galiryeya	9.8, 11.7
article	статья́ *(f)*	stat'ya	11.3
artist	худо́жник *(m)*;	khudozhnik;	2.14,
	челове́к *(m)* иску́сства	chilavyek iskusstva	11.7
as … as …	так же … как и …	tak zhe … kak i …	15.2
as soon as	как то́лько	kak tol'ka	19.3
as well as	та́кже	takzhi	19.3
as you wish	как хоти́те	kak khatite	4.2
Ashkhabad (Turkmenistan)	Ашхаба́д *(m)*	Ashkhabat	3.4
ashtray	пе́пельница *(f)*	pyepil'nitsa	5.12
Asia	А́зия *(f)*	Aziya	9.2
ask, to	спра́шивать	sprashivat'	12.8, 13.2
asleep, to be; sleep, to	спать	spat'	2.4
asparagus	спа́ржа *(f)*	sparzha	5.6
assembly	собра́ние *(n)*	sabraniye	12.6
assistant principal	за́вуч *(m)*	zavuch	12.3
at	на *(+ acc./prep.)*	na	19.4
at last	наконе́ц	nakanyets	17.1
at once *(immediately)*	неме́дленно	nimyedlinna	17.1
at that time	в то вре́мя	v to vryemya	17.1
athlete	спортсме́н *(m)*	sportsmyen	14.4
Atlantic Ocean	Атланти́ческий океа́н *(m)*	Atlantichiskiy akian	9.4
attend church, to	ходи́ть в це́рковь	khadit' f tserkaf'	11.6
attend school, to	учи́ться в шко́ле	uchit'sa f shkolye	12.1
attendance	посеща́емость *(f)*	pasishchaimast'	12.6
attention	внима́ние *(n)*	vnimaniye	12.6
attitudes	отноше́ния *(pl)*	atnasheniya	2.9
attractiveness	привлека́тельность *(f)*	privlikatil'nast'	15.7
August	а́вгуст *(m)*	avgust	17.7
aunt	тётя *(f)*	tyotya	2.12
Australia	Австра́лия *(f)*	Avstraliya	9.2
autumn; fall	о́сень *(f)*	osen'	17.6

English	Russian	Transliteration	Section
auxiliary verbs	вспомога́тельные глаго́лы (*pl*)	vspamagatil'niye glagoly	19.1
avalanche	сне́жный обва́л (*m*)	snyezhniy abval	1.5
Azerbaijan	Азербайджа́н (*m*)	Azirbaidzhan	3.4
baby	младе́нец (*m*)	mladyenits	2.1
back	наза́д	nazat	16.3
back entrance	запа́сной вход (*m*)	zapasnoy vkhot	8.5
backyard	двор (*m*)	dvor	8.4
bad	плохо́й	plakhoy	2.9
bad luck	неуда́ча (*f*)	niudacha	2.9
badminton	бадминто́н (*m*)	badminton	14.5
bag; handbag	су́мка (*f*)	sumka	6.3
bag of	мешо́к (*m*) с (+ *inst.*)	mishok s	18.8
bake	печь	pyech'	5.10
bakery (*bread*)	бу́лочная (*f*)	bulachnaya	7.1
bakery (*sweets*)	конди́терская (*f*)	kanditerskaya	5.3
Baku (Azerbaijan)	Баку́ (*m*)	Baku	3.4
balcony	балко́н (*m*)	balkon	8.5
ballet	бале́т (*m*)	balyet	3.2
ballpoint pen	ша́риковая ру́чка (*f*)	sharikavaya ruchka	13.5
Baltic Sea	Балти́йское мо́ре (*n*)	Baltiyskaye morye	3.4, 9.4
banana	бана́н (*m*)	banan	5.5
bank	банк (*m*)	bank	7.1, 9.8, 10.10
bankruptcy	банкро́тство (*n*)	bankrotstvo	10.6
bar	бар (*m*)	bar	5.3
barber	парикма́хер (*m*)	parikmakher	2.14
barber shop	парикма́херская (*f*)	parikmakherskaya	7.1
bargain, to	торгова́ться	targavat'sa	7.2
bark, to	ла́ять	layet'	1.8
baseball	бейсбо́л (*m*)	beysbol	14.5
basic	элемента́рный	elimintarniy	15.3
basket of	корзи́на (*f*) с (+ *inst.*)	karzina s	18.8
basketball	баскетбо́л (*m*)	basketbol	14.5
batch (of)	па́чка (*f*) (+ *gen.*)	pachka	18.8
bathroom	ва́нная (*f*)	vannaya	8.2
bathtub	ва́нна (*f*)	vanna	8.5
bay	зали́в (*m*)	zalif	1.2
be, to	есть	yest'	19.1
beach	пляж (*m*)	plyazh	1.3
bear	медве́дь (*m*)	midvyet'	1.9
beard	борода́ (*f*)	barada	2.2
beautiful	краси́вый	krasiviy	15.7
because	потому́	patamu	15.5, 19.3
become, to	станови́ться	stanavit'sa	15.1

bed	крова́ть (f)	kravat'	8.3
bedroom	спа́льня (f)	spal'nya	8.2
bedspread	покрыва́ло (n)	pakryvala	8.3
bee	пчела́ (f)	pchila	1.9
beef	говя́дина (f)	govyadina	5.4
beer	пи́во (n)	piva	5.9
before	пе́ред, до	pyerit, do	19.3
begin, to	начина́ть	nachinat'	12.1, 17.2
beginning	нача́ло (n)	nachala	17.1, 17.2
behind	сза́ди (+ gen.)	szadi	19.4
beige	бе́жевый	bezhiviy	6.5
Belarus	Белару́сь (f)	Bilarus'	3.4
believe, to	ве́рить	vyerit'	11.6
believer	ве́рующий	verayushchiy	11.6
below	под (+ acc./inst.)	pot	16.3
bend, to	сгиба́ть	sgibat'	8.9
besides	поми́мо	pamima	19.3
better than	лу́чше чем	luchshe chem	15.2
between	ме́жду (+ inst.)	mezhdu	16.3, 16.5
beyond	вне; по ту сто́рону	vnye; pa tu storanu	16.5
Bible	Би́блия (f)	Bibliya	11.6
bicycle	велосипе́д (m)	vilasipyed	9.5
bill	счёт (m)	schyot	7.2
biology	биоло́гия (f)	bialogiya	12.5
bird	пти́ца (f)	ptitsa	1.9
birthday	день (m) рожде́ния	dyen' razhdyeniye	2.3
Bishkek (Kyrgyzstan)	Бишке́к (m)	Bishkyek	3.4
bite, to	куса́ть	kusat'	1.8
bitter	го́рький	gor'kiy	5.8
black	чёрный	chyorniy	6.5
black caviar with blinis	чёрная икра́ (f) с блина́ми	chyornaya ikra s blinami	5.7
Black Sea	Чёрное мо́ре (n)	Chyornoye morye	3.4, 9.4
blackboard	доска́ (f)	daska	12.6
blanket	одея́ло (n)	adiyala	8.3
blood	кровь (f)	krov'	2.2
blood pressure	давле́ние (n)	davlyeniye	2.6
blouse	блу́зка (f)	bluzka	6.2
blow, to	дуть	dut'	1.4
blue	голубо́й	galuboy	6.5
blunt	тупо́й	tupoy	8.8
boarding school	шко́ла-интерна́т (m)	shkola-internat	12.2
boast, to	хва́статься	khvastatsa	2.9
boat	ло́дка (f)	lotka	9.5

body	тéло *(n)*	tyela	
boiled water	кипячёная водá *(f)*	kipachyonaya vada	
Bolshoi Theater	Большóй теáтр *(m)*	Bol'shoi tiatr	
bon voyage!; have a good trip!	счастлńвого путń!	schastlivava puti!	
bone	кость *(f)*	kost'	
book	кнńга *(f)*	kniga	
bookcase	кнńжный шкаф *(m)*	knizhniy shkaf	
bookshelf	кнńжная пóлка *(f)*	knizhnaya polka	
bookstore	кнńжный магазńн *(m)*	knizhniy magazin	7.1, 9.8,
boots	сапогń *(pl)*	sapagi	
boring	скýчный	skuchniy	
born, to be	родńться	radit'sa	
borrow, to	одолжńть	adalzhit'	7.2, 10
borshch	борщ *(m)*	borshch	
botanical garden	ботанńческий сад *(m)*	batanichiskiy sat	1.7,
bottle (of)	бутńлка *(f) (+ gen.)*	butylka	1
Boulevard Ring	Садóвое кольцó *(n)*	Sadovaye kal'tso	
bowl; bowl (of)	мńска *(f); (+ gen.)*	miska	5.11, 1
box (of)	корóбка *(f) (+ gen.)*	karopka	1
boy	мáльчик *(m)*	mal'chik	
boyfriend	друг *(m)*	druk	14
boys	мáльчики *(pl)*	mal'chiki	2.
bracelet	браслéт *(m)*	braslyet	6
brain	мозг *(m)*	mozg	2.
branches	вéтки *(pl)*	vyetki	1.
brandy	брéнди *(n)*	brendi	5.
Brazil	Бразńлия *(f)*	Braziliya	9.2
bread	хлеб *(m)*	khlep	5.4
break	перемéна *(f)*	pirimyena	12.6
break down, to	сломáть(ся) *(perf.)*	slomat'(sa)	9.5
break, to	ломáть	lamat'	8.9
breakfast	зáвтрак *(m)*	zaftrak	5.2
breast	грудь *(f)*	grud'	2.2
brick	кирпńч *(m)*	kirpich	8.8
bricklayer	кáменщик *(m)*	kamin'shchik	2.14
bridge	мост *(m)*	most	9.3
bright	ńркий	yarkiy	1.1
bring along, to	приносńть	prinasit'	15.4
broad	широ́кий	shirokiy	18.1
broadcast	передáча *(f)*	piridacha	11.4
broadcast, to	передавáть	piridavat'	11.4
broken *(damaged)*	слóманный	slomanniy	8.9
broken *(out of order)*	не рабóтает	ni rabotayet	8.9

broken into pieces	разби́тый на кусо́чки	razbitiy na kusochki	8.9
broom	метла́ *(f)*	mitla	8.7
brother	брат *(m)*	brat	2.12
brown	кори́чневый	karichniviy	6.5
brush	ки́сточка *(f)*	kistachka	13.5
brush one's teeth, to	чи́стить зу́бы	chistit' zuby	2.5
bucket	ведро́ *(n)*	vidro	8.7
buckle	пря́жка *(f)*	pryazhka	6.1
buckle up, to	пристёгивать(ся)	pristyogivat'(sya)	9.5
Buddhism	будди́зм *(m)*	Budizm	11.6
budget	бюдже́т *(m)*	byudzhyet	10.6
buffet	шве́дский стол *(m)*	shvyetskiy stol	5.1
build, to	стро́ить	stroit'	8.1
building	зда́ние *(n)*	zdaniye	8.1
bunch (of)	пучо́к *(m) (+ gen.)*	puchok	18.8
burn, to	горе́ть	garyet'	1.5
bus	авто́бус *(m)*	aftobus	9.5
bush	куст *(m)*	kust	1.7
businessman	бизнесме́н *(m)*	biznismyen	2.14
busy	за́нятый	zanyatiy	10.7
but	но	no	15.8, 19.3
butcher shop	мясно́й магази́н *(m)*	myasnoy magazin	7.1
butter	ма́сло *(n)*	masla	5.4
buttocks	я́годицы *(f)*	yagaditsy	2.2
button	пу́говица *(f)*	pugavitsa	6.1
button, to	застёгивать	zastyogivat'	6.1
buy, to	покупа́ть	pakupat'	7.2
by	при *(+ prep.)*	pri	19.4
cabbage	капу́ста *(f)*	kapusta	5.6
café	кафе́ *(n)*	kafye	5.3
cafeteria	кафете́рий *(m)*	kafityeriy	5.3
cake	пиро́г *(m)*	pirok	5.4
calendar	календа́рь *(m)*	kalindar'	17.5
call	звоно́к	zvanok	13.7
call, to	звони́ть	zvanit'	13.7
camera	фотоаппара́т *(m)*	fotaaparat	14.3
camping, to go	ходи́ть в похо́д	khadit' f pakhot	14.3
can of	консе́рвная ба́нка *(f)* с *(+ inst.)*	kansyervnaya banka s	18.8
Canada	Кана́да *(f)*	Kanada	9.2
Canadian	кана́дец *(m)*, кана́дка *(f)*	kanadyets, kanadka	9.2
candy	конфе́та *(f)*	kanfyeta	5.4
canvas	полотно́ *(n)*	palatno	11.7
capabilities	спосо́бности *(pl)*	spasobnasti	2.11

capable	спосо́бный	spasobniy	2.11
capital (*city*)	столи́ца (*f*)	stalitsa	3.4
capital (*money*)	капита́л (*m*)	kapital	10.6
capitalism	капитали́зм (*m*)	kapitalizm	10.3
car	маши́на (*f*)	mashina	9.5
car accident	автомоби́льная ава́рия (*f*)	aftamabil'naya avariya	9.6
careful	осторо́жный	astarozhniy	2.8, 2.11
careful; carefully	осторо́жно	astarozhna	9.6
careless	беззабо́тный	bizzabotniy	2.11
carpet	ковёр (*m*)	kavyor	8.5
carrots	морко́вь (*f*)	morkov'	5.6
carton of	коро́бка (*f*) с (+ *inst.*)	karopka s	18.8
case (*grammar*)	падёж (*m*)	padyezh	3.3
case of	я́щик (*m*) с (+ *inst.*)	yashchik s	18.8
cash	нали́чные де́ньги (*pl*)	nalichniye dyen'gi	7.3
cashier	касси́р (*m*), касси́рша (*f*)	kasir, kasirsha	2.14, 7.2
Caspian Sea	Каспи́йское мо́ре (*n*)	Kaspiyskaya morye	9.4
cassette tape	кассе́та (*f*)	kassyeta	11.4
cat	ко́шка (*f*)	koshka	1.9
catch a cold, to	простуди́ться (*perf.*)	prastudit'sa	2.6
catch fire, to	загоре́ться (*perf.*)	zagaryet'sa	1.5
Caucasus Mountains	Кавка́зские го́ры (*pl*)	Kavkazskiye gory	3.4
CD (compact disc)	компа́кт-диск (*m*)	kampakt-disk	11.4
ceiling	потоло́к (*m*)	patalok	8.5
celebrate the New Year, to	пра́здновать Но́вый год	praznavat' Noviy got	17.5
celery	сельдере́й (*m*)	sildiryey	5.6
cement	цеме́нт (*m*)	tsimyent	8.8
cent	цент (*m*)	tsyent	7.3
centimeter	сантиме́тр (*m*)	santimyetr	18.2
central heating	центра́льное отопле́ние (*n*)	tsentral'naye ataplyeniye	8.6
Central Puppet Theater	Центра́льный теа́тр (*m*) ку́кол	Tsintral'niy tiatr kukal	3.2
century	век (*m*)	vyek	17.5
certain	определённый	apridilyonniy	15.8
certainly	определённо	apridilyonna	15.8
certainty	уве́ренность (*f*)	uvyerinnast'	15.8
chair	стул (*m*)	stul	8.3
chairman	председа́тель (*m*)	pridsidatel'	10.3
chalk	мел (*m*)	myel	12.6
change	ме́лочь (*f*); сда́ча (*f*); измене́ния (*pl*)	myeloch; sdacha; izmenyeniya	7.3 10.2
change (*clothes*), to	переоде́ть	piriadyet'	6.1

change, to	меня́ть	minyat'	15.1
character	хара́ктер (m)	kharakter	2.11
chat, to	болта́ть	baltat'	13.2
check; bill	счёт (m); чек (m)	schyot; chyek	5.3, 7.3
cheers!	на здоро́вье!	na zdarov'ye!	4.2
cheese	сыр (m)	syr	5.4
chemistry	хи́мия (f)	khimiya	12.5
chest	грудна́я кле́тка (f)	grudnaya klyetka	2.2
chewing gum	жва́чка (f)	zhvachka	5.4
chicken	ку́рица (f)	kuritsa	1.9, 5.4
child	ребёнок (m)	rebyonak	2.1
Chile	Чи́ли (n)	Chili	9.2
China	Кита́й (m)	Kitay	9.2
chocolate	шокола́д (m)	shikalat	5.4
choose, to	выбира́ть	vibirat'	15.2
Christianity	христиа́нство (n)	khristianstva	11.6
Christmas	Рождество́ (n)	Razhdistvo	11.6
Christmas tree	рожде́ственская ёлка (f)	razhdyestvinskaya yolka	11.6
church	це́рковь (f)	tserkaf'	9.8, 11.6
cigarettes	сигаре́ты (pl)	sigaryety	5.12
cigars	сига́ры (pl)	sigary	5.12
city	го́род (m)	gorat	3.1, 9.2
civil engineer	инжене́р-строи́тель (m)	inzhinyer-straityel'	2.14
classical music	класси́ческая му́зыка (f)	klassichiskaya muzyka	11.8
classmate	однокла́ссник (m)	adnaklassnik	14.1
classroom	кла́сс (m)	klass	12.6
clean	чи́стый; чи́сто	chistiy; chista	6.1, 8.7
clean, to	убира́ть	ubirat'	8.7
cleaning	убо́рка (f)	uborka	8.7
clear	я́сно; я́сный	yasna; yasniy	1.4, 2.10
clever; intelligent	у́мный	umniy	2.11
climate	кли́мат (m)	klimat	1.4
clinic	поликли́ника (f)	paliklinika	2.7
close	ря́дом	ryadom	8.4
close, to	закры́ть (perf.)	zakrit'	8.4
closet	шкаф (m)	shkaf	8.3
cloth; fabric	ткань (f)	tkan'	6.4
clothes	оде́жда (f)	adyezhda	6.1
clothing	оде́жда (f)	adyezhda	6.1
cloud	о́блако (n)	oblaka	1.4
cloudy	о́блачно	oblachna	1.4
coat	пальто́ (n)	pal'to	6.2
Coca-Cola®	ко́ка-ко́ла (f)	koka-kola	5.9
coffee table	журна́льный стол (m)	zhurnal'niy stol	8.3

cold	хо́лодно	kholadna	1.4, 8.6, 17.6
cold appetizers	холо́дные заку́ски *(pl)*	khalodnye zakuski	5.1, 5.7
cold dish	холо́дное блю́до *(n)*	khalodnaye blyuda	5.1
cold drink	холо́дный напи́ток *(m)*	khalodniy napitak	5.9
cold water	холо́дная вода́ *(f)*	khalodnaya vada	2.5
collar	воротни́к *(m)*	varatnik	6.1
colleague	колле́га *(m, f)*	kalyega	14.1
college	институ́т *(m);*	institut;	9.8,
	колле́дж *(m)*	kalyedzh	12.2
colloquial expressions	разгово́рные выраже́ния *(pl)*	razgavorniye vyrazhyeniya	4.2
colon	двоето́чие *(n)*	dvayetochiye	11.2
color	цвет *(m)*	tsvet	6.5
color television	цветно́й телеви́зор *(m)*	tsvyetnoy tilivizar	11.4
comb one's hair, to	причёсывать во́лосы	prichyosyvat' volasy	2.5
come back, to	возвраща́ться	vazvrashchat'sa	16.1
come down, to	сойти́ вниз	sayti vniz	16.1
come in, to	войти́	vayti	16.1
come out, to	вы́йти	viyti	16.1
come up, to	подня́ться *(perf.)*	padnyat'sa	16.1
come, to	приходи́ть	prikhadit'	16.1
comedy	коме́дия *(f)*	kamyediya	11.9
comfortable; contented	дово́льный	davol'niy	2.9
comics	коми́ческие расска́зы *(pl)*	komichiskiye rasskazy	11.3
comma	запята́я *(f)*	zapitaya	11.2
commerce	комме́рция *(f)*	kammyertsiya	10.10
common	обы́чный	abbychniy	15.7
Commonwealth of Independent States (CIS)	Содру́жество *(n)* Незави́симых Госуда́рств (СНГ)	Sadruzhistva Nizavisimykh Gasudarstf (SNG)	3.1, 3.4
communism	коммуни́зм *(m)*	kammunizm	10.3
community	общи́на *(f)*	abshchina	9.2
comparatively	сравни́тельно	sravnityel'na	18.6
compare, to	сра́внивать	sravnivat'	15.2
compared to	сра́внивая с (+ instr.)	sravnivaya s	19.4
comparison	сравне́ние	sravnyeniye	15.2
compete, to	соревнова́ться	sarivnavat'sa	14.4
competition	соревнова́ние *(n)*	sarivnavaniye	10.6, 14.4
completed	зако́нчен	zakonchin	8.9
completely	по́лностью	polnast'yu	18.7
complicated	сло́жный, тру́дный	slozhniy, trudniy	15.6
complications	тру́дности, сло́жности *(pl)*	trudnasti, slozhnasti	15.6
composition	сочине́ние *(n)*	sachinyeniye	12.6

computer specialist	специали́ст (m) по компью́терам	spitsialist pa kamp'uteram	2.14
concerning	относи́тельно (+ gen.)	otnasitil'no	19.4
concert	конце́рт (m)	kantsert	11.8
concert hall	конце́ртный зал (m)	kantsyertniy zal	9.8, 11.8
conductor (of orchestra/band)	дирижёр (m)	dirizhyor	2.14, 11.8
conductor (ticket seller)	конду́ктор (m), конду́кторша (f)	kanduktar, kanduktarsha	2.14
congratulations	поздравля́ем	pazdravlyayem	4.2
connecting words	свя́зки (pl)	svyazki	19.3
conscientious	созна́тельный	saznatel'niy	2.11
consider, to	учи́тывать	uchityvat'	2.10
consonant: hard, soft, voiced, unvoiced	согла́сный (m) звук: твёрдый, мя́гкий, зво́нкий, глухо́й	saglasniy zvuk: tvyordiy, myakhkiy, zvonkiy, glukhoy	3.3
construction site	строи́тельная площа́дка (f)	straitel'naya plashchatka	8.1
consulate	ко́нсульство (n)	konsul'stva	10.11
contact, to	контакти́ровать	kantaktiravat'	13.6
continent	контине́нт (m)	kantinyent	1.2
continue, to	продолжа́ть	pradalzhat'	17.1
contractor	подря́дчик (m)	padryadchik	2.14
conversation	разгово́р (m)	razgavor	13.2
cook	по́вар (m)	povar	2.14
cook, to	вари́ть	varit'	8.4, 14.3
cook a meal, to	пригото́вить еду́	prigatovit' yedu	5.10
cookbook	пова́ренная кни́га (f)	pavarennaya kniga	5.10
cooking	приготовле́ние (n) пи́щи	prigatavlyeniye pishchi	5.10
copy	ко́пия (f)	kopiya	12.6
copy, to	спи́сывать	spisyvat'	12.6
corn	кукуру́за (f)	kukuruza	5.6
corner	у́гол (m)	ugal	9.3
correct	пра́вильный, ве́рный	pravil'niy, vyerniy	12.7
corridor	коридо́р (m)	karidor	8.2
cotton	хло́пок (m)	khlopak	6.4
cough, to	ка́шлять	kashlyat'	2.6
country	страна́ (f)	strana	9.1
countryside	се́льская ме́стность (f)	syel'skaya myestnost'	9.2
county	гра́фство (n)	grafstva	9.2
course (of food)	блю́до (n) (+ gen.)	blyuda	18.8
courtesy expressions	выраже́ния ве́жливости	vyrazhyeniya vezhlivasti	13.3
cow	коро́ва (f)	karova	1.9

cream	крем *(m)*; крéмовый	kryem; kryemaviy	5.4, 6.5
credit card	кредúтная кáрточка *(f)*	kriditnaya kartochka	7.3
creek	ручéй *(m)*	ruchyei	1.3
cross the street, to	переходúть ýлицу	pikhadit' ulitsu	9.3
cry, to	кричáть; плáкать	krichat'; plakat'	2.8
Cuba	Кýба *(f)*	Kuba	9.2
cucumber	огурéц *(m)*	aguryets	5.6
cucumber salad	салáт *(m)* из огурцóв	salat iz agurtsof	5.7
cufflinks	зáпонки *(pl)*	zapanki	6.3
cuisine	кýхня *(f)*	kukhnya	5.7
cultural	культýрный	kul'turniy	11.1
culture	культýра *(f)*	kul'tura	10.1, 11.1
cup	чáшка *(f)*	chashka	5.11, 18.8
currency	валюта *(f)*	valyuta	7.3
curtain	занавéс *(m)*	zanavyes	8.5
cushion	подýшка *(f)* для дивáна	padushka dlya divana	8.5
custom	обы́чай *(m)*	abychay	10.1, 11.1
customer	покупáтель *(m)*	pakupatil'	7.2
cut off, to	обрывáть	abryvat'	13.7
cut, to	рéзать	ryezat'	8.9
cute	симпатúчный	simpatichniy	15.7
dad	пáпа *(m)*	papa	2.12
daily paper	ежеднéвная газéта *(f)*	ezhidnyevnaya gazyeta	11.3
dance hall	танцевáльный зал *(m)*	tantsival'niy zal	9.8
dance, to	танцевáть	tantsivat'	14.2, 14.3
danger	опáсность *(f)*	apasnast'	1.5, 9.6
dark	тёмный	tyomniy	1.1, 6.5
dash	тирé *(n)*	tire	11.2
data	дáнные *(pl)*	danniye	11.5
date	свидáние *(n)*	svidaniye	14.2
daughter	дочь *(f)*	doch	2.12
day	день *(m)*	dyen'	1.1, 2.4, 17.9
day after tomorrow	послезáвтра	poslyezaftra	17.8
day before yesterday	позавчерá	pozafchera	17.8
daylight saving time	лéтнее врéмя *(n)*	lyetniye vryemya	17.1
days	дни *(pl)*	dni	17.8
daytime	дневнóе врéмя *(n)*	dnivnoye vryemya	17.10
dead	мёртвый	myortviy	1.7, 2.3
dear friends	дорогúе друзья́ *(pl)*	daragiye druz'ya	2.15
December	декáбрь *(m)*	dikabr'	17.7
Decembrist Revolt	восстáние *(n)* декабрúстов	vasstaniye dikabristaf	3.5
decide, to	решáть	rishat'	10.4
decision	решéние *(n)*	rishyeniye	10.4

decorate, to	обставля́ть	apstavlyat'	8.4
decrease, to	уменьша́ть	umin'shat'	18.1
deep	глубоко́	glubako	18.2
deer	оле́нь *(m)*	alyen'	1.9
defend, to	защища́ть	zashishchat'	10.4
delicacies	деликате́сы *(pl)*	dilikatyesy	5.1
delicious	вку́сный	fkusniy	5.8
deliver	доставля́ть	dastavlyat'	7.2
democracy	демокра́тия *(f)*	dimakratiya	3.5, 10.3
demonstration	демонстра́ция *(f)*	dimanstratsiya	10.9
dentist	зубно́й врач *(m)*	zubnoy vrach	2.7, 2.14
depart, to	отъезжа́ть	at"yezhat'	9.7
Department of Education	Министе́рство *(n)* образова́ния	Ministyerstva abrazavaniya	10.3
Department of Foreign Affairs	Министе́рство *(n)* иностра́нных дел	Ministyerstva inastrannykh dyel	10.3
department store	универса́льный магази́н *(m)*	universal'niy magazin	7.1, 9.8
departure	отъе́зд *(m)*	at"yezd	9.7
departure time	вре́мя *(n)* отъе́зда	vryemye at"yezda	9.7
descend to; come down, to	спуска́ться	spuskat'sa	8.4
desert	пусты́ня *(f)*	pustynye	1.2
desk	пи́сьменный стол *(m)*; рабо́чий стол *(m)*	pis'menniy stol; rabochiy stol	8.3, 10.7
desk lamp	насто́льная ла́мпа *(f)*	nastol'naya lampa	8.5
detach, to; separate, to	отделя́ть	atdelyat'	16.1
detention	наказа́ние *(n)*	nakazaniye	12.6
develop, to	развива́ть	razvivat'	2.2, 10.6
dialect	диале́кт *(m)*	dialyekt	13.1
diarrhea	поно́с *(m)*	panos	2.6
dictation	дикта́нт *(m)*	diktant	12.6
dictatorship	диктату́ра *(f)*	diktatura	3.5
dictionary	слова́рь *(m)*	slavar'	11.2
die, to	умере́ть *(perf.)*	umiryet'	2.3
difficulties	тру́дности *(pl)*	trudnasti	15.6
dining room *(in a home)*	столо́вая *(f)* *(дома)*	stalovaya *(doma)*	5.3, 8.2
dining hall *(in a school)*	столо́вая *(f)* *(в школе)*	stalovaya *(f shkole)*	5.3
dinner	обе́д *(m)*	abyet	5.2
dinner party	зва́ный обе́д *(m)*	zvaniy abyet	14.2
diplomacy	дипломатия *(f)*	diplamatiya	10.11
diplomat	диплома́т *(m)*	diplamat	2.14, 10.11
direction	направле́ние *(n)*	napravlyeniye	16.4, 16.5
director	дире́ктор *(m)*	diryektar	11.9
dirty	гря́зный; гря́зно	gryazniy; gryazna	6.1, 8.7

disappoint, to	разочаровáть *(perf.)*	razachiravat'	2.8
disaster	бéдствие *(n)*	byetstviye	1.5
disco	дискотéка *(f)*	diskatyeka	9.8, 11.8
discount	скúдка *(f)*	skitka	7.2
discover, to	открывáть	atkrivat'	11.5
discovery	открúтие *(n)*	otkritiye	11.5
dish	блюдо *(n)*	blyuda	5.1, 18.8
dishcloth	посýдное полотéнце *(n)*	pasudnaye palatyentse	8.7
distribute, to	распределя́ть	raspridilyat'	15.4
divide into, to	делúть на *(+ acc.)*	dilit' na	18.1
divorce, to	разводúться	razvodit'sa	2.3
do well (on an exam), to	хорошó сдать экзáмен	kharasho sdat' ekzamin	12.8
do, to; make, to	дéлать	dyelat'	15.1
doctor; physician	дóктор *(m)*; врач *(m)*	doktar; vrach	2.7, 2.14
documentary	документáльный фильм *(m)*	dakumintal'niy fil'm	11.9
dollar	дóллар *(m)*	dollar	7.3
domestic life	жизнь в дóме	zhizn' v domye	8.4
don't mention it	не стóит благодáрности	ni stoit blagadarnasti	4.3
door	дверь *(f)*	dvyer'	8.5
doorbell	двернóй звонóк *(m)*	dvernoy zvanok	8.5
double room *(in a hotel)*	нóмер *(m)* на двоúх	nomir na dvoikh	8.2
down	вниз *(+ gen.)*	vniz	19.4
downstairs	внизý	vnizu	8.5
downtown	центр *(m)*	tsyentr	3.1
dozen	дю́жина *(f)*	dyuzhina	18.8
drafting	черчéние *(n)*	chirchyeniye	12.5
drama	дрáма *(f)*	drama	11.9
drawer	я́щик *(m)*	yashchik	8.5
dream, to	мечтáть	michtat'	2.4
dress	плáтье *(n)*	plat'ye	6.2
drill, to	зубрúть	zubrit'	12.7
drink to, to	пить за *(+ acc.)*	pit' za	5.1
drinks	напúтки *(pl)*	napitki	5.9
drive safely	ведúте машúну осторóжно	viditye mashinu astarozhna	4.5
drive, to	вестú машúну	visti mashinu	9.6
driver	водúтель *(m)*	vaditil'	9.6
drizzle	морося́щий дождь *(m)*	marasyashchiy dozhd'	1.4
drunk; tipsy	пья́ный	p'yaniy	5.9
dry	сýхо; сухóй	sukha; sukhoy	1.4, 5.8
dry cleaner's	химчúстка *(f)*	khimchistka	7.1
dry cleaning	химчúстка *(f)*	khimchistka	6.1
dry in the sun, to	сушúть на сóлнце	sushit' na sontse	8.7

dryer	су́шка *(f)*	sushka	8.7
duck	у́тка *(f)*	utka	1.9
Duma *(parliament)*	Ду́ма *(f)*	Duma	3.1
Dushanbe (Tajikistan)	Душанбе́ *(m)*	Dushanbe	3.4
dust	пыль *(f)*	pyl'	8.7
dust, to	вытира́ть пыль	vitirat' pyl'	8.7
duty	обя́занность *(f)*	abyazannast'	10.1
dynasty	дина́стия *(f)*	dinastiya	3.5
each year	ка́ждый год *(m)*	kazhdiy got	17.5
ear	у́хо *(n)*	ukha	2.2
early	ра́но	rana	17.1, 17.4
earrings	се́рьги *(pl)*	ser'gi	6.3
earth; land	земля́ *(f)*	zimlya	1.2
earthquake	землетрясе́ние *(n)*	zimlitrisyeniye	1.5
east	восто́к *(m)*	vastok	16.4
Easter	Па́сха *(f)*	Paskha	11.6
eat	есть	yest'	5.1
economics; economy	эконо́мика *(f)*	ekanomika	10.6, 12.5
edge	край *(m)*	kray	16.5
editor	реда́ктор *(m)*	ridaktar	11.3
education	образова́ние *(n)*	obrazavaniye	12.1
education system	систе́ма *(f)* образова́ния	sistyema abrazavaniya	12.1
egg	яйцо́ *(n)*	yaitso	5.4
eggplant	баклажа́н *(m)*	baklazhan	5.6
eight	во́семь	vosim'	18.1
eighteen	восемна́дцать	vosemnatsat'	18.1
eighty	во́семьдесят	vosem'desat	18.1
elect, to	выбира́ть	vybirat'	10.3
election(s)	вы́боры *(pl)*	vybary	10.3
electric fan	электри́ческий вентиля́тор *(m)*	eliktrichiskiy vintilyatr	8.6
electrician	эле́ктрик *(m)*	elyektrik	2.14
electronic music	электро́нная му́зыка *(f)*	eliktronnaya muzyka	11.8
elementary school	нача́льная шко́ла *(f)*	nachal'naya shkola	12.2, 12.4
elementary school student	шко́льник, учени́к *(m)*	shkol'nik, uchinik	12.3
elephant	слон *(m)*	slon	1.9
elevator	лифт *(m)*	lift	8.5
eleven	оди́ннадцать	adinatsat'	18.1
embarrass, to	смуща́ть	smushchat'	2.8
embassy	посо́льство *(n)*	pasol'stva	10.11
emotions	эмо́ции *(pl)*	imotsii	2.8
emperor	импера́тор *(m)*	impiratar	3.5
employee	слу́жащий *(m)*	sluzhashchiy	10.10
end	коне́ц *(m)*	kanyets	17.2

end of school day	конéц *(m)* шкóльного дня	kanyets shkol'nava dnya	12.6
ending	окончáние *(n)*	akanchaniye	3.3
engineer	инженéр *(m)*	inzhinyer	2.14
England	Áнглия *(f)*	Angliya	9.2
English (language)	англи́йский язы́к *(m)*	anglyskiy yezyk	12.5, 13.1
English-Russian dictionary	áнгло-рýсский словáрь *(m)*	anglo-russkiy slavar'	11.2
Englishman, Englishwoman	англичáнин *(m)*, англичáнка *(f)*	anglichanin, anglichanka	9.2
enjoy, to	получáть удовóльствие	poluchat' udavol'stviye	14.2
enough	достáточно	dastatachna	18.6
enter, to	входи́ть	vkhadit'	8.4
entertainment	развлечéние *(n)*	razvlichyeniye	14.3
enthusiasm	энтузиáзм *(m)*	entuziazm	2.9
entirely	весь	vyes'	15.2
entrance	вход *(m)*	vkhot	8.5
entrance examination	вступи́тельный экзáмен *(m)*	vstupitel'niy ekzamin	12.8
envelope	конвéрт *(m)*	kanvyert	13.5
eraser	лáстик *(m)*	lastik	13.5
escalator	эскалáтор *(m)*	eskalatar	8.5
escape	побéг *(m)*	pabyek	10.5
especially	специáльно	spitsial'na	2.11
essay	сочинéние *(n)*, рассκáз *(m)*	sachinyeniye, rasskaz	11.2, 12.6
essential	сущéственный	sushchestvenniy	15.3
estimates	оцéнки *(pl)*	otsenki	18.4
Estonia	Эстóния *(f)*	Estoniya	3.4
Europe	Еврóпа *(f)*	Yevropa	9.2
evacuation	эвакуáция *(f)*	evakuatsiya	3.5
even	дáже	dazhe	19.3
even more	дáже бóльше	dazhi bol'she	15.2
evening	вéчер *(m)*	vyechir	17.10
evening gown	вечéрнее плáтье *(n)*	vichyerniye plat'ye	6.2
evening paper	вечéрняя газéта *(f)*	vichyernyaya gazyeta	11.3
event	собы́тие *(n)*	sabytiye	10.4
every day	кáждый день *(m)*	kazhdiy dyen'	17.8
every month	кáждый мéсяц *(m)*	kazhdiy myesats	17.6
every morning	кáждое ýтро *(n)*	kazhdaye utra	17.10
every time	кáждый раз *(m)*	kazhdiy raz	17.1
every week	кáждая недéля *(f)*	kazhdaya nidyelya	17.8
everyone	кáждый	kazhdiy	2.13
everywhere	вездé	vezdye	16.3

exam	экза́мен (m)	ekzamin	12.1, 12.8
examine, to	иссле́довать	isslyedavat'	11.5,
	экзаменова́ть	ekzaminavat'	12.8
exceedingly	чрезвыча́йно	chrezvychaina	18.7
except	кро́ме (+ gen.)	kromye	19.4
excessively	чрезме́рно	chryezmyerna	18.7
exchange	обме́н (m)	abmyen	7.3
exchange, to	меня́ть	minyat'	7.2
excite, to	возбужда́ть	vazbuzhdat'	2.8
exclamation point	восклица́тельный знак (m)	vasklitsatil'niy znak	11.2
excuse me	извини́те	izvinitye	4.2
exercise, to	упражня́ться	uprazhnyat'sa	14.4
exhaust, to	истоща́ть	istashchat'	2.8
exhibition	вы́ставка (f)	vistavka	11.7
expensive	дорого́й	daragoy	7.3
experience	о́пыт (m)	opyt	10.7
experienced	о́пытный	opytniy	10.7
experiment	экспериме́нт (m)	ekspirimyent	11.5
explain, to	объясня́ть	ab"yesnyat'	13.2
explanation	объясне́ние	ab"yesnyeniye	13.2
export, to	экспорти́ровать	ekspartiravat'	10.10
expression	выраже́ние (n)	vyrazheniye	13.1
extracurricular activities	дополни́тельные заня́тия (pl)	dapalnityel'niye zanyatiya	12.6
extremely	о́чень	ochin'	15.3, 18.7
eye	глаз (m)	glaz	2.2
eyebrow	бровь (f)	brov'	2.2
fabric	материа́л (m); ткань (f)	matirial; tkan'	6.4
face	лицо́ (n)	litso	2.2
facing	лицо́м к (+ dat.)	litsom k	16.4
factory	фа́брика (f), заво́д (m)	fabrika, zavot	10.9
fail an exam, to	не сдать (perf.) экза́мен	ni sdat' ekzamin	12.8
fairly	дово́льно	davol'na	18.6
fall	о́сень (f)	osen'	1.6
fall down, to	упа́сть (perf.)	upast'	16.1
false	ло́жный, фальши́вый	lozhniy, fal'shiviy	15.8
family	семья́ (f)	sem'ya	2.12
famous	изве́стный	izvyestniy	11.1
farm	фе́рма (f)	fyerma	10.8
farmer	фе́рмер (m)	fyermer	2.14
fashionable	мо́дный	modniy	6.1
fast	бы́стро	bystra	17.1, 17.4
fasten, to	прикрепля́ть	prikreplyat'	8.9

fat	то́лстый	tolstiy	2.2, 18.1
father	оте́ц (*m*)	atyets	2.12
fax	телефа́кс (*m*)	tilifaks	13.7
February	февра́ль (*m*)	fivral'	17.7
feel, to	чу́вствовать	chustvavat'	2.6, 2.8
fence	забо́р (*m*)	zabor	8.5
festival	фестива́ль (*m*)	festival'	11.6
fever	жар (*m*)	zhar	2.6
few	немно́го	nimnoga	18.5
field	по́ле (*n*)	polye	10.8
fifteen	пятна́дцать	pitnatsat'	18.1
fifth (*day of the month*)	пя́тый	pyatiy	17.9
fifth year	пя́тый год (*m*)	pyatiy got	12.4
fifty	пятьдеся́т	pyatdyesyat	18.1
film (*movie*)	кино́ (*n*), фильм (*m*)	kino, fil'm	11.9
fine	прекра́сно	prikrasna	13.3
finish class, to	зако́нчить (*perf.*) уро́к	zakonchit' urok	12.6
finish, to	зака́нчивать	zakanchivat'	17.2
fire	пожа́р (*m*)	pazhar	1.5
first	пе́рвый	pyerviy	17.2, 17.9
first month	пе́рвый ме́сяц (*m*)	pyerviy myesats	17.7
first name	и́мя (*n*)	imya	2.12
first of all	пре́жде всего́	pryezhdye vsivo	17.2
first time	пе́рвый раз (*m*)	pyerviy raz	17.3
first year	пе́рвый год (*m*)	pyerviy got	12.4
fish	ры́ба (*f*)	ryba	1.9, 5.4
fish shop	ры́бный магази́н (*m*)	ribniy magazin	7.1
fish soup	ры́бный суп (*m*)	ribniy sup	5.7
fish, to	лови́ть ры́бу	lavit' ribu	14.3
fisherman	рыба́к (*m*)	rybak	2.14
fit, to	хорошо́ сиде́ть;	kharasho sidyet';	6.1
	подходи́ть	padkhadit'	15.1
fitting room	приме́рочная (*f*)	primyerachnaya	7.2
five	пять	pyat'	18.1
fix, to	чини́ть	chinit'	8.9
flatter, to	льстить	l'stit'	2.9
flesh	плоть (*f*)	plot'	2.2
flood	наводне́ние (*n*)	navadnyeniye	1.5
floor	эта́ж (*m*)	etazh	8.1
flow, to	течь	tyech'	1.3
flower	цвето́к (*m*)	tsvitok	1.7
fly	лета́ть	litat'	1.8
fog	тума́н (*m*)	tuman	1.4
folk music	наро́дная му́зыка (*f*)	narodnaya muzyka	11.8

food	еда́ (f)	yeda	5.1
foot (body part)	нога́ (f)	naga	2.2
foot (measurement)	фут (m)	fut	18.2
football	америка́нский футбо́л (m)	amirikanskiy futbol	14.5
footpath	доро́жка (f)	darozhka	9.3
for	за (+ acc./inst.)	za	19.4
for a long time	давно́	davno	17.1
for example	наприме́р	naprimyer	19.3
for sure	безусло́вно	bizuslovna	15.8
for the first time	в пе́рвый раз	v pyerviy raz	17.2
for the most part	в большинстве́ слу́чаев	v bal'shinstvye sluchayev	15.3
forceful	си́льный; убеди́тельный	sil'niy; ubiditel'niy	2.11
foreign language	иностра́нный язы́к (m)	inastranniy yezyk	12.5, 13.1
foreign trade	междунаро́дная торго́вля (f)	mezhdunarodnaya targovlya	10.10
foreigner	иностра́нец (m), иностра́нка (f)	inastranyets, inastranka	9.1
forest	лес (m)	lyes	1.7
forget, to	забыва́ть	zabyvat'	12.7
forgive, to	проща́ть	prashchat'	2.9
fork	ви́лка (f)	vilka	5.11
format	форма́т (m)	farmat	15.1
forty	со́рок	sorak	18.1
four	четы́ре	chityre	18.1
four seasons	четы́ре вре́мени го́да	chityri vryemini goda	1.6
fourteen	четы́рнадцать	chityrnatsat'	18.1
fourth	четвёртый	chitvyortiy	17.9
fourth year	четвёртый год (m)	chitvyortiy got	12.4
fracture (of the bone)	перело́м (m)	pirilom	2.7
France	Фра́нция (f)	Frantsiya	9.2
freedom	свобо́да (f)	svaboda	10.2, 10.3
freeway	шоссе́ (n)	shasse	9.3
frequency	частота́ (f)	chastota	17.3
Friday	пя́тница (f)	pyatnitsa	17.9
fried eggs	яи́чница (f)	yaichnitsa	5.4
friend	друг (m)	druk	14.1
friendly	дружелю́бный	druzhilyubniy	2.11
friendship	дру́жба (f)	druzhba	14.1
from	от (+ gen.)	ot	19.4
front	фаса́д (m); пере́дняя сторона́ (f)	fasat; peryednyaya starana	16.3, 16.5
front entrance	пара́дный вход (m)	paradniy vkhot	8.5

front, in front	пе́ред (+ *inst.*), спе́реди (+ *gen.*)	pyeret, spyeredi	19.4
frozen	заморо́женный	zamarozhenniy	5.4
fruit drink	фрукто́вый напи́ток (*m*)	fruktoviy napitak	5.9
fruit(s)	фру́кты (*pl*)	frukty	5.5, 10.8
fry, to	жа́рить	zharit'	5.10
full	по́лный	polniy	18.7
full name	по́лное и́мя (*n*)	polnaye imya	2.12
funny	смешно́й	smishnoy	2.8
furniture	ме́бель (*f*)	myebil'	8.3
furniture store	ме́бельный магази́н (*m*)	myebil'niy magazin	7.1
gain weight, to	поправля́ться	papravlyat'sa	2.2
gallon	галло́н (*m*)	galon	18.4
garage	гара́ж (*m*)	garazh	8.1
garden	сад (*m*)	sat	1.7, 8.4
gardener	садо́вник (*m*)	sadovnik	2.14
garden, to	рабо́тать в саду́	rabotat' f sadu	14.3
gargle, to	полоска́ть го́рло	palaskat' gorla	2.5
garlic	чесно́к (*m*)	chisnok	5.4
gas	газ (*m*)	gaz	8.6
gas station	запра́вочная ста́нция (*f*)	zapravachnaya stantsiya	9.5
gender:	род (*m*):	rot:	3.3
masculine, feminine, neuter	мужско́й, же́нский, сре́дний	muzhskoi, zhenskiy, sredniy	
general	о́бщее	opshchiye	3.1, 5.1
generally	вообще́	vaapshche	18.4
generation	поколе́ние (*n*)	pakalyeniye	2.12
gentle	мя́гкий; кро́ткий	myakhkiy; krotkiy	2.11
geography	геогра́фия (*f*)	giagrafiya	3.4, 12.5
geometry	геоме́трия (*f*)	giamyetriya	12.5
Georgia	Гру́зия (*f*)	Gruziya	3.4
Germany	Герма́ния (*f*)	Germaniya	9.2
get off, to	выходи́ть	vykhadit'	9.6
get on, to	входи́ть	vkhadit'	9.6
get up, to	встава́ть; встать (*perf.*)	vstavat'; vstat'	2.4, 16.1
get used to, to	привы́кнуть (*perf.*)	privyknut'	2.11
gift; present	пода́рок (*m*)	padarak	4.3
girl	де́вочка (*f*); де́вушка (*f*)	dyevachka; dyevushka	2.1
girlfriend	подру́га (*f*)	padruga	14.1
girls	де́вочки (*pl*)	dyevachki	2.15
give a present, to	дари́ть пода́рок	darit' padarak	15.4
give a talk/lecture, to	чита́ть ле́кцию	chitat' lyektsiyu	11.4
give back, to	возвраща́ть	vazvrashchat'	15.4
give my regards to …	переда́йте приве́т …	piridaite privyet …	4.5

give, to	дава́ть	davat'	15.4
glass (tumbler)	стака́н (m)	stakan	5.11
glass (material)	стекло́ (n)	stiklo	8.8
glasses	очки́ (pl)	achki	6.3
gloves	перча́тки (pl)	pirchatki	6.3
glue	клей (m)	klyey	8.9
go on a picnic, to	ходи́ть на пикни́к	khadit' na piknik	14.3
go on a trip, to	уе́хать (perf.) в путеше́ствие	yekhat' f putishyestviye	14.3
go to a restaurant, to	пойти́ (perf.) в рестора́н	paiti v ristaran	5.3
go to bed, to	ложи́ться спать	lazhit'sa spat'	2.4
go to sleep, to	засыпа́ть	zasypat'	2.4
go to the bathroom, to	идти́ в туале́т	iti f tualyet	2.5
go to the doctor, to	идти́ к врачу́	iti k vrachu	2.6
go to the movies, to	ходи́ть в кино́	khadit' f kino	14.3
go to the opera, to	ходи́ть на о́перу	khadit' na operu	14.3
go to the theater, to	ходи́ть в теа́тр	khadit' f tiatr	14.3
go, to	идти́	idti	16.1
God	Бог (m)	Bok	11.6
goulash	гуля́ш (m)	gulyash	5.7
golden	золото́й	zalatoy	6.5
Golden Ring	Золото́е кольцо́ (n)	Zalatoye kal'tso	3.2
golf	гольф (m)	gol'f	14.5
golubtsi (stuffed cabbage)	голубцы́ (pl)	golubtsy	5.7
good	хоро́ший; хорошо́	kharoshiy; kharasho	2.9, 13.3
good afternoon	до́брый день (m)	dobriy dyen'	4.1
good evening	до́брый ве́чер (m)	dobriy vyecher	4.1
good luck	уда́ча (f)	udacha	2.9
good morning	до́брое у́тро (n)	dobraye utra	4.1
good night	споко́йной но́чи	spakoynoy nochi	4.1
good spirits/mood	хоро́шее настрое́ние (n)	kharoshiye nastrayeniye	2.6
good-looking	прия́тный	priyatniy	15.7
good-bye	до свида́ния	da svidaniya	4.5
government	прави́тельство (n)	pravitel'stva	3.5, 10.3
gradually	постепе́нно	pastipyenna	17.4
graduate, to	ока́нчивать шко́лу	akanchivat' shkolu	12.1
graduation	оконча́ние (n) шко́лы	akanchaniye shkoly	12.1
gram	грамм (m)	gramm	18.3
grammar	грамма́тика (f)	grammatika	13.1
granddaughter	вну́чка (f)	vnuchka	2.12
grandfather	де́душка (m); дед (m)	dyedushka; dyed	2.12, 2.15
grandmother	ба́бушка (f)	babushka	2.15
grandpa	дед (m)	dyed	2.12
grandson	внук (m)	vnuk	2.12

grapes	виногра́д (m)	vinagrat	5.5
grass	трава́ (f)	trava	1.7
gray	се́рый	seriy	6.5
Great Patriotic War	Вели́кая Оте́чественная война́ (f)	Velikaya Atechistvinnaya voina	3.5
Greece	Гре́ция (f)	Gryetsiya	9.2
green	зелёный	zilyoniy	6.5
green peas	зелёный горо́шек (m)	zilyoniy garoshik	5.6
greet, to	приве́тствовать	privyetstvavat'	14.2
greetings	приве́тствия (pl)	privyetstviya	4.1
grocery store	гастроно́м (m)	gastranom	7.1
group of	гру́ппа (f) из (+ gen.)	gruppa iz	18.8
grow, to	расти́; выра́щивать	rasti; vyrashchivat'	2.2, 10.8
guest	гость (m)	gost'	14.2
guest room	ко́мната (f) для госте́й	komnata dlya gostey	8.2
guide	гид (m)	git	2.14
guilty	вино́вный	vinovniy	10.4
guitar	гита́ра (f)	gitara	11.8
guys; kids	ребя́та (pl)	ribyata	2.15
gymnastics	гимна́стика (f)	gimnastika	12.5
had	име́л, име́ла, име́ло	imyel, imyela, imyela	19.1
hail	град (m)	grat	1.4
hair	во́лосы (pl)	volosy	2.2
hairdresser	парикма́хер (m)	parikmakher	2.14
half	полови́на (f)	palavina	17.1, 18.1
half a day	полови́на (f) дня	palavina dnya	17.1
half a month	полови́на (f) ме́сяца	palavina myesatsa	17.6
half a week	полови́на (f) неде́ли	palavina nidyeli	17.1
half year	полови́на (f) го́да	palavina goda	17.5
half-an-hour	полчаса́	polchasa	17.11
ham	ветчина́ (f)	vichina	5.4
hammer	молото́к (m)	malatok	8.8
hand	рука́ (f)	ruka	2.2
hand over, to	вруча́ть	vruchat'	15.4
handkerchief	носово́й плато́к (m)	nasavoy platok	6.3
hang out the laundry, to	ве́шать бельё	vyeshat' bil'yo	8.7
hang, to	ве́шать	vyesht'	8.4
happen, to	случа́ться	sluchat'sa	1.5
happy	счастли́вый	schastliviy	2.8
hard-boiled egg	яйцо́ вкруту́ю	yaitso vkrutuyu	5.4
hard; difficult	тру́дный	trudniy	15.6
hard; firm	твёрдый	tvyordiy	8.8
hard sign	твёрдый знак (m)	tvyordiy znak	3.3

hardly any	почти́ никто́; почти́ ничего́	pochti nikto; pochti nichivo	18.5
hardware store	хозя́йственный магази́н *(m)*	khazyaistvenniy magazin	7.1
hardworking	трудолюби́вый	trudalyubiviy	2.11, 10.7
have	име́ли	imyeli	19.1
have, to	име́ть	imyet'	19.1
haven't seen you for ages	я вас сто лет не ви́дел	ya vas sto lyet ni vidil	4.1
he, him, (to) him	он, его́, ему́	on, yevo, yemu	2.13
headache	головна́я боль *(f)*	galavnaya bol'	2.6
headmaster	дире́ктор *(m)* ча́стной шко́лы	diryektar chastnoy shkoly	12.3
health	здоро́вье *(n)*	zdarov'ye	2.6
healthy	здоро́вый	zdaroviy	2.6
hear, to	слы́шать	slyshat'	2.10, 13.2
heart	се́рдце *(n)*	sertse	2.2
heater	отопи́тельный прибо́р *(m)*	atapityel'niy pribor	8.6
heating	отопле́ние	ataplyeniye	8.6
heaven	рай *(m)*	ray	11.6
heavy	тяжёлый	tizholiy	18.3
hectare	гекта́р *(m)*	giktar	18.2
height	высота́ *(f)*	vysata	18.2
hell	ад *(m)*	at	11.6
hello	здра́вствуйте; алё, алло́	zdrastvuite; alyo, allo	4.1, 13.7
help yourself	угоща́йтесь	ugashchaytes'	5.1
help, to	помога́ть	pamagat'	14.1
helper	помо́щник *(m)*	pamoshnik	14.1
here	здесь	zdyes'	16.3
Hermitage Museum	Эрмита́ж *(m)*	Ermitazh	3.2
hide	шку́ра *(f)*	shkura	1.8
high	высоко́	vysoko	18.2
high jump	прыжки́ *(pl)* в высоту́	prizhki v vysatu	14.5
high school first year	пе́рвый год *(m)* в шко́ле	perviy got v shkole	12.4
high school student	шко́льник, учени́к *(m)*	shkol'nik, uchinik	12.3
hiking, to go	ходи́ть пешко́м	khadit' peshkom	14.3
hill	холм *(m)*	kholm	1.2
historical period	истори́ческий пери́од *(m)*	istarichiskiy piriot	3.5
history	исто́рия *(f)*	istoriya	12.5
hobby	хо́бби *(n)*	khobbi	14.3
hockey	хокке́й *(m)*	khakkey	14.5
hold a meeting, to	проводи́ть собра́ние	pravadit' sabraniye	10.1

hold, to	держа́ть	derzhat'	15.4
holidays	пра́здники *(pl)*	prazniki	12.1
home owner	владе́лец *(m)* до́ма	vladyelets doma	8.4
homework	дома́шняя рабо́та *(f)*	damashnyaya rabota	12.6
honest	че́стный	chyestniy	2.11
Hong Kong	Гонко́нг *(m)*	Gankonk	9.2
hope, to	наде́яться	nadyeyatsa	2.8
horror movie	фильм *(m)* у́жасов	fil'm uzhasov	11.9
horse race	ска́чки *(pl)*	skachki	14.5
horseback riding	верхова́я езда́ *(f)*	virkhavaya yezda	14.5
hospital	больни́ца *(f)*	bol'nitsa	2.7, 9.8
host, to	принима́ть	prinimat'	14.2
host, to be a	быть хозя́йкой	byt' khazyaykay	5.1
hot	жа́рко; горячо́	zharka; garacho	1.4, 8.6
hot *(boiling)*	горя́чий	garyachiy	5.8
hot *(spicy)*	о́стрый	ostriy	5.8
hot tea	горя́чий чай *(m)*	garyachiy chay	5.9
hot water	горя́чая вода́ *(f)*	garyachaya vada	2.5
hotel	гости́ница *(f)*	gastinitsa	9.7, 9.8
hour	час *(m)*	chas	17.11
house	дом *(m)*	dom	8.1
housewife	домохозя́йка *(f)*	damakhazyaika	2.14
how	как	kak	19.2
how about you?	а как вы?	a kak vy?	4.1
how are things?	как дела́?	kak dela?	4.1
how are you?	как вы пожива́ете?	kak vy pazhivaite?	4.4
how far?	как далеко́?	kak daliko?	19.2
how long?	как до́лго?	kak dolga?	17.1, 18.4
how many subjects?	ско́лько предме́тов?	skol'ka pridmyetof?	12.5
how many?	ско́лько?	skol'ka?	18.4
how much is it?	ско́лько сто́ит?	skol'ka stoit?	7.3, 18.4, 19.2
how old?	ско́лько лет?	skol'ka lyet?	19.2
how terrible	как ужа́сно	kak uzhasna	2.9
hundred	сто	sto	18.1
hungry	голо́дный	galodniy	5.1
hurricane	урага́н *(m)*	uragan	1.5
hurry	быстре́е; поспеши́	bystryeye; paspishi	17.1
hurry up, to	торопи́ться	tarapit'sa	17.4
husband	муж *(m)*	muzh	2.12
hygiene	гигие́на *(f)*	gigiyena	2.5
I don't deserve it	я э́того не заслу́живаю	ya etova ni zasluzhivayu	4.2
I'm glad to see you	рад вас ви́деть	rat vas vidit'	4.2
I, me, (to) me	я, меня́, мне	ya, minya, mnye	2.13
ice	лёд *(m)*	lyot	5.9

English	Russian	Transliteration	Section
ice cream	мороженое (n)	marozhinaye	5.4
ice-skating	катание (n) на коньках	kataniye na kon'kakh	14.5
iced tea	чай со льдом	chay sa l'dom	5.9
ideal	идеальный	idial'niy	10.2
if	если	yesli	19.3
import, to	импортировать	impartiravat'	10.10
important	важный	vazhniy	2.9, 2.11, 15.3
in	в (+ prep.)	v	19.4
in a moment	через минуту	chyeriz minutu	17.1
in a short time	в короткое время	v karotkaye vryemya	17.1
in fact	фактически	faktichiski	19.3
in other words	другими словами	drugimi slavami	19.3
in the beginning	в начале	v nachlye	17.2
in the future	в будущем	v budushchim	17.1
in the past	в прошлом	v proshlom	17.1
inch	дюйм (m)	dyuim	18.2
incident	случай (m)	sluchay	10.4
increase, to	увеличивать	uvilichivat'	18.1
Indian Ocean	Индийский океан (m)	Indiyskiy akian	9.4
Indonesia	Индонезия (f)	Indanyeziya	9.2
industry	промышленность (f)	promyshlinnost'	10.9
influence	влияние (n)	vliyaniye	15.1
influenza	грипп (m)	gripp	2.6
inform, to	информировать	informirovat'	13.2, 13.6
injure, to	ранить; повредить (perf.)	ranit'; pavridit'	2.6
injured	раненый	raniniy	1.5
ink	чернила (pl)	chirnila	13.5
innocent	невиновный	nivinovniy	10.4
inside	внутри (+ gen.)	vnutri	16.3, 16.5
institute	институт (m)	institut	12.2
intellectual	интеллектуал (m)	intiliktual	2.14
intelligent	умный	umniy	2.11
intensity	интенсивность	intensivnast'	15.3
intention	намерение (n)	namyereniye	2.8
interest, to; to be interested in	интересоваться	intirisavat'sa	14.3
interesting	интересный	intiryesniy	2.9
internal	внутренний	vnutriniy	2.7
international	международный	mezhdunarodniy	10.11
international call	международный разговор (m)	mizhdunarodniy razgavor	13.7
International Woman's Day	Международный женский день (m)	Mezhdunarodniy zhenskiy dyen'	3.1
intersection	перекрёсток (m)	pirikryostak	9.3

introduce, to	предста́вить *(perf.)*;	pridstavit';	4.4, 14.2
	представля́ть	pridstavlyat'	10.3
invent, to	изобрета́ть	izabritat'	11.5
invention	изобрете́ние *(n)*	izabrityeniye	11.5
investigate	рассле́довать	raslyedavat'	11.3
invitation	приглаше́ние *(n)*	priglashyeniye	14.1
invite to dinner, to	пригласи́ть *(perf.)* на обе́д	priglasit' na abyet	5.1
invite, to	приглаша́ть	priglashat'	14.1
Ireland	Ирла́ндия *(f)*	Irlandiya	9.2
iron *(for clothes)*	утю́г *(m)*	utyuk	8.7
iron *(element)*	желе́зо *(n)*	zhilyeza	8.8
iron *(clothes)*, to	гла́дить	gladit'	8.7
is it all right?	э́то хорошо́?	eta kharasho?	4.2
island	о́стров *(m)*	ostraf	1.2
it smells good	хорошо́ па́хнуть	kharasho pakhnut'	5.8
Italy	Ита́лия *(f)*	Italiya	9.2
jail	тюрьма́ *(f)*	tyur'ma	10.5
jam	пови́дло *(n)*	pavidla	5.4
January	янва́рь *(m)*	yanvar'	17.7
Japan	Япо́ния *(f)*	Yaponiya	9.2
jealous	ревни́вый	rivniviy	2.8
jeans	джи́нсы *(pl)*	dzhinsy	6.2
jewelry	ювели́рные изде́лия *(pl)*	yuvilirnye izdyeliya	6.3
jewelry shop	ювели́рный магази́н *(m)*	yuvelirniy magazin	7.1
job	рабо́та *(f)*	rabota	10.7
journal; assignment book	дневни́к *(m)*	dnevnik	12.6
Judaism	иудаи́зм *(m)*	iudaizm	11.6
judge	судья́ *(m)*	sud'ya	2.14, 10.4
July	ию́ль *(m)*	iyul'	17.7
June	ию́нь *(m)*	iyun'	17.7
just	то́лько что	tol'ka chto	17.1
Kazakhstan	Казахста́н *(m)*	Kazakhstan	3.4
kettle	ча́йник *(m)*	chaynik	5.11
keys	ключи́ *(pl)*	klyuchi	8.5
kids	ребя́та *(pl)*	ribyata	2.15
Kiev (Ukraine)	Ки́ев *(m)*	Kiyef	3.4
Kievan Rus	Ки́евская Русь *(f)*	Kiyevskaya Rus'	3.5
kill, to	убива́ть	ubivat'	10.5
kilogram	килогра́мм *(m)*	kilagramm	18.3
kilometer	киломе́тр *(m)*	kilamyetr	18.2
kind	до́брый	dobriy	2.11
kind; type	вид *(m)*, тип *(m)*	vit; tip	15.1, 18.8
kindergarten	де́тский сад *(m)*	dyetskiy sat	12.2

king	коро́ль *(m)*	karol'	10.3
Kishinev (Moldova)	Кишинёв *(m)*	Kishinyov	3.4
kitchen	ку́хня *(f)*	kukhnya	8.2
knife	нож *(m)*	nozh	5.11
knock, to	стуча́ть	stuchat'	8.4
know, to	знать	znat'	2.10, 12.7
knowledge	зна́ние *(n)*	znaniye	12.7
Korea	Коре́я *(f)*	Koryeya	9.2
Kremlin	Кремль *(m)*	Kreml'	3.2
kulibyaka *(cabbage bread)*	кулебя́ка *(f)*	kulibyaka	5.7
Kyrgyzstan	Кыргызста́н *(m)*	Kyrgystan	3.4
Labor Day	День *(m)* Труда́	Den' Truda	3.1
laboratory	лаборато́рия *(f)*	labaratoriya	11.5
lace	кру́жево *(n)*	kruzhivo	6.4
lake	о́зеро *(n)*	ozira	1.3
Lake Baikal	о́зеро *(n)* Байка́л	ozero Baikal	3.4
lamb	бара́нина *(f)*	baranina	5.4
land	земля́ *(f)*	zyemlya	10.8
lane *(highway)*	полоса́ *(f)*, ли́ния *(f)*	palasa, liniya	9.3
language	язы́к *(m)*	yezyk	13.1
large	большо́й	bal'shoy	18.1
last month	после́дний ме́сяц *(m)*	paslyedniy myesats	17.6
last name	фами́лия *(f)*	familiye	2.12
last one	после́дний	paslyedniy	17.2
last time	после́дний раз *(m)*	paslyedniy raz	17.3
last week	после́дняя неде́ля *(f)*	paslyednyaya nidyelya	17.8
last year	про́шлый год *(m)*	proshliy got	17.5
late	по́здно	pozdna	17.1, 17.4
later on	пото́м	patom	17.1, 19.3
Latin America	Лати́нская Аме́рика *(f)*	Latinskaya Amyerika	9.2
Latvia	Ла́твия *(f)*	Latviya	3.4
laugh, to	смея́ться	smiyatsa	2.8
launder, to	стира́ть	stirat'	8.7
laundry	пра́чечная *(f)*	prachichnaya	8.2
laundry detergent	стира́льный порошо́к *(m)*	stiral'niy parashok	8.7
law	зако́н *(m)*	zakon	10.4
lawn	газо́н *(m)*	gazon	1.7, 8.4
lawnmower	коси́лка *(f)* для травы́	kasilka dlya travy	8.8
lawyer	юри́ст *(m)*	yurist	2.14, 10.4
lazy	лени́вый	liniviy	2.11, 10.7
leaf	лист *(m)*	list	1.7
learn, to	учи́ть	uchit'	12.1, 12.7
learning process	уче́бный проце́сс *(m)*	uchebniy pratses	12.1

English	Russian	Transliteration	Reference
leather	ко́жа (f)	kozha	6.4
leave, to	оставля́ть; уходи́ть; уезжа́ть	astavlyat'; ukhadit'; uyezhat'	8.4, 9.7, 16.1
lecturer	ле́ктор (m)	lyektar	2.14, 12.3
left	сле́ва	slyeva	16.3, 16.5
leg	нога́ (f)	naga	2.2
lemon	лимо́н (m)	limon	5.5
lemonade	лимона́д (m)	limanat	5.9
lend, to	дава́ть взаймы́	davat' vzaimy	10.10
length	длина́ (f)	dlina	18.1, 18.2
lengthen, to	удлиня́ть	udlinyat'	18.1
Lenin's tomb	Мавзоле́й (m) Ле́нина	Mavzalyei Lenina	3.2
less than	ме́ньше чем	myen'she chyem	18.4
lesson	уро́к (m)	urok	12.6
let me help you	разреши́те вам помо́чь	razrishiti vam pamoch	4.2
let me pay	я заплачу́	ya zaplachu	7.2
letter (of the alphabet)	бу́ква (f)	bukva	3.3, 13.1
letter (missive)	письмо́ (n)	pis'mo	13.6
letter paper	бума́га (f) для письма́	bumaga dlya pis'ma	13.5
lettuce	сала́т (m)	salat	5.6
liberalism	либерали́зм (m)	libiralizm	10.3
liberation	освобожде́ние (n)	asvabazhdyeniye	3.5
librarian	библиоте́карь (m), библиоте́карша (f)	bibliatyekar', bibliatyekarsha	2.14
library	библиоте́ка (f)	bibliatyeka	9.8, 11.2
library book	библиоте́чная кни́га (f)	bibliatyechnaya kniga	11.2
lie down, to	ложи́ться	lazhitsa	2.4
life	жизнь	zhizn'	2.3
light	свет (m); све́тлый; лёгкий	svyet; svetliy; lyokhkiy	1.1, 6.5, 8.5, 18.3
light a fire, to	заже́чь (perf.) ого́нь	zazhyech agon'	8.6
lighter	зажига́лка (f)	zazhigalka	5.12
lightning	мо́лния (f)	molniya	1.4
like, to; I like	нра́виться; мне нра́вится	nravit'sa; mnye nravitsa	2.9, 14.3
line	строка́ (f)	straka	11.2
linen	лён (m)	lyon	6.4
listen, to	слу́шать	slushat'	2.10, 13.2
listen to the radio, to	слу́шать ра́дио	slushat' radio	14.3
listen to records, to	слу́шать пласти́нки	slushat' plastinki	14.3
liter	литр (m)	litr	18.3
literature	литерату́ра (f)	litiratura	11.2, 12.5
Lithuania	Литва́ (f)	Litva	3.4
little	ма́ло	mala	18.5

little by little	понемно́гу	panimnogu	18.6
little (of)	немно́го	nimnoga	18.8
live, to	жить	zhit'	8.4
lively	живо́й	zhivoy	2.11
living room	гости́ная (f)	gastinaya	8.2
local residents	ме́стные жи́тели (pl)	myestniye zhitili	9.1
location	местонахожде́ние (n)	mestonakhozhdyeniye	16.3
lock	замо́к (m)	zamok	8.5
lock the door, to	запира́ть дверь	zapirat' dvyer'	8.4
lonely	одино́кий	adinokiy	2.8
long	дли́нный	dlinniy	6.1
long distance call	междугоро́дный разгово́р (m)	mizhdugarodniy razgavor	13.7
long distance running	бег (m) на дли́нные диста́нции	beg na dlinniye distantsii	14.5
long for, to	тоскова́ть	taskavat'	2.8
long jump	прыжки́ (pl) в длину́	pryzhki v dlinu	14.5
long time ago, (a)	давно́	davno	17.1
look for work, to	иска́ть рабо́ту	iskat' rabotu	10.7
look for, to	иска́ть	iskat'	16.1
loose	свобо́дный	svabodniy	6.1
lose weight, to	худе́ть	khudyet'	2.2
lose, to	теря́ть; проигра́ть	tiryat'; praigrat'	2.8, 14.4
loss	поте́ря (f)	patyerya	10.6
loud voice	гро́мкий го́лос (m)	gromkiy golas	13.2
lovable	ми́лый	miliy	2.9, 2.11, 15.7
love	любо́вь (f)	lyubov'	2.9
love, to	люби́ть	lyubit'	2.9
low	ни́зко	nizka	18.2
lower part	ни́жняя часть (f)	nizhnyaya chast'	16.5
luck; success	уда́ча (f)	udacha	2.9
luggage	бага́ж (m)	bagazh	9.7
lunar calendar	лу́нный календа́рь (m)	lunniy kalendar'	17.5
lung cancer	рак (m) лёгких	rak lyokhkikh	5.12
lungs	лёгкие (pl)	lyokiye	2.2
machine	маши́на (f)	mashina	10.9
madam	мада́м (f)	madam	2.15
made of …	сде́ланный из … (+ gen.)	sdelanniy iz …	6.1
magazine	журна́л (m)	zhurnal	11.3
mail	по́чта (f)	pochta	13.6
mail, to	отправля́ть по по́чте	atpravlyat' pa pochte	13.6
mailbox	почто́вый я́щик (m)	pachtoviy yashchik	13.6
mailman	почтальо́н (m)	pachtal'yon	2.14, 13.6
mainland	матери́к (m)	matirik	1.2

majority	большинство́ (n)	bal'shinstvo	18.1
make, to	де́лать	dyelat'	15.1
make a copy, to	сде́лать (perf.) ко́пию	sdyelat' kopiyu	12.6
make a list, to	записа́ть (perf.)	zapisat'	7.2
make a mistake, to	де́лать оши́бку	dyelat' ashipku	13.2
make a presentation, to	де́лать докла́д	dyelat' daklat	11.4
make a speech, to	произноси́ть речь	praiznasit' ryech'	13.2
make a toast, to	предложи́ть (perf.) тост	pridlazhit' tost	4.2
make coffee, to	вари́ть ко́фе	varit' kofe	5.9
make friends, to	подружи́ться	padruzhit'sa	14.1
make tea, to	пригото́вить (perf.) чай	prigatovit' chay	5.9
make the bed, to	убира́ть крова́ть	ubirat' kravat'	8.4
Maly Theater	Ма́лый теа́тр (m)	Maliy tiatr	3.2
man	мужчи́на (m)	muzhchina	2.1
manager	нача́льник (m)	nachal'nik	10.10
mandarin (orange)	мандари́н (m)	mandarin	5.5
mango	ма́нго (n)	manga	5.5
many; much	мно́го	mnoga	18.7
map	ка́рта (f)	karta	9.1
March	март (m)	mart	17.7
market	ры́нок (m)	rinak	7.1
marry, to	жени́ться	zhinit'sa	2.3
master, to	усоверше́нствоваться	usavirshyenstvavat'sya	12.7
matches	спи́чки (pl)	spichki	5.12
materials	материа́лы (pl)	materialy	8.8
mathematics	матема́тика (f)	matimatika	12.5
May	май (m)	may	17.7
may I introduce …	разреши́те предста́вить …	mozhna pridstavit' …	14.2
may I trouble you?	мо́жно вас побеспоко́ить?	mozhna vas pabispakoit'?	4.2
meal	еда́ (f)	yeda	5.1, 18.8
mealtimes	вре́мя приёма пи́щи	vryemya priyoma pishchi	5.2
meaning	значе́ние (n)	znachyeniye	13.1
measures	измере́ния (pl)	izmeryeniya	18.8
meat	мя́со (n)	myasa	5.4
meat salad	мясно́й сала́т (m)	misnoy salat	5.7
mechanic	меха́ник (m)	mikhanik	2.14
medicine	медици́на (f)	miditsina	2.7
Mediterranean Sea	Средизе́мное мо́ре (n)	Sridizyemnaya morye	9.4
medium	сре́дний	sryednii	18.6
meet, to	встре́тить (perf.)	vstryetit'	14.2
meeting	собра́ние (n)	sabraniye	10.1
melon	ды́ня (f)	dynya	5.5

English	Russian	Transliteration	Ref
memorize, to	запомина́ть	zapaminat'	12.7
menu	меню́ (n)	minyu	5.3
meter	метр (m)	myetr	18.2
method	ме́тод (m)	myetot	11.5
methodical	методи́чный	mitadichniy	2.11
metro	метро́ (n)	metro	3.1
Mexico	Ме́ксика (f)	Myeksika	9.2
microwave oven	ми́кроволно́вая печь (f)	mikravalnovaya pech	5.11
middle-aged person	челове́к (m) сре́днего во́зраста	chilavyek sryedneva vozrasta	2.1
midnight	по́лночь (f)	polnach'	17.10
miles	ми́ли (pl)	mili	18.2
military	вое́нный	vayenniy	10.11
milk	молоко́ (n)	malako	5.9, 10.8
milk, to	дои́ть	dait'	10.8
millimeter	миллиме́тр (m)	millimyetr	18.2
mine	ша́хта (f)	shakhta	10.9
miner	шахтёр (m)	shakhtyor	2.14
mineral water	минера́льная вода́ (f)	miniral'naya vada	5.9
mining industry	у́гольная промы́шленность (f)	ugal'naya pramyshlinnost'	10.9
minister	свяще́нник (m)	svishchyennik	10.3
minority	меньшинство́ (n)	men'shinstvo	18.1
Minsk (Belarus)	Минск (m)	Minsk	3.4
minutes	мину́ты (pl)	minuty	17.11
mirror	зе́ркало (n)	zyerkala	8.5
mischievous	озорно́й	azarnoy	2.11
Miss	де́вушка (f)	dyevushka	2.15
mist	мгла (f)	mgla	1.4
mistake	оши́бка (f)	ashipka	12.7
modern literature	совреме́нная литерату́ра (f)	savremyennaya lityeratura	11.2
modest	скро́мный	skromniy	2.11
Moldova	Молдо́ва (f)	Maldova	3.4
mom	ма́ма (f)	mama	2.12
Monday	понеде́льник (m)	panidyelnik	17.9
money	де́ньги (pl)	dyen'gi	7.3
money exchange	обме́н де́нег	abmyen dyenig	7.3
monk	мона́х (m)	manakh	11.6
month	ме́сяц (m)	myesats	17.6, 17.7
moon	луна́ (f)	luna	1.1
more and more	бо́льше и бо́льше	bol'she i bol'she	19.3
more than	бо́льше чем	bol'she chyem	18.4, 18.7
(the) more, the better	чем бо́льше тем лу́чше	chem bol'she tyem luchshe	19.3

morning	у́тро *(n)*	utra	17.10
morning paper	у́тренняя газе́та *(f)*	utrinnyaya gazyeta	11.3
Moscow (Russia)	Москва́ *(f)*	Maskva	3.1, 3.4
Moscow University	Моско́вский университе́т *(m)*	Maskofskiy univirsityet	3.2
Moskva River	Москва́-река́ *(f)*	Maskva-rika	3.4
most	наибо́льший	naibol'shiy	18.1
most of all	бо́льше всего́	bol'she vsyevo	15.2
mother	мать *(f)*	mat'	2.12
motorcycle	мотоци́кл *(m)*	matatsikl	9.5
mountain	гора́ *(f)*	gora	1.2
mountain climbing	альпини́зм *(m)*	al'pinizm	14.3
mouth	рот *(m)*	rot	2.2
move, to	дви́гаться; переезжа́ть	dvigat'sa; pereyezhat'	16.1
movement	движе́ние *(n)*	dvizhyeniye	16.1
movie	кино́ *(n)*, фильм *(m)*	kino, fil'm	11.9
movie star	кинозвезда́ *(f)*	kinozvezda	11.9
movie theater	кинотеа́тр *(m)*	kinatiatr	9.8, 11.9
Mr.	господи́н *(m)*	gaspadin	2.15
Mrs.	госпожа́ *(f)*	gaspazha	2.15
much	мно́го	mnoga	18.7
muscle	му́скул *(m)*	muskl	2.2
museum	музе́й *(m)*	muzyey	9.8
mushrooms	грибы́ *(pl)*	griby	5.6, 5.7
music	му́зыка *(f)*	muzyka	11.8
music fan	люби́тель *(m)* му́зыки	lyubitel' muzyki	11.8
music lesson	уро́к *(m)* му́зыки	urok muzyki	11.8
musical instrument	музыка́льный инструме́нт *(m)*	muzykal'niy instrumyent	11.8
musician	музыка́нт *(m)*	muzykant	2.14, 11.8
my name is …	меня́ зову́т …	minya zavut …	4.4
nail *(finger/toe)*	но́готь *(m)*	nogat'	2.2
nail *(metal)*	гвоздь *(m)*	gvozd'	8.8
napkin	салфе́тка *(f)*	salfyetka	5.11
narrow	у́зкий	uzkiy	18.1
natural	приро́дный	prirodniy	1.5
natural disasters	стихи́йные бе́дствия *(pl)*	stikhiyniye byetstviya	1.5
navy	вое́нно-морски́е си́лы *(pl)*	vayenna-marskiye sily	10.11
near	бли́зко	blizka	18.2
necessary	необходи́мый	niabkhadimiy	15.3
necklace	цепо́чка *(f)*	tsipochka	6.3
need, to	нужда́ться	nuzhdat'sa	15.3
needle	игла́ *(f)*	igla	6.1
neighborhood	сосе́дство *(n)*	sasyetstva	16.3

neighbors	сосе́ди (pl)	sasyedi	8.4
nerves	не́рвы (pl)	nyervy	2.2
nervous	не́рвный	nyervniy	2.8, 15.3
Neva (river)	Нева́ (f)	Neva	3.4
never mind, that's all right	ничего́	nichivo	4.2
new	но́вый	noviy	17.1
New Zealand	Но́вая Зела́ндия (f)	Novaya Zilandiya	9.2
news	но́вости (pl)	novasti	11.3, 11.4
newspaper	газе́та (f)	gazyeta	11.3
New Year('s)	Но́вый год (m)	Noviy got	17.5
next month	сле́дующий ме́сяц (m)	slyeduyushchiy myesats	17.6
next time	сле́дующий раз (m)	slyeduyushchiy raz	17.3
next week	сле́дующая неде́ля (f)	slyeduyushchaya nidyelya	17.8
next year	сле́дующий год	slyeduyushchiy got	17.5
nice	ми́лый	miliy	2.11
nine	де́вять	dyevat'	18.1
nineteen	девятна́дцать	devatnatsat'	18.1
ninety	девяно́сто	divanosta	18.1
no	нет	nyet	4.2, 13.3
no more	бо́льше нет	bol'she nyet	4.2
no problem	нет пробле́м	nyet prablyem	4.2
nobleman	дворяни́н (m)	dvarinin	3.5
noon	по́лдень (m)	poldyen'	17.10
north	се́вер (m)	syever	16.4
North Sea	Се́верное мо́ре (n)	Syevernoye morye	9.4
nose	нос (m)	nos	2.2
not as good as	не так хорошо́ как	ni tak kharasho kak	15.2
not much	немно́го	nimnoga	18.5
not yet	ещё нет	ishcho nyet	17.1
notebook	тетра́дь (f)	tetrat'	12.6
novel	рома́н (m)	raman	11.2
November	ноя́брь (m)	nayabr'	17.7
now	сейча́с	siychas	17.1
nowadays	в настоя́щее вре́мя	v nastayashchiye vryemya	17.1
number	но́мер (m)	nomir	9.3, 18.1
nun	мона́хиня (f)	manakhinya	11.6
nurse	медсестра́ (f)	medsistra	2.7, 2.14
nuts	оре́хи (pl)	aryekhi	5.4
nylon	нейло́н (m)	neilon	6.4
O.K.	хорошо́	kharasho	4.2
obedient	послу́шный	paslushniy	2.11
occupation	оккупа́ция (f); заня́тие (n); профе́ссия (f)	akupatsiya; zanyatiye; prafessiya	3.5, 10.7

ocean	океа́н (m)	akian	1.3, 9.4
October	октя́брь (m)	aktyabr'	17.7
October Revolution	Октя́брьская революция (f)	Aktyabr'skaya rivalutsiya	3.5
October Revolution Day	День (m) Октя́брьской Револю́ции	Den' Oktyabr'skoy Revolyutsie	3.1
of course	коне́чно	kanyeshna	15.8
office	кабине́т (m), бюро́ (n)	kabinyet, byuro	9.8, 10.7
office hours	часы́ (pl) приёма	chasy priyoma	17.1
often	ча́сто	chasta	17.3
oil (cooking)	расти́тельное ма́сло (n)	rastitel'naye masla	5.4
oily	жи́рный	zhirniy	5.8
old	ста́рый	stariy	17.1
old age	пожило́й во́зраст (m)	pazhiloy vozrast	2.3
old person	пожило́й челове́к (m)	pazhiloy chilavyek	2.1
on the contrary	наоборо́т	naoborot	15.2
once again	ещё раз	ishcho raz	17.3
once in a while	иногда́	inagda	17.1
once upon a time	давны́м-давно́	davnym-davno	17.1
one	оди́н	adin	18.1
one day	оди́н день	adin dyen'	17.8
one month	оди́н ме́сяц	adin myesats	17.6
onion	лук (m)	luk	5.6
only	то́лько	tol'ka	19.3
open, to	открыва́ть	atkryvat'	8.4
opera	о́пера (f)	opira	3.2, 11.8
operation	опера́ция (f)	apiratsiya	2.7
operator	опера́тор (m)	apiratr	2.14
opinion	мне́ние (n)	mnyeniye	10.3
opportunity	возмо́жность (f)	vazmozhnast'	15.1
oppose, to	возража́ть	vazrazhat'	10.3
opposite	противополо́жный	protivopolozhniy	16.3
opposite side	противополо́жная сторона́ (f)	prativapalozhnaya starana	16.4
or	и́ли	ili	19.3
orange	апельси́н (m); ора́нжевый	apil'sin; aranzhiviy	5.5, 6.5
orange drink	апельси́новый напи́ток (m)	apil'sinaviy napitak	5.9
orange juice	апельси́новый сок (m)	apil'sinaviy sok	5.9
orchard	фрукто́вый сад (m)	fruktoviy sat	1.7
orchestra	орке́стр (m)	arkyestr	11.8
order food, to	заказа́ть (perf.) еду́	zakazat' yedu	5.3

order, to	заказа́ть *(perf.)*; прика́зывать; зака́зывать	zakazat'; prikazyvat'; zakazyvat'	7.2, 15.4
other day, the	друго́й день	drugoy dyen'	17.8
others	други́е	drugiye	15.2
otherwise	ина́че	inache	19.3
ounce	у́нция *(f)*	untsiya	18.3
out	из *(+ gen.)*	iz	19.4
outside	снару́жи	snaruzhi	16.5
own, to	владе́ть	vladyet'	15.1
Pacific Ocean	Ти́хий океа́н *(m)*	Tichiy akian	9.4
pack, to	упако́вывать	upakovyvat'	9.7
packet	паке́т *(m)* с *(+ inst.)*	pakyet s	18.8
page	страни́ца *(f)*	stranitsa	11.2
pain	боль *(f)*	bol'	2.6
painfully	бо́льно	bol'na	2.6
painter	худо́жник *(m)*	khudozhnik	11.7
painting	карти́на *(f)*	kartina	11.7
pair	па́ра *(f)*	para	6.3, 18.8
pajamas	пижа́ма *(f)*	pizhama	6.2
Palace of Congresses	Дворе́ц *(m)* съе́здов	Dvaryets s"yezdof	3.2
pan of	сковорода́ *(f)* с *(+ inst.)*	skavarada s	18.8
paper	бума́га *(f)*	bumaga	13.5
paper money	бума́жные де́ньги *(pl)*	bumazhniye dyen'gi	7.3
paragraph	пара́граф *(m)*	paragraf	11.2
parcel	посы́лка *(f)*	pasylka	13.6
parents	роди́тели *(pl)*	raditili	2.12
park	парк *(m)*	park	9.8
park, to	оставля́ть маши́ну	astavlyat' mashinu	9.5
parliament	парла́мент *(m)*	parlament	10.3
part, section	часть *(f)*, се́кция *(f)*	chast', syektsiya	16.5
parts of the body	ча́сти *(pl)* те́ла	chasti tyela	2.2
part, to	расстава́ться	rasstavat'sa	14.1
participate, to	принима́ть уча́стие	prinimat' uchastiye	10.1
party	ве́чер *(m)*, вечери́нка *(f)*	vyecher, vyechirinka	14.2
pass an exam, to	сдать экза́мен	sdat' ekzamin	12.8
patch, to	ста́вить запла́ту	stavit' zaplatu	8.9
path	тропи́нка *(f)*	trapinka	8.4
patient *(noun)*	пацие́нт *(m)*, пацие́нтка *(f)*	patsiyent, patsiyentka	2.7
patient *(adj.)*	терпели́вый	tirpiliviy	2.11
pay attention, to	уделя́ть внима́ние	udilyat' vnimaniye	12.7
pay, to	плати́ть	platit'	5.3, 7.2
peace	мир *(m)*	mir	10.11

peach	пе́рсик *(m)*	persik	5.5
pear	гру́ша *(f)*	grusha	5.5
peasant	крестья́нин *(m)*, крестья́нка *(f)*	krist'yanin, krist'yanka	2.14
pedestrian	пешехо́д *(m)*	pishikhot	9.3, 9.6
pedestrian crossing	перехо́д *(m)* для пешехо́дов	pirikhot dlya pishikhodof	9.3
pelmeni *(ravioli)*	пельме́ни *(pl)*	pil'myeni	5.7
pen	ру́чка *(f)*	ruchka	13.5
pencil	каранда́ш *(m)*	karandash	13.5
pencil case	пена́л *(m)*	penal	13.5
pencil sharpener	точи́лка *(f)*	tochilka	13.5
pen pals	друзья́ *(pl)* по перепи́ске	druz'ya pa piripiski	14.1
people	лю́ди *(pl)*	lyudi	2.1
pepper	пе́рец *(m)*	pyerits	5.4
percent off	… проце́нтов ски́дка *(f)*	… pratsyentaf skitka	7.2
perceptions	восприя́тия *(pl)*	vaspriyatiya	2.10
perhaps	вероя́тно	virayatna	15.8
person	челове́к *(m)*	chilavyek	2.1
person in charge	отве́тственный	atvyetstvenniy	10.10
personal hygiene	ли́чная гигие́на *(f)*	lichnaya gigiyena	2.5
pet	дома́шнее живо́тное *(n)*	damashniye zhivotnaye	1.8
Petrodvorets	Петродворе́ц *(m)*	Pitradvaryets	3.2
pharmacy; drugstore	апте́ка *(f)*	aptyeka	2.7, 7.1
Philippines	Филиппи́ны *(pl)*	Filippiny	9.2
philosophy	филосо́фия *(f)*	filasofiya	12.5
photo shop	фототова́ры	fototavary	7.1
photographer	фото́граф *(m)*	fatograf	2.14
photograph, to	фотографи́ровать	fatografiravat'	14.3
phrase	фра́за *(f)*	fraza	11.2, 13.1
physical therapy	физиотерапи́я *(f)*	fizioterapiya	2.7
physics	фи́зика *(f)*	fizika	12.5
piano	пиани́но *(n)*	pianino	11.8
pick up, to	зайти́ за *(+ acc.)*	zayti za	16.1
pictorial	иллюстри́рованный	illyustriravanniy	11.3
picture	карти́на *(f)*	kartina	8.5
piece (of)	кусо́к *(m)* *(+ gen.)*	kusok	18.8
pile (of)	па́чка *(f)* *(+ gen.)*	pachka	18.8
pillow	поду́шка *(f)*	padushka	8.3
pilot	пило́т *(m)*	pilot	2.14
pineapple	анана́с *(m)*	ananas	5.5
Ping-Pong	пинг-по́нг *(m)*	pink-ponk	14.5
pink	ро́зовый	rozaviy	6.5
pipe	тру́бка *(f)*	trupka	5.12

pirogi with meat	пироги́ (pl) с мя́сом	piragi s myasam	5.7
pirogi with mushrooms	пироги́ с гриба́ми	piragi s gribami	5.7
pirogi with potatoes	пироги́ с карто́шкой	piragi s kartoshkoy	5.7
place	ме́сто (n)	myesta	16.3
places of interest	достопримеча́тельности (pl)	dastaprimichatel'nasti	9.7
plan	план (m)	plan	10.6
plant	расте́ние (n)	rastyeniye	1.7
plant, to	сажа́ть	sazhat'	10.8
plastic	пла́стик (m)	plastik	6.4
plate	таре́лка (f)	taryelka	5.11, 18.8
play	пье́са (f), спекта́кль (m)	p'yesa, spektakl'	11.9
play, to; act, to	игра́ть	igrat'	11.9
play an instrument, to	игра́ть на инструме́нте	igrat' na instrumyente	14.3
play cards, to	игра́ть в ка́рты	igrat' f karty	14.2
play checkers, to	игра́ть в ша́шки	igrat' f shashki	14.3
play chess, to	игра́ть в ша́хматы	igrat' f shakhmaty	14.3
play electronic games, to	игра́ть в электро́нные и́гры	igrat' v iliktronniye igry	14.3
player	игро́к (m)	igrok	14.4
playground	игрова́я площа́дка (f)	igravaya plashchatka	12.6
playing field	игрово́е по́ле (n)	igravoye polye	14.4
please	пожа́луйста	pazhalsta	4.3
please come in	пожа́луйста, заходи́те	pazhalsta, zakhaditye	4.2
pleased to meet you	прия́тно познако́миться	priyatna paznakomit'sa	4.4
plug	розе́тка (f)	razyetka	8.5
plum	сли́ва (f)	sliva	5.5
plural	мно́жественное число́ (n)	mnozhistvennoye chislo	3.3
pocket	карма́н (m)	karman	6.1
poem	стихотворе́ние (n)	stikhatvaryeniye	11.2
poetry	поэ́зия (f)	paeziya	11.2
Poland	По́льша (f)	Pol'sha	9.2
police	мили́ция (f), поли́ция (f)	militsiya, politsiya	10.5
police car	полице́йская маши́на (f)	politseyskaya mashina	10.5
police officer	полице́йский (m)	palitsyeyskiy	10.5
police station	мили́ция (f); отделе́ние (n) поли́ции	militsiya; atdyelyenie politsii	9.8, 10.5
policeman	милиционе́р (m)	militsianyer	2.14
polite	ве́жливо	vyezhliva	4.3
politeness	ве́жливость (f)	vyezhlivast'	4.3
political party	полити́ческая па́ртия (f)	palitichiskaya partiya	10.3
politician	поли́тик (m)	palitik	2.14, 10.3

politics	поли́тика *(f)*	palitika	10.3, 12.5
polo	по́ло *(n)*	pola	14.5
pond	пруд *(m)*	prut	1.3
pool	билья́рд *(m)*	bil'yard	14.5
pool room	билья́рдная *(f)*	bil'yardnaya	8.2
poor	бе́дный	byedniy	10.2
pop music	поп-му́зыка *(f)*	pop-muzyka	11.8
popular	популя́рный	papulyarniy	15.7
population	населе́ние *(n)*	nasilyeniye	9.1, 10.2
pork	свини́на *(f)*	svinina	5.4
post office	по́чта *(f)*;	pochta;	7.1, 9.8,
	почто́вое отделе́ние *(n)*	pachtovaye atdelyeniye	13.6
post office box	абонеме́нтный я́щик *(m)*	abanimyentniy yashchik	13.6
postage stamp	почто́вая ма́рка *(f)*	pachtovaya marka	13.6
postcard	почто́вая откры́тка *(f)*	pachtovaya atkrytka	13.6
pot (of)	кастрю́ля *(f) (+ gen.)*	kastryulya	18.8
potato	карто́шка *(f)*	kartoshka	5.4, 5.6
pound	фунт *(m)*	funt	18.3
practice, to	практикова́ться	praktikavat'sa	11.8, 14.4
praise, to; commend, to	хвали́ть	khvalit'	2.9
pray, to	моли́ться	malit'sa	11.6
prepare, to	подгото́вить *(perf.)*	padgatovit'	9.7
prepositions	предло́ги *(pl)*	pridlogy	19.4
prescription	реце́пт *(m)*	ritsept	2.6
presentation	презента́ция *(f)*,	prizintatsiya,	11.4
	докла́д *(m)*	daklat	
president	президе́нт *(m)*	prezidyent	3.1, 10.3
president *(university)*	ре́ктор *(m)* университе́та	ryektar universityeta	12.3
press, (the)	пре́сса *(f)*	pryessa	11.3
previous time	пре́жде	pryezhdye	17.3
previously	пре́жде	pryezhdye	17.1
price	цена́ *(f)*	tsina	7.3
priest	свяще́нник *(m)*	svashchyenik	11.6
prime minister	премье́р-мини́стр *(m)*	prim'yer ministr	10.3
principal	дире́ктор *(m)* шко́лы	diryektar shkoly	12.3
print, to	печа́тать	pichatat'	11.3
prisoner	заключённый *(m)*	zaklyuchyonniy	10.5
problem	пробле́ма *(f)*	prablyema	10.2
produce	проду́кты *(pl)*	pradukty	10.8
produce, to	производи́ть	praizvadit'	10.8
professions	профе́ссии *(pl)*	prafyesii	2.14
professor	профе́ссор *(m)*	prafyessar	12.3
profit	при́быль *(f)*	pribyl'	10.6
program	програ́мма *(f)*	pragramma	11.4

progress	прогре́сс (m)	pragress	10.2
progressive	прогресси́вный	pragressivniy	10.2
prohibit, to	запреща́ть	zaprishchat'	10.2
pronouns	местоиме́ния (pl)	mistaimyeniya	2.13
pronunciation	произноше́ние (n)	praiznasheniye	13.1
prosecute, to	обвиня́ть	obvinyat'	10.4
province	прови́нция (f), о́бласть (f)	pravintsiya, oblast'	9.2
public telephone	телефо́н-автома́т (m)	tilifon-avtamat	9.8, 13.7
public toilets; restrooms	туале́ты (pl)	tualyety	9.8
publisher	изда́тель (m)	izdatil'	2.14
pull, to	тяну́ть	tanut'	8.9
pullover	пуло́вер (m)	pulovyer	6.2
pumpkin	ты́ква (f)	tykva	5.6
punctually	пунктуа́льно	punktual'na	15.8
punctuation	пунктуа́ция (f)	punktuatsiya	11.2
pupil	учени́к (m)	uchinik	12.3
purple	фиоле́товый	fialyetaviy	6.5
purse	су́мка (f)	sumka	7.2
push, to	толка́ть	talkat'	8.9
Pushkin Museum	музе́й (m) Пу́шкина	muzey Pushkina	3.2
put down, to	опусти́ть (perf.)	apustit'	16.1
put into, to	вста́вить (perf.); положи́ть (perf.)	vstavit'; palazhit'	16.1
put out a fire, to	погаси́ть (perf.) ого́нь	pagasit' agon'	8.6
put the garbage out, to	выноси́ть му́сор	vynasit' musar	8.7
quantity	коли́чество (n)	kalichistva	18.5
quarter	че́тверть (f)	chyetvert'	18.1
quarter hour	че́тверть (f) часа́	chyetvert' chasa	17.11
question	вопро́с (m)	vapros	12.8
question mark	вопроси́тельный знак (m)	vaprasitil'niy znak	11.2
question words	вопроси́тельные слова́	vaprasitel'niye slava	19.2
radiator	радиа́тор (m)	radiatar	8.6
radio	ра́дио (n)	radio	11.4
rain	дождь (m)	dozhd'	1.4
raincoat	плащ (m)	plashch	6.2
rainy	дождли́вый	dazhdliviy	1.4
rainy season	дождли́вый сезо́н (m)	dazhdliviy sizon	1.4
raise animals, to	выра́щивать живо́тных	vyrashchivat' zhivotnykh	1.8
raspberry	мали́на (f)	malina	5.5
rayon	виско́за (f)	viskoza	6.4
read, to	чита́ть	chitat'	12.7, 13.4
read a book, to	чита́ть кни́гу	chitat' knigu	14.3

read a magazine, to	чита́ть журна́л	chitat' zhurnal	14.3
read aloud, to	чита́ть вслух	chitat' vslukh	13.4
read silently, to	чита́ть про себя́	chitat' prosebya	13.4
read the newspapers, to	чита́ть газе́ту	chitat' gazyetu	14.3
reading	чте́ние (n)	chtyeniye	13.4
real; actual	действи́тельный	distvitil'niy	15.8
reality	действи́тельность (f)	distvitil'nast'	15.8
realize, to	осознава́ть	asaznavat'	2.10
rear	за́дний	zadniy	16.5
reason	причи́на (f)	prichina	15.5
reasonable	разу́мный	razumniy	2.11
receipt	квита́нция (f)	kvitantsiya	7.2
receive, to	получа́ть	paluchat'	7.2, 15.4
recently	неда́вно	nidavna	17.1
record, to	запи́сывать на магнитофо́н	zapisyvat' na magnitafon	11.4
record player	прои́грыватель (m)	praigryvatel'	11.4
red	кра́сный	krasniy	6.5
red caviar with blinis	кра́сная икра́ (f) с блина́ми	krasnaya ikra s blinami	5.7
Red Sea	Кра́сное мо́ре (n)	Krasnaye morye	9.4
region	райо́н (m)	rayon	9.2
regret, to	сожале́ть	sazhalyet'	2.8
regrettable	приско́рбный	priskorbniy	2.8
relations; relationships	отноше́ния (pl)	atnashyeniya	15.1
relative; relation	ро́дственник (m)	rotstvennik	2.12
release, to	отпуска́ть	atpuskat'	10.5
reliable	надёжный	nadyozhniy	2.11
relieve, to	облегча́ть	ablikhchat'	2.8
religion	рели́гия (f)	riligiya	11.6, 12.5
remove, to	устрани́ть (perf.)	ustranit'	16.1
rent	пла́та (f) за кварти́ру	plata za kvartiru	8.4
rent, to	сдава́ть	sdavat'	8.4
repair, to	чини́ть	chinit'	8.9
repairs	ремо́нт (m), почи́нка (f)	rimont, pachinka	8.9
reporter	репортёр (m)	ripartyor	2.14, 11.3
represent, to	представля́ть	pridstavlyat'	10.3
representative	представи́тель (m)	pridstavitil'	10.3, 15.2
republic	респу́блика (f)	rispublika	3.5
request	про́сьба (f)	pros'ba	13.2
research	иссле́дование (n)	isslyedovaniye	12.7
research, to	иссле́довать	isslyedavat'	12.7
researcher	иссле́дователь (m)	isslyedavatil'	2.14
resemble, to	походи́ть на …	pakhadit' na …	15.2

English	Russian	Transliteration	Ref
reserve a room (in a hotel)	заказа́ть *(perf.)* ко́мнату (в гости́нице)	zakazat' komnatu (v gastinitse)	9.7
responsibility	обя́занность *(f)*	abyazannast'	10.1
rest	о́тдых *(m)*	otdykh	14.3
rest, to	отдыха́ть	atdykhat'	14.3
restrooms	туале́ты *(pl)*	tualyety	9.8
restaurant	рестора́н *(m)*	ristaran	5.3, 9.8
result	результа́т *(m)*	risul'tat	12.8
retiree	пенсионе́р *(m)*	pinsianyer	2.14
review	повторе́ние *(n)*	paftaryeniye	12.7
review, to	повторя́ть	paftaryat'	12.7
revolt	восста́ние *(n)*	vasstaniye	3.5
revolution	револю́ция *(f)*	rivalutsiya	3.5
rich	бога́тый	bagatiy	10.2
ride, to	е́здить	yezdit'	9.5
Riga (Latvia)	Ри́га *(f)*	Riga	3.4
right	спра́ва	sprava	16.3, 16.5
right now	сейча́с же	siychas zhe	17.1
right; correct	пра́вильный, ве́рный	pravil'niy, vyerniy	12.7
ring	кольцо́ *(n)*	kal'tso	6.3
ring the doorbell, to	звони́ть в две́рь	zvanit' v dvyer'	8.4
river	река́ *(f)*	rika	1.3
road	доро́га *(f)*	daroga	9.3
rock music	рок-му́зыка *(f)*	rok-muzyka	11.8
roll (of)	руло́н *(m) (+ gen.)*	rulon	18.8
Roman Catholic	католи́ческая це́рковь *(f)*	katalichiskaya tserkaf'	11.6
Romanov dynasty	дина́стия *(f)* Рома́новых	dinastiya Romanavykh	3.5
roof	кры́ша *(f)*	krysha	8.5
room (in a hotel)	но́мер *(m)*	nomir	8.2
room (in a house)	ко́мната *(f)*	komnata	8.2
root	ко́рень *(m)*	koren'	1.7
row (of)	ряд *(m) (+ gen.)*	ryat	18.8
rowing	гре́бля *(f)*	gryeblya	14.5
ruble	рубль *(m)*	rubl'	7.3
rule, to	пра́вить	pravit'	3.5
ruler	лине́йка *(f)*	linyeika	13.5
run, to	бе́гать *(indeterminate)*; бежа́ть *(determinate)*	byegat'; bizhat'	14.4, 1.8
Russia	Росси́я *(f)*	Rassiya	3.4, 9.2
Russian	ру́сский *(m)*, ру́сская *(f)*	russkiy, russkaya	9.2
Russian (language)	ру́сский язы́к *(m)*	russkiy yezyk	3.3, 12.5
Russian currency	ру́сская валю́та *(f)*	russkaya valyuta	7.3
Russian grammar	ру́сская грамма́тика *(f)*	russkaya grammatika	12.5
Russian literature	ру́сская литерату́ра *(f)*	russkaya litiratura	12.5

Russian Orthodox	правосла́вная це́рковь (f)	pravaslavnaya tserkaf'	11.6
sad	гру́стный	grustniy	2.8
safety	безопа́сность (f)	bezapasnost'	9.6
sailboat	па́русная ло́дка (f)	parusnaya lotka	14.5
sailor	матро́с (m)	matros	2.14
salad	сала́т (m)	salat	5.4
sale	распрода́жа (f)	raspradazha	7.2
salesclerk	продаве́ц (m), продавщи́ца (f)	pradavyets, pradavshchitsa	2.14
salesperson	продаве́ц (m)	pradavyets	7.2
salt	соль (f)	sol'	5.4
salty	солёный	salyoniy	5.8
same, (the)	тако́й же	takoy zhe	15.2
sandals	санда́лии (pl)	sandalii	6.3
sandwich	бутербро́д (m)	buterbrot	5.4
satin	сати́н (m)	satin	6.4
Saturday	суббо́та (f)	subbota	17.9
sauce	блю́дце (n)	blyutse	5.11
say, to	сказа́ть	skazat'	13.2
scarf	шарф (m)	sharf	6.3
schedule	расписа́ние (n)	raspisaniye	9.7, 12.6
scholarship	стипе́ндия (f)	stipyendiya	12.1
school	шко́ла (f)	shkola	9.8, 12.2
school day	шко́льный день (m)	shkol'niy dyen'	12.6
science	нау́ка (f)	nauka	11.5
science film	нау́чный фильм (m)	nauchniy fil'm	11.9
scientific	нау́чный	nauchniy	11.5
scientist	учёный (m)	uchyoniy	2.14, 11.5
scissors	но́жницы (pl)	nozhnitsy	6.1, 8.8
Scotland	Шотла́ндия (f)	Shatlandiya	9.2
screwdriver	отвёртка (f)	atvyortka	8.8
scrubbing brush	щётка (f)	shchyotka	8.7
sculptor	ску́льптор (m)	skul'ptar	11.7
sculpture	скульпту́ра (f)	skul'ptura	11.7
sea	мо́ре (n)	morye	9.4
season	вре́мя (n) го́да	vryemye goda	1.6, 17.6
seat belt	реме́нь (m)	rimyen'	9.5
second	второ́й	vtoroy	17.9
second year	второ́й год (m)	ftoroy got	12.4
seconds	секу́нды (pl)	sikundy	17.11
secretary	секрета́рь (m), секрета́рша (f)	sikritar', sikritarsha	2.14
section of	се́кция (f) (+ gen.)	syektsiya	18.8
see someone off, to	провожа́ть	pravazhat'	9.7

see you soon	до ско́рого	da skorava	4.5
see you tomorrow	до за́втра	da zaftra	4.5
see, to	ви́деть	vidit'	2.10
seeds	семена́ *(pl)*	simina	1.7
seem as if, to	ка́жется как бу́дто	kazhitsya kak budta	15.2
seldom	ре́дко	ryetka	17.3
sell, to	продава́ть	pradavat'	7.2
semicolon	то́чка *(f)* с запято́й	tochka s zapitoy	11.2
send a telegram, to	посыла́ть телегра́мму	pasylat' tiligrammu	13.7
send back, to	возвраща́ть	vazvrashchat'	16.1
send, to	посыла́ть	pasylat'	13.6
sentence	предложе́ние *(n)*	pridlazhyeniye	11.2
separate, to	отделя́ть	atdelyat'	16.1
September	сентя́брь *(m)*	sentyabr'	17.7
serfdom	крепостно́е пра́во *(n)*	kripastnoye prava	3.5
set (of)	набо́р *(m)* *(+ gen.)*	nabor	18.8
set the table, to	накрыва́ть на стол	nakryvat' na stol	5.1
seven	семь	syem'	18.1
seventeen	семна́дцать	semnatsat'	18.1
seventy	се́мьдесят	syem'desat	18.1
several	не́сколько	nyeskol'ko	18.1
severe	сло́жный	slozhniy	15.3
sew, to	шить	shit'	6.1
sewing machine	швейная маши́на *(f)*	shveynaya mashina	6.1
shallow	ме́лко	myelka	18.2
shampoo	шампу́нь *(m)*	shampun'	8.7
shampoo one's hair, to	мыть го́лову	myt' golavu	2.5
share, to	дели́ться	dilit'sa	18.1
sharp	проница́тельный;	pranitsatel'niy;	8.8,
	о́стрый	ostriy	2.11
shave, to	бри́ться	britsa	2.5
shchi *(fish soup)*	щи *(pl)*	shchi	5.7
she, her, (to) her	она, её, ей	ana, yeyo, yey	2.13
shelves	по́лки *(pl)*	polki	8.3
shine, to	свети́ть	svitit'	1.1
ship	кора́бль *(m)*	karabl'	9.5
shirt	руба́шка *(f)*	rubashka	6.2
shoe polish	крем *(m)* для боти́нок	kryem dlya batinak	6.3
shoe shop	о́бувь *(f)*	obuv'	7.1
shoelaces	шну́рки *(pl)*	shnurki	6.3
shoes	о́бувь *(f)*	obuf'	6.3
shop; store	магази́н *(m)*	magazin	7.1, 7.2, 9.8
shopping	поку́пки *(pl)*	pakupki	7.2
shore	бе́рег *(m)*	berik	1.3

short	коро́ткий, ма́ленький	karotkiy, malin'kiy	2.2, 6.1, 18.2
shorts	шо́рты (*pl*)	shorty	6.2
shoulder	плечо́ (*n*)	plicho	2.2
shower	душ (*m*)	dush	8.5
shower, to	принима́ть душ (*m*)	prinimat' dush	2.5
shrewd	хи́трый	khitriy	2.11
Siberia	Сиби́рь (*f*)	Sibir'	3.4
sick, to be	быть больны́м	byt' bol'nym	2.6
sickness; illness	боле́знь (*f*)	balyezn'	2.6
side	сторона́ (*f*)	starana	16.3
sightsee, to	смотре́ть достопримеча́тельности	smatryet' dastaprimichatyel'nasti	9.7
significant	ва́жный	vazhniy	15.3
silk	шёлк (*m*)	shyolk	6.4
silver	сере́бряный	siryebriniy	6.5
simmer, to	туши́ть	tushit'	5.10
sing, to	петь	pyet'	11.8, 14.3
Singapore	Сингапу́р (*m*)	Singapur	9.2
singer	певе́ц (*m*), певи́ца (*f*)	pivyets, pivitsa	2.14, 11.8
single room (*in a hotel*)	но́мер (*m*) на одного́	nomir na adnovo	8.2
singular	еди́нственное число́ (*n*)	yedinstvinnoye chislo	3.3
sink	ра́ковина (*f*)	rakovina	8.5
sister	сестра́ (*f*)	sistra	2.12
six	шесть	shyest'	18.1
sixteen	шестна́дцать	shestnatsat'	18.1
sixth year	шесто́й год (*m*)	shistoy got	12.4
sixty	шестьдеся́т	shestdesyat	18.1
size	разме́р (*m*)	razmyer	6.1, 18.1
skiing	ката́ние (*n*) на лы́жах	kataniye na lyzhakh	14.5
skill	уме́ние (*n*), о́пыт (*m*)	umyeniye, opyt	10.9
skin	ко́жа (*f*)	kozha	1.8, 2.2
skirt	ю́бка (*f*)	yupka	6.2
sky	не́бо (*n*)	nyeba	1.1
skyscraper	небоскрёб (*m*)	nibaskryop	8.1
Slavic language family	гру́ппа (*f*) славя́нских языко́в	gruppa slavyanskikh yezykov	3.3
sleeping pill	снотво́рное (*n*)	snatvornaye	2.7
sleepy	со́нный	sonniy	2.4
sleeve	рука́в (*m*)	rukaf	6.1
slice of	кусо́к (*m*) (+ *gen.*)	kusok	18.8
slippers	та́почки (*pl*)	tapachki	6.3
slow	ме́дленно; ме́дленный	myedlinna; myedlinniy	17.1, 17.4

slowly	ме́дленно	myedlinna	17.4
small	ма́ленький	malin'kiy	18.1
smell, to	па́хнуть	pakhnut'	5.8
smoke	дым *(m)*	dym	5.12
smoke, to	кури́ть	kurit'	5.12
smoking	куре́ние *(n)*	kuryeniye	5.12
snack, to have a	перекуси́ть	pirikusit'	5.1
snackbar	заку́сочная *(f)*	zakusochnaya	9.8
snap	застёжка *(f)*	zastyozhka	8.9
snow	снег *(m)*	snyek	1.4
so-so	так себе́	tak sibye	4.2
soap	мы́ло *(n)*	myla	2.5, 8.7
soccer	футбо́л *(m)*	futbol	14.5
social order	обще́ственный поря́док *(m)*	abshchestvinniy paryadak	10.5
social science	обще́ственные нау́ки *(pl)*	abshchestvinniye nauki	12.5
socialism	социали́зм *(m)*	satsializm	10.3
society	о́бщество *(n)*	opshistva	10.1
socks	носки́ *(pl)*	naski	6.2
soda water	со́довая вода́ *(f)*	sodavaya vada	5.9
sofa	софа́ *(f)*; дива́н *(m)*	safa; divan	8.3
soft	мя́гкий	myakhkiy	8.8
soft sign	мя́гкий знак *(m)*	myakhkiy znak	3.3
soft voice	ти́хий го́лос *(m)*	tikhiy golas	13.2
soil	по́чва *(f)*	pochva	1.2
solar calendar	со́лнечный календа́рь *(m)*	solnechniy kalendar'	17.5
sold out	распро́дан	rasprodan	7.2
soldier	солда́т *(m)*	saldat	2.14
sometimes	иногда́	inagda	17.1, 17.3
son	сын *(m)*	syn	2.12
song	пе́сня *(f)*	pyesnya	11.8
sore throat, to have a	боли́т го́рло *(n)*	balit gorla	2.6
sorry	прости́те	prastite	4.3
sound	звук *(m)*	zvuk	3.3, 13.1, 13.2
soup	суп *(m)*	sup	5.4
sour	ки́слый	kisliy	5.8
south	юг *(m)*	yuk	16.4
South Africa	Ю́жная А́фрика *(f)*	Yuzhnaya Afrika	9.2
souvenir	сувени́р *(m)*	suvinir	4.3
souvenir shop	сувени́ры *(pl)*	suviniry	7.1
Soviet Union	Сове́тский Сою́з *(m)*	Savetskii Sayuz	3.4
Spain	Испа́ния *(f)*	Ispaniya	9.2
spare room	свобо́дная ко́мната *(f)*	svabodnaya komnata	8.2
speak, to	говори́ть	gavarit'	13.2

speaking	у́стная речь (f)	ustnaya ryech'	13.2
special	специа́льный	spitsial'niy	15.3
speech	речь (f)	ryech	13.1
speed	ско́рость	skorast'	17.4
spend, to	тра́тить	tratit'	10.6
spinach	шпина́т (m)	shpinat	5.6
spoiled	избало́ванный	izbalovanniy	2.11
spoon	ло́жка (f)	lozhka	5.11, 18.8
sport(s)	спорт (m)	sport	14.4
sporting goods store	спорти́вные това́ры (pl)	spartivniye tavary	7.1
spread out, to	расстила́ться	rasstilat'sa	18.1
spring	весна́ (f)	vesna	1.6, 17.6
stairs	ле́стница (f)	lyesnitsa	8.5
stamp	ма́рка (f)	marka	13.6
stamp collection	колле́кция (f) ма́рок	kallyektsiya marak	13.6
star	звезда́ (f)	zvyezda	1.1
start	нача́ло (n)	nachala	17.2
start, to	начина́ть	nachinat'	17.1, 17.2
state	штат (m)	shtat	9.2
station (radio)	програ́мма (f)	pragramma	11.4
stationery shop	канцеля́рские това́ры (pl)	kantsilyarskiye tavary	7.1
steal, to	красть	krast'	10.5
steam, to	вари́ть на пару́	varit' na paru	5.10
stepfather	о́тчим (m)	ochim	2.12
stepmother	ма́чеха (f)	machikha	2.12
stereo	сте́рео (n)	styerio	11.4
stern	неумоли́мый	niumalimiy	2.11
still	ещё; до сих пор	ishcho; da sikh por	15.8
sting, to	ужа́лить (perf.)	uzhalit'	1.8
stockings	чулки́ (pl)	chulki	6.2
stomach	желу́док (m)	zhiludak	2.2
stone	ка́мень (m)	kamin'	1.2
stool	табуре́тка (f)	taburyetka	8.3
stop (bus, trolley, etc.)	остано́вка (f)	ostanofka	9.5, 17.2
stop, to	остана́вливаться; прекраща́ть; останови́ться (perf.)	astanavlivat'sya; prikrashchat'; astanavit'sa	9.5, 17.1, 17.2
store	магази́н (m)	magazin	7.1, 7.2, 9.8
storm	шторм (m)	shtorm	1.5
story	эта́ж (m)	etazh	8.1
stove	плита́ (f)	plita	5.11
straight	пря́мо	pryama	16.4
straightforward	прямо́й	primoi	2.11
strawberry	клубни́ка (f)	klubnika	5.5

street	у́лица (*f*)	ulitsa	9.3
streetcar	трамва́й (*m*)	tramvay	9.5
strength	си́ла (*f*)	sila	15.3
stress	ударе́ние (*n*)	udaryeniye	3.3, 13.1
strict	стро́гий	strogiy	2.11
string	нить (*f*)	nit'	18.8
strong	кре́пкий; си́льный	krepkiy; sil'niy	5.8, 15.3
strong wind	си́льный ве́тер (*m*)	sil'niy vyetir	1.5
student (*university*)	студе́нт (*m*), студе́нтка (*f*)	studyent, studyentka	12.3
studies	учёба	uchyoba	12.4
studious	приле́жный	prilyezhniy	2.11
study	кабине́т (*m*)	kabinet	8.2
study (*a subject*), to	учи́ть (*предме́т*)	uchit' (*predmyet*)	12.7
study abroad, to	учи́ться за грани́цей	uchit'sa za granitsey	12.1
study by correspondence	зао́чное обуче́ние (*n*)	zaochnaye abuchyeniye	12.2
stupid	глу́пый	glupiy	2.11
subject	предме́т (*m*)	pridmyet	12.5
subsequently	впосле́дствии	vpaslyetstvii	17.1
substitute, to	заменя́ть	zaminyat'	15.1
subtract, to	отнима́ть	atnimat'	18.1
suburb	при́город (*m*)	prigarat	9.2
subway	метро́ (*n*)	mitro	9.5
success	уда́ча (*f*)	udacha	2.9
suddenly	вдруг	fdruk	17.4
suffer, to	страда́ть	stradat'	1.5
sufficient	доста́точно	dastatachna	18.6
sugar	са́хар (*m*)	sakhar	5.4
suit	костю́м (*m*)	kastyum	6.2
suit yourself	как вам подхо́дит	kak vam padkhodit	4.2
suitable	подходя́щий	padkhadyashchiy	15.1
sultry	ду́шный	dushniy	1.4
summer	ле́то (*n*)	lyeta	1.6, 17.6
Summer Palace	Ле́тний дворе́ц (*m*)	Letniy dvaryets	3.2
summer vacation	ле́тние кани́кулы (*pl*)	lyetniye kanikuly	12.1
sun	со́лнце (*n*)	sontse	1.1
Sunday	воскресе́нье (*n*)	voskrisyen'ye	17.9
sunglasses	очки́ (*pl*) от со́лнца	achki at sontsa	6.3
sunlight	со́лнечный свет (*m*)	solnichniy svyet	1.1
supermarket	суперма́ркет (*m*)	supermarkit	7.1
supper	у́жин (*m*)	uzhin	5.2
surgeon	хиру́рг (*m*)	khirurk	2.14
surgery	опера́ция (*f*)	apiratsiya	2.7
sweat suit	спорти́вный костю́м (*m*)	spartivniy kastyum	6.2
sweep, to	подмета́ть	padmitat'	8.7

sweet	сла́дкий	slatkiy	5.8
sweets	сла́дости *(pl)*	sladasti	5.4
swim, to	пла́вать	plavat'	14.4
swimming	пла́вание *(n)*	plavaniye	14.5
swimming pool	бассе́йн *(m)*	bassyeyn	14.4
swimsuit	купа́льный костю́м *(m)*	kupal'niy kostyum	14.4
switch	выключа́тель *(m)*	vyklyuchatel'	8.5
switch off, to	выключа́ть	vyklyuchat'	8.4, 11.4
switch on, to	включа́ть	vklyuchat'	8.4, 11.4
syllable	слог *(m)*	slok	3.3
synagogue	синаго́га *(f)*	sinagoga	11.6
synthetic	синте́тика *(f)*	sintyetika	6.4
system	систе́ма *(f)*	sistyema	10.1
T-shirt	ма́йка *(f)*	mayka	6.2
table	стол *(m)*	stol	8.3
table tennis	насто́льный те́ннис *(m)*	nastol'niy tyennis	14.5
Tadjikistan	Таджикиста́н *(m)*	Tazhikistan	3.4
taiga	тайга́ *(f)*	taiga	3.4
tailor	портно́й *(m)*	partnoy	2.14, 6.1
tailor's	ателье́ *(n)*	atel'ye	7.1
take a bath, to	принима́ть ва́нну	prinimat' vannu	2.5
take a seat, please	сади́тесь пожа́луйста	saditis' pazhalsta	4.2
take a walk, to	ходи́ть на прогу́лку	khadit' na pragulku	14.3
take away, to	забра́ть *(perf.)*	zabrat'	15.4, 16.1
take care of, to	забо́титься	zabotitsa	2.8
take into account, to	принима́ть во внима́ние	prinimat' va vnimaniye	15.5
take medicine, to	принима́ть лека́рство	prinimat' likarstva	2.7
take notes, to	конспекти́ровать	kanspiktirovat'	13.4
take off *(undress)*, to	раздева́ть	razdivat'	6.1
take your time	не торопи́тесь	ni tarapityes'	17.1
tall	высо́кий	vysokiy	2.2
Tallinn (Estonia)	Та́ллин *(m)*	Tallin	3.4
Tanzania	Танза́ния *(f)*	Tanzaniya	9.2
tape	плёнка *(f)*	plyonka	11.4
tape recorder	магнитофо́н *(m)*	magnitafon	11.4
Tashkent (Uzbekistan)	Ташке́нт *(m)*	Tashkent	3.4
tastes	вкусовы́е ощуще́ния *(pl)*	fkusaviye ashchushchyeniya	5.8
tasty	вку́сный	fkusniy	5.8
tasty, it's	вку́сно	fkusna	5.1
taxi	такси́ *(n)*	taksi	9.5
Tbilisi (Georgia)	Тбили́си *(m)*	Tbilisi	3.4
Tchaikovsky Concert Hall	Конце́ртный зал *(m)* и́мени Чайко́вского	Kantsertniy zal imini Chaikovskava	3.2
tea	чай *(m)*	chay	5.9

teacher	учи́тель (m),	uchitil',	2.14,
	учи́тельница (f)	uchitil'nitsa	12.3
teacup	ча́шка (f)	chashka	5.11
team	кома́нда (f)	kamanda	14.4, 18.8
teapot	ча́йник (m)	chaynik	5.9
tear, to	разорва́ть (perf.)	razarvat'	8.9
technical school	техни́ческая шко́ла (f)	tikhnichiskaya shkola	12.2
technician	те́хник (m)	tyekhnik	2.14
teeth	зу́бы (pl)	zuby	2.2
telegram	телегра́мма (f)	tiligramma	13.7
telephone	телефо́н (m)	tilifon	13.7
telephone booth	телефо́нная бу́дка (f)	tilifonnaya butka	9.8
telephone directory (book)	телефо́нная кни́га (f)	tilifonnaya kniga	13.7
telephone number	но́мер (m) телефо́на	nomir tilifona	13.7
telephone, to	звони́ть по телефо́ну	zvanit' pa tilifonu	13.7
television	телеви́дение (n)	tilividiniye	11.4
television (set)	телеви́зор (m)	tilivizar	11.4
tell a story, to	расска́зывать ска́зки	rasskazyvat' skazki	13.2
tell, to	расска́зывать	rasskazyvat'	13.2
temperament	темпера́мент (m)	temperament	2.8
temperature	температу́ра (f)	timpiratura	1.4, 2.6
ten	де́сять	dyesat'	18.1
ten thousand	де́сять ты́сяч	dyesat' tysach	18.1
tender	мя́гкий	myakhkiy	5.8
tennis	те́ннис (m)	tyennis	14.5
tennis shoes	ке́ды (pl)	kyedy	6.3
tenth	деся́тый	disyatiy	17.9
terrible	ужа́сный	uzhasniy	2.8
terrific	великоле́пный	vilikalyepniy	2.9
test	контро́льная рабо́та (f)	kantrol'naya rabota	12.1, 12.8
textbook	уче́бник (m)	uchebnik	12.6
thank, to	благодари́ть	blagadarit'	4.3
thank you	спаси́бо	spasiba	4.2
thank you for your hospitality	спаси́бо за гостеприи́мство	spasiba za gastipriimstva	4.5
thank you very much	большо́е спаси́бо	bal'shoye spasiba	4.2
thanks (gratitude)	благода́рность (f)	blagadarnast'	4.3
that	тот (m)	tot	16.2
that side	та сторона́ (f)	ta starana	16.3
theater	теа́тр (m)	tiatr	9.8
then	пото́м, зате́м	patom, zatyem	19.3
there is; there are	вот есть	vot yest	15.1
therefore	поэ́тому	paetomu	15.5, 19.3
thermometer	термо́метр (m)	termometr	1.4

thermos	тéрмос *(m)*	tyermos	5.11
these	эти *(pl)*	eti	16.2
these days	эти дни *(pl)*	eti dni	17.1, 17.8
they, them, (to) them	они́, их, им	ani, ikh, im	2.13
thick	тóлстый	tolstiy	18.1
thief	вор *(m)*	vor	10.5
thigh	бедрó *(n)*	bidro	2.2
thin	худóй; тóнкий	khudoy; tonkiy	2.2, 18.1
thing	вещь *(f)*	veshch	15.1
think, to	дýмать	dumat'	2.10
third	трéтий	tryetiy	17.9
third year	трéтий год *(m)*	tretiy got	12.4
thirsty, to be	хотéть пить	khatyet' pit'	5.1, 5.9
thirteen	тринáдцать	trinatsat'	18.1
thirteenth	тринáдцатый	trinatsatiy	17.9
thirty	три́дцать	tritsat'	18.1
thirty-first	три́дцать пéрвый	tritsat' pyerviy	17.9
thirty-one days	три́дцать оди́н день *(m)*	tritsat' adin dyen'	17.8
this	этот *(m)*	etot	16.2
this day	этот день *(m)*	etat dyen'	17.10
this evening	этот вéчер *(m)*	etat vyechir	17.10
this kind	этот вид *(m)*	etat vit	16.2
this morning	это ýтро *(n)*	eta utra	17.10
this one	вот этот *(m)*	vot etat	16.2
this side	эта сторонá *(f)*	eta starana	16.3
this time	в этот раз *(m)*	v etot raz	17.1
this way	так (прáвильно); сюдá	tak (pravil'na); syuda	16.2
this week	эта недéля *(f)*	eta nidyelya	17.8
this year	этот год *(m)*	etat got	17.5
those	те *(pl)*	tye	16.2
thousand	ты́сяча *(f)*	tysacha	18.1
thread	ни́тка *(f)*	nitka	6.1
three	три	tri	18.1
three days later	чéрез три дня	chyeriz tri dnya	17.1
throat	гóрло *(n)*	gorla	2.2
throw, to	вы́бросить	vybrasit'	16.1
thunder	гром *(m)*	grom	1.4
Thursday	четвéрг *(m)*	chitvyerk	17.9
tie	гáлстук *(m)*	galstuk	6.3
tie, to	завязáть *(perf.)*;	zavyazat';	6.3,
	привя́зывать	privyazivat'	8.9
time	врéмя *(n)*	vryemya	17.1, 17.3
timid; shy	рóбкий	robkiy	2.11
tip	чаевы́е *(pl)*	chaiviye	5.3, 7.2

tired	уста́лый	ustaliy	2.4
to (direction), into	в (+ acc.)	v	19.4
toast	тост (m)	tost	5.4
tobacco	таба́к (m)	tabak	5.12
tobacco shop	таба́чная лавка (f)	tabachnaya lafka	7.1
today	сего́дня	sivodnya	17.8
together with	вме́сте с (+ inst.)	vmyestye s	14.1, 19.4
toilet	туале́т (m)	tualyet	8.2, 8.5
toilet paper	туале́тная бума́га (f)	tualyetnaya bumaga	2.5, 8.5
tomato	помидо́р (m)	pamidor	5.6
tomato juice	тома́тный сок (m)	tamatniy sok	5.7
tomato salad	сала́т (m) из помидо́р	salat iz pamidor	5.7
tomorrow	за́втра	zaftra	17.8
ton	то́нна (f)	tonna	18.3
tongue	язы́к (m)	yezyk	2.2
too much	сли́шком мно́го	slishkam mnoga	18.7
tool	инструме́нт (m)	instrumyent	8.8
toothbrush	зубна́я щётка (f)	zubnaya shchyotka	2.5
toothpaste	зубна́я па́ста (f)	zubnaya pasta	2.5
topic	те́ма (f)	tyema	12.8
torn	разо́рванный	razorvanniy	8.9
torte	торт (m)	tort	5.4
tough	твёрдый	tvyordiy	5.8
tour bus	тури́стский авто́бус (m)	turistkiy avtobus	9.7
tour group	тури́стская гру́ппа (f)	turiskaya grupa	9.7
tour guide	гид (m)	git	9.7
tourism	тури́зм (m)	turizm	3.2
toward	по направле́нию к (+ dat.)	po napravlyeniyu k	19.4
towel	полоте́нце (n)	palatyentse	2.5, 8.7
toy store	игру́шки (pl)	igrushki	7.1
trade	торго́вля (f)	targovlya	10.10
trade union	профсою́зы (pl)	profsayuzy	10.9
trading hours	поменя́ться часа́ми	paminyat'sa chisami	17.1
tradition	тради́ция (f)	traditsiya	10.1, 11.1
traditional	традицио́нный	traditsionniy	11.1
traffic	движе́ние (n)	dvizhyeniye	9.6
traffic light	светофо́р (m)	svitafor	9.3
tragedy	траге́дия (f)	tragyediya	11.9
train	по́езд (m)	poyezd	9.5
tram	трамва́й (m)	tramvay	9.5
transport; transportation	тра́нспорт (m)	transport	9.6
trash can	му́сорное ведро́ (n)	musarnaye vidro	8.5
travel	путеше́ствия (pl)	putishyestviya	9.7
travel, to	путеше́ствовать	putishyestvavat'	9.7

traveler	путеше́ственник *(m)*	putishyestvinik	9.7
tree	де́рево *(n)*	dyereva	1.7
Tretyekov Art Gallery	Третья́ковская галере́я *(f)*	Tret'yakofskaya galeryeya	3.2
trial	проце́сс *(m)*	protsess	10.4
trip, to; stumble, to	споткну́ться *(perf.)*	spatykhnut'sa	16.1
trolley	тролле́йбус *(m)*	traleybus	9.5
trouble	неприя́тности *(pl)*	nipriyatnasti	2.9
trousers	брю́ки *(pl)*	bryuki	6.2
tsar	царь *(m)*	tsar'	3.5
Tsar Bell	Царь-ко́локол	Tsar'-kolakal	3.2
Tsar Cannon	Царь-пу́шка	Tsar'-pushka	3.2
tsarina	цари́ца *(f)*	tsaritsa	3.5
Tuesday	вто́рник *(m)*	ftornik	17.9
tundra	ту́ндра *(f)*	tundra	3.4
tune in, to	настра́ивать	nastraivat'	11.4
Turkmenistan	Туркмениста́н *(m)*	Turkministan	3.4
turn	поворо́т *(m)*	pavarot	16.1
turn left, to	поверну́ть *(perf.)* нале́во	pavirnut' na lyevo	16.1
turn right, to	поверну́ть *(perf.)* напра́во	pavirnut' na pravo	16.1
turn, to	поверну́ть *(perf.)*	pavirnut'	16.1
turnip	ре́па *(f)*	ryepa	5.6
TV channel	телевизио́нный кана́л *(m)*	tilivizionniy kanal	11.4
twelfth month	двена́дцатый ме́сяц *(m)*	dvinatsatiy myesats	17.7
twelve	двена́дцать	dvenatsat'	18.1
twentieth	двадца́тый	dvatsatiy	17.9
twenty	два́дцать	dvatsat'	18.1
twenty-one	два́дцать оди́н	dvatsat' adin	18.1
twins	близнецы́ *(pl)*	bliznitsy	2.12
two	два	dva	18.1
two days	два дня	dva dnya	17.8
typewriter	пи́шущая маши́нка *(f)*	pishushchaya mashinka	13.5
typical	типи́чный	tipichniy	15.2
ugly	некраси́вый	nikrasiviy	6.1, 15.7
Ukraine	Украи́на *(f)*	Ukraina	3.4
umbrella	зонт *(m)*	zont	6.3
unable to find, to be	не мочь найти́	ne moch' nayti	16.1
uncle	дя́дя *(m)*	dyadya	2.12
underground	подзе́мный	padzyemniy	9.5
underpants	трусы́ *(pl)*	trusy	6.2
underpass	подзе́мный перехо́д *(m)*	padzyemniy pirikhot	9.3
undershirt	ма́йка *(f)*	mayka	6.2
understand, to	понима́ть	panimat'	2.10
underwear	бельё *(n)*	bel'yo	6.2

unemployed	безрабо́тный *(m)*	bezrabotniy	2.14
unexpected	неожи́данный	niazhidanniy	1.5, 2.8
uniform	фо́рма *(f)*	forma	6.1
unimportant	нева́жный	nivazhniy	2.9
United Nations	Организа́ция *(f)* Объединённых На́ций	Arganizatsiya Ab"yedinyonykh Natsiy	10.11
university	университе́т *(m)*	universityet	9.8, 12.2
university first year	пе́рвый год *(m)* университе́та	pyerviy got universityeta	12.4
unscrew, to	отвёртывать	atvyortyvat'	8.9
unsuccessful	неуда́чный	niudachniy	2.9
until now	до настоя́щего вре́мени	da nastayashchiva vryemini	17.1
untrustworthy	ненадёжный	ninadyozhniy	2.11
upper part	ве́рхняя часть *(f)*	vyerkhnyaya chast'	16.5
upstairs	наверху́	naverkhu	8.5
Ural Mountains	Ура́льские го́ры *(pl)*	Ural'skiye gory	3.4
urgent	сро́чный	srochniy	15.3
USA	США *(pl)*	SShA	9.2
use, to	испо́льзовать	ispol'zavat'	8.9
useful	ну́жный	nuzhniy	15.1
usually	обы́чно	abychna	17.3
utensils	прибо́ры *(pl)*	pribory	5.11
Uzbekistan	Узбекиста́н *(m)*	Uzbekistan	3.4
vacation	кани́кулы *(pl)*	kanikuly	12.1
vacuum cleaner	пылесо́с *(m)*	pylisos	8.7
valid	действи́тельный	deystvitel'niy	10.4
vase	ва́за *(f)*	vaza	8.5
vegetable dish	овощно́е блю́до *(n)*	avoshchnoye blyuda	5.6
vegetables	о́вощи *(pl)*	ovashchi	5.6, 10.8
velvet	ба́рхат *(m)*	barkhat	6.4
veranda	вера́нда *(f)*	veranda	8.5
verb tense	вре́мя *(n)* глаго́ла	vryemya glagola	3.3
very	о́чень	ochen'	15.3, 18.7
very bad	о́чень пло́хо	ochin' plokha	2.9
video recorder	ви́деомагнитофо́н *(m)*	vidiomagnitafon	11.4
videotape	видеокассе́та *(f)*	vidiokassyeta	11.4
village	дере́вня *(f)*	deryevnya	3.1, 9.2
Vilnius (Lithuania)	Ви́льнюс *(m)*	Vil'nyus	3.4
vinegar	у́ксус *(m)*	uksus	5.4
violin	скри́пка *(f)*	skripka	11.8
visit, to	посеща́ть	pasishchat'	9.7, 14.2
Volga River	река́ Во́лга *(f)*	rika Volga	3.4
volleyball	волейбо́л *(m)*	valeybol	14.5

volume	объём *(m)*	ob"yom	18.3
vowel:	гла́сный звук *(m):*	glasniy zvuk:	3.3
stressed, unstressed	уда́рный, безуда́рный	udarniy, bezudarniy	
waist	та́лия *(f)*	taliya	2.2
wait a minute	подожди́те мину́тку	padazhditye minutku	4.2
wait a moment	подожди́те мину́тку	padazhditi minutku	17.1
waiter	официа́нт *(m)*	afitsiant	5.3
wake up, to	буди́ть	budit'	2.4
walk the dog, to	прогу́ливать соба́ку	pragulivat' sabaku	1.8
walk, to	ходи́ть	khadit'	16.1
wall	стена́ *(f)*	styena	8.5
wallet	бума́жник *(m)*	bumazhnik	6.3
war	война́ *(f)*	vayna	10.11
war memorial	па́мятник *(m)* же́ртвам войны́	pamyatnik zhertvam voyny	9.8
warm	тепло́	tiplo	1.4, 8.6, 17.6
warm water	тёплая вода́ *(f)*	tyoplaya vada	2.5
warmhearted	добросерде́чный	dabrasirdyechniy	2.11
was	был, была́, бы́ло	byl, byla, byla	19.1
wash dishes, to	мыть посу́ду	myt' pasudu	8.7
wash one's face, to	умыва́ться; мыть лицо́	umyvat'sya; myt' litso	2.5
wash the car, to	мыть маши́ну	myt' mashinu	8.4
wash, to	мыть; стира́ть	myt'; stirat'	6.1, 8.7
washing	сти́рка *(f)*	stirka	8.7
washing machine	стира́льная маши́на *(f)*	stiral'naya mashina	8.7
watch	часы́ *(pl)*	chasy	6.3
watch television, to	смотре́ть телеви́зор	smatryet' tilivizar	14.3
watches	часы́ *(pl)*	chisy	7.1
water	вода́ *(f)*	vada	1.3, 5.9
waterskiing	во́дные лы́жи *(pl)*	vodnye lyzhi	14.5
water, to	полива́ть	palivat'	10.8
water the plants, to	полива́ть цветы́	palivat' tsvyety	8.4
watermelon	арбу́з *(m)*	arbuz	5.5
wave	волна́ *(f)*	valna	1.3
we, us, (to) us	мы, нас, нам	my, nas, nam	2.13
weak	сла́бый	slabiy	15.3
weak *(of a drink)*	сла́бый	slabiy	5.8
wear, to	носи́ть	nasit'	6.1
weather	пого́да *(f)*	pagoda	1.4
weather report	сво́дка *(f)* пого́ды	svotka pagody	1.4
Wednesday	среда́ *(f)*	sryeda	17.9
week	неде́ля *(f)*	nidyelya	17.8, 17.9
weekend	выходно́й	vikhadnoy	17.9

English	Russian	Transliteration	Ref
weigh, to	взве́шивать	vzvyeshivat'	13.6
weight	вес *(m)*	vyes	18.3
welcome	добро́ пожа́ловать	dabro pazhalavat'	4.4
well, to be/feel	чу́вствовать себя́ хорошо́	chustvavat' sebya kharasho	2.6
were	бы́ли	byli	19.1
west	за́пад *(m)*	zapat	16.4
Western medicine	за́падная медици́на *(f)*	zapadnaya miditsina	2.7
wet	мо́крый	mokriy	1.4
wharf	верфь *(f)*	vyerf'	9.5
what	что	shto	19.2
what happened?	что случи́лось?	shto sluchilas'?	4.2
what is your name?	как вас зову́т?	kak vas zavut?	4.4
what time is it?	кото́рый час?	katoriy chas?	17.11
when	когда́	kagda	17.1, 19.2
when the time comes	когда́ придёт вре́мя	kagda pridyot vryemya	17.1
where	где	gdye	16.3, 19.2
where are you from?	отку́да вы?	atkuda vy?	4.1
which	како́й *(m)*	kakoy	16.2, 19.2
which one	кото́рый *(m)*	katoriy	16.2
which subject?	како́й предме́т?	kakoy pridmyet?	12.5
while (during)	в то вре́мя как	f to vryemya kak	17.1
whiskey	ви́ски *(n)*	viski	5.9
white	бе́лый	beliy	6.5
who	кто	kto	19.2
who, whom, (to) whom	кто, кого́, кому́	kto, kavo, kamu	2.13
whole day, (the)	весь день *(m)*	vyes' dyen'	17.10
whose	чей	chey	19.2
why	почему́	pachemu	15.5, 19.2
wicked	зло́бный	zlobniy	2.11
wide	широ́кий	shirokiy	18.1
wife	жена́ *(f)*	zhina	2.12
wild animals	ди́кие живо́тные *(pl)*	dikiye zhivotniye	1.8
win, to	вы́играть *(perf.)*	vyigrat'	14.4
wind	ве́тер *(m)*	vyetir	1.5
window	окно́ *(n)*	akno	8.5
wine:	вино́ *(n)*:	vino:	5.9
red wine,	кра́сное вино́,	krasnaye vino,	
white wine	бе́лое вино́	byelaye vino	
winter	зима́ *(f)*	zima	1.6, 17.6
Winter Palace	Зи́мний дворе́ц *(m)*	Zimniy dvaryets	3.2
winter vacation	зи́мние кани́кулы *(pl)*	zimniye kanikuly	12.1
wipe, to	вытира́ть	vytirat'	8.7
with	с *(+ inst.)*	s	19.4
within	внутри́	vnutri	16.5, 18.6

woman	жéнщина (f)	zhenshchina	2.1
wonderful	прекрáсный	prikrasniy	2.9, 13.3
wood	дéрево (n)	dyereva	8.8
wool	шерсть (f)	sherst'	6.4
word	слóво (n)	slova	13.1
work	рабóта (f)	rabota	10.7
worker	рабóчий (m)	rabochiy	2.14
world	мир (m)	mir	9.1
World War I	Пéрвая мировáя войнá (f)	Pervaya miravaya vaina	3.5
World War II	Вторáя мировáя войнá (f)	Vtaraya miravaya vaina	3.5
worry, to	беспокóиться	bispakoitsa	2.8
wrap, to	завёртывать; заворáчивать	zavyortyvat'; zavarachivat'	7.2, 13.6
write, to	писáть	pisat'	12.7, 13.4
write a letter, to	писáть письмó	pisat' pis'mo	13.4
writer	писáтель (m), писáтельница (f)	pisatel', pisatel'nitsa	2.14, 11.2
wrong; incorrect	непрáвильный, невéрный	nepravil'niy, nivyerniy	12.7
X ray	рентгéн (m)	rentgen	2.7
Yasnaya Polyana Estate Museum	музéй-усáдьба (f) Ясная Поляна	muzey-usat'ba Yasnaya Palyana	3.2
year	год	got	17.5
year after next (in 2 years)	чéрез два гóда	chyeriz dva goda	17.5
year before last (2 years ago)	два гóда назáд	dva goda nazat	17.5
five years old	пять лет	pyat' let	17.5
yellow	жёлтый	zhyoltiy	6.5
Yellow Sea	Жёлтое мóре (n)	Zhyoltaye morye	9.4
Yerevan (Armenia)	Еревáн (m)	Yerivan	3.4
yes	да	da	4.2, 13.3
yesterday	вчерá	fchera	17.8
you (pl), you, (to) you	вы, вас, вам	vy, vas, vam	2.13
you (polite), you, (to) you	Вы, Вас, Вам	vy, vas, vam	2.13
you (sing), you, (to) you	ты, тебя, тебé	ty, tibya, tibye	2.13
you are too kind	вы óчень добры́	vy ochin' dabry	4.3
young	молодóй	maladoy	2.3
young person	молодóй человéк (m)	maladoy chilavyek	2.1
zero; nothing	ноль; нуль; ничегó	nol'; nul'; nichivo	18.1, 18.5
Zimbabwe	Зимбáбве (n)	Zimbabve	9.2
zoo	зоопáрк (m)	zaapark	1.8, 9.8